From
Nell & Stanley.
Deer. 25ᵗʰ 1953

1953
£6.50

X
+10

19 MAY 1986
Bq
16. MAY 1986
6 JAN 1988
PS
ROBSON.
14 JAN 1988
6/3/89
Fulwood & Cadley
CP school.
25. MAY 1990
PP

AUTHOR	CLASS
COLLINS. H C	E01

TITLE	No
Lancashire plain and seaboard	08472205

LANCASHIRE PLAIN AND SEABOARD

N. Wolstenholme

The shrimper

LANCASHIRE
PLAIN AND SEABOARD

BY HERBERT C. COLLINS

ILLUSTRATED BY
H. HARTE

LONDON: J. M. DENT AND SONS LTD

L0000042579
0142297

TO

ETHEL

08472205

CONTENTS

v

ILLUSTRATIONS

PHOTOGRAPHS

LINE DRAWINGS

I

THE BACKGROUND PLAN
EXPLAINED

WE are apt to regard the development of western Lancashire as of comparatively recent origin. It is recognized that the area was cut off from the rest of England by marsh and bog, and that influence from that direction was meagre, but there was another and very important influence springing from early developments in Ireland.

Into this arc of Lancashire coastline came a variety of races: adventurers, traders, and missionaries from Ireland. The land routes of Lancashire may have been sparse and difficult, but the sea afforded an open gateway. The wide mouth of Morecambe Bay with its many rivers provided, in the first place, all that was necessary for settlement, and to plot the oldest settlements on the map is to show an inhabited coastline around each of the estuaries.

Place-names provide a further clue to the Celtic, Norse, and Anglo-Saxon groupings which went to form a chain of settlements strung out from north to south along the higher ridges of land and linked by a route crossing the estuaries and running the whole length of western Lancashire, from Mersey to Duddon. This route is strewn with neolithic remains and the bones of extinct animals, and is overlooked by circles of standing stones and the cave-dwellings of its earliest inhabitants.

It can be no coincidence that Burscough Priory, Upholland Priory, Lytham Priory, Cockersand Abbey, Cartmel Priory, and Conishead Priory are on this route, or that isolated Stanlawe Abbey on the Cheshire side of the Mersey lies in a direct line with this route if we extend it to Chester, for by the time the abbey was built Chester was the great city of the west, and one Norman de Lacy, whose family were patrons of Stanlawe Abbey, was also constable of Chester.

A trodden trackway along the ridges and over the estuaries

appears to have been the means of communication between the earlier groups of settlers. Not until the days of written documents do we learn that the wide Mersey estuary was crossed by ferries with tolls payable to the religious communities who had been granted the right to operate them, and it is not possible to know for certain whether they were carrying on a service which was already old when they were founded. Certainly these communities also undertook the protection of travellers crossing the estuaries of the Ribble and Morecambe Bay, and we can be sure of the continuous use of this track from the twelfth to the fourteenth centuries. In 1296, the 'Inquisitio post mortem' of Lord Edmund, brother of King Edward I, shows that he died possessed of 'passagium ultra Mersey,' and a Duchy of Lancaster lease, dated 1485, describes the ferry as 'the passage or ferry over the water of Mersey between the town of Liverpool and the County of Chester.'

There was a ferry from Eastham to Liverpool operated by the Abbey of St Werburgh at Chester which passed to the Stanleys after the Dissolution, and the Runcorn ferry seems to have been operated by John FitzRichard who died in 1190, for in that year the Knights Hospitallers granted lands to Richard de la More in return for a rent on condition that he kept in repair the vessel which John, Constable of Chester, for the love of God, had formerly provided for the convenience of those wishing to cross the stream. A map of about A.D. 1300, quoted by Harrison but not named (Lancashire and Cheshire Antiquarian Society, *Transactions*, vol. iv), shows a road from Chester across the Wirral and over the River Mersey to Liverpool (ten miles). Celia Fiennes crossed from Burton to the ferry opposite Liverpool and Daniel Defoe crossed from Neston to the same point. The Chester–Neston road is mentioned earlier, in 1687, when a carriage stuck in the sand.

After crossing the Duddon estuary the old route was directed to the heart of Scotland, for it is interesting to note that Blackpool, on the west coast of Lancashire, is about the same degree of longitude as Edinburgh on the east coast of Scotland, making this route across the west of Lancashire a direct road to the north. From the south there is a concentration of roads converging on Chester to cross the narrow Wirral peninsula to Stanlawe Abbey for the Mersey ferry, and so to the north.

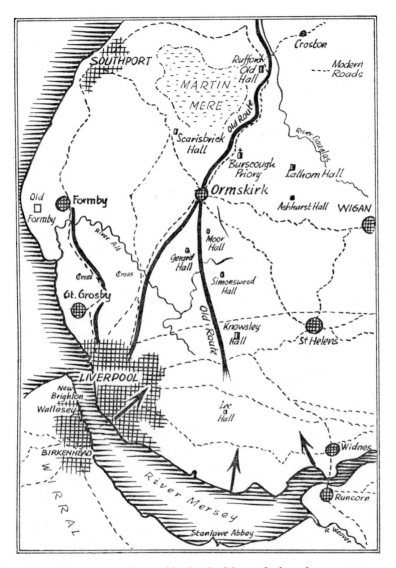

The old route enters Lancashire by the Mersey fords and concentrates
on Ormskirk to follow the ridgeway through the mosses

The Romans, invading Britain from the south and driving new roads to the north, exerted another influence in this district, and provided a new conception of the construction of permanent ways. If the Mersey ferries existed in their time, they disregarded them. They used the fords, the first of which was at Warrington, so that their new road out of Chester kept further eastward, skirting the marsh by way of Wigan to Preston and Lancaster. All northerly roads went through Lancaster, for here was the only place to ford or bridge the River Lune in a narrow bottle-neck between the sea and the hills.

The Romans also advanced through Manchester to their great camp at Ribchester and thence again struck northward to Lancaster, in addition to using the Hodder valley to cross to the east of the Pennines. The Lancaster–Ribchester Roman road has been obliterated close to Ribchester, for after the early destruction of that fortress in the Scottish raids there was no other use for it. But the Warrington ford—Wigan–Preston–Lancaster Roman road remained the chief route through Lancashire, as indeed it is to this day. It now has its dangers in bottle-necks and congested towns—seventeenth- and eighteenth-century complications which produce an alarming number of accidents, and to overcome them it is planned to replace the straight line of the Roman pavement by the wavy line of the by-pass, at present operating only at Garstang.

Meanwhile the more westerly routes survived in parts to serve a local population, and accounts of its separate portions have been handed down to us by local historians. The unsatisfactoriness of the Ribble estuary crossing caused a deviation to be made at Tarleton to join the road into Preston, and from that town travellers went north by the Roman road to Lancaster.

The crossing of Morecambe Bay sands, however, remained, for no overland route, short of travelling north to Kendal before turning south-west, could be found until the coming of the railway in 1857. This part of the route, therefore, remains the most vivid in memory. Later the creation of the town of Barrow and the railway crossing of the Duddon estuary effaced the old land route over the Furness peninsula. On the other hand the growth of Liverpool and Southport gave greater value to the old road between Ormskirk and Preston, and to-day it shows as an important red line on the map.

The early life-stream of Christianity also found its way along the old route. The first men of religion sailed into Morecambe Bay, founding the most ancient of Lancashire chapels at Heysham, and so the word of God followed the high road into the settlements. You may trace its course up the Lune valley where, at Halton, are crosses carved so early in the era of Christian thought that you can feel the sculptor groping amongst his older beliefs to find suitable symbols to mark conversion to the new religion, so that Beowulf and the old gods had perforce to serve to picture the story of the new God.

The pioneers of religion had naturally travelled to areas where there were people to convert. It was therefore surely no accident that the monks of Lindisfarne carried St Cuthbert's body across Lancashire, for their goal was no unpopulated wilderness but safety amongst a friendly people. And likewise the monks of Furness and Cartmel would not have come to settle and exert their influence except where there was an already settled population.

All these activities and many more were dependent upon movement, and were partly conditioned by the old road which went out of the Morecambe Bay area north and south to disperse the new arrivals and to bring in fresh influences. But we have seen how it faded after the Roman occupation, and it was cut into little pieces by the industrial era, when the great easterly manufacturing towns created resorts made in their own image for holiday-making by the sea, and these demanded new linking roads, this time running from east to west.

The long-standing influence of sea and river must not be forgotten. Hilaire Belloc once made a map of England and marked upon each river the first bridge upstream from the sea, then, above this bridge, the highest point to which a small vessel could carry with the tide, and again the very highest point to which a loaded boat could reach. He then joined the latter points, and shaded the area beyond them and so demonstrated how little of England remained cut off from water traffic.

To-day we have largely lost this approach by river to the countryside. Roads are well engineered and plentiful. But it is a point to remember when considering Lancashire.   The safe anchorage of the River Wyre created the ports of Wardleys and Skippool.   In 1590 an extensive trade with Russia was done through these ports.   In 1708 there were six customs officers stationed at Poulton to check cargoes of timber from America, flax and tallow from the Baltic, and so on.   There were three pilots at Knott End to give passage to Wardleys.

Along the banks of the rivers we find those early industries which were later to succumb before the cheap power-machines of south Lancashire.   Backbarrow on the River Leven had its six-storey cotton-mill worked by water power, with two hundred and fifty employees, its famous furnace, still in operation, and the Low Wood gunpowder works established in 1799.

The Leven afforded communication with the mines and quarries of old Coniston.   There was a time when the beautiful countryside round the third largest lake in England was a black country, like the Weald and the Forest of Dean.   Smoke and flame rose from furnace after furnace dotted among woods, which were being chopped down by the colliers to provide charcoal fuel.   On the lake was a constant procession of boats with cargoes of slate, iron, timber, copper, and food.   As late as 1815 the Muckle Gill copper vein was worked by a Staffordshire firm which took the metal to the midlands to make wire and sheets for coppering the bottom of ships.

Caton on the River Lune had a population of over a thousand at the beginning of the nineteenth century of whom some three hundred or three hundred and fifty were employed in local cotton-, flax-, and silk-mills. Isaac Hodgson's cotton-mill employed one hundred and fifty, including seventy apprentices wholly maintained by him, and turned out 3,000 lb. of yarn every week.   A schoolmaster was kept to give daily instruction to the apprentices, who were fed on meat and potato pies, broth, beef and cabbage, lobscouse (a dialect word still understood and also used by sailors for a dish of meat stew and potatoes), rice pudding, and salt herrings with oatmeal bread to fill up.   The cost to Isaac Hodgson was 2s. 8½d. each week per person, and for seventy-five people he used 570 lb. of oatmeal, 545½ quarts of milk, and 448 lb. of potatoes.   He had also to find clothing which averaged 5s. 6d. per head per week.

The Goree Piazzas, Liverpool, before the blitz of World War II

At Dolphinholme on the River Wyre was a large worsted-mill, and top hats were made in the village. It has been reported that black slaves were employed here until the Act of Liberation (1833). The next water-driven mill was at Cleveleys and there were others at Garstang. The tributary Calder drove the Calderdale Mill and the Pyrmont cotton works, and there were several mills on the seventeen miles of the tributary Brock, which joins the Wyre at St Michael's.

At Seathwaite on the River Duddon there was a water-powered carding mill and the Heckle stream turned much cotton machinery and a fulling-mill at Broughton. The River Lune provided the power for cotton-mills at Force Bank and Halton, while a silk-mill at Wray was driven by the water of the River Roeburn. The River Condor turned two silk-mills at Ellel, and Inglewhite depended on water power for a considerable amount of silk and cotton manufacture.

Ulverston and Warrington turned out much sailcloth for sailing ships at the ports in their area, and we find the same trade at Poulton-le-Fylde. There were also two flax-mills for this trade at Caton, a number at Ulverston, and in 1836 it was the principal trade of Kirkham 'from whence considerable supplies are sent to Naval depots.'

Sir Alexander Rigby built himself a town house at Poulton-le-Fylde in 1693, and this later became a manufactory of flax dressing and twine spinning. There was a dye house where the railway now runs. Even Sunderland Point had its rope-making industry to supply the demand from shipping.

A census of Lancashire manufacturers in the 1790s would run somewhat as follows: cotton, silk, and woollen goods, hats, stockings, pins, needles, nails, small wares, tobacco and tobacco pipes, snuff, earthenware, English porcelain, clocks and watches and their special tools, long bows and steel bows, paper, smelting of iron and copper, casting plate glass, blown glass, white lead, lamp black, vitriolic acid, fossil alkali, refining of sugar, wooden swills, bobbins, gunpowder, and the building of boats. At that date very few of these goods came from the areas which manufacture them to-day.

The transport of these goods, together with food, was by water, so the industries remained close to the rivers. Cotton and silk were landed at small ports and manufactured as close to them as might be.   The nearest stream with a fall of water sufficient to drive a small mill was all that these early industrialists required.   Cotton delivered at Sunderland Point was spun on the River Lune and transported to Kendal for final manufacture into dyed goods, which were brought back to the ports by pack-horse for reshipment overseas.   Wool was the only textile manufactured locally.   It was made up into goods on the hills, among the sheep which supplied the raw material, and then taken by pack-horse to the ports where the cotton was already being unloaded which, hand in hand with the newly discovered power of steam, was to transform the industrial scene.   These country, water-driven mills shut their doors as the coal-fields of south-east Lancashire acted like a magnet to industry demanding the new power.   Once again there came a complete change of scene in the Lancashire countryside.

Further north, in the Furness peninsula, the coppice woods provided baskets and bobbins for industry situated further south until they were ousted by cheaper products.   The local iron deposits which had led to the creation of industrial Barrow were replaced to an increasing extent by imported raw material as the local supply became exhausted.   But local industry stretched its fingers even to Walna Scar in the mountains, where bracken burning was carried on to supply large quantities of potash.   There are still the remains of bracken ovens on the moor.

Because the Industrial Revolution produced more goods than the small ships and pools and creeks could accommodate, trade by sea was eventually concentrated into the ports of Liverpool and Preston, which were able to meet the demand for bigger ships and docks.   In 1720 the River Douglas was made navigable to Wigan to get coal to Liverpool by way of the Ribble, and the River Weaver in Cheshire was deepened to provide a passage from the saltfields to Liverpool.   The deepening of the Sankey Brook to the Mersey became the first canal.

In a previous age the monks of Furness had exported their wool from the Pile of Foudrey, and this isolated port was later used by some woollen manufacturers to escape the payment of duties on exports.   Such ports supplied the local requirements of a coastal trade.   Poulton-le-Fylde, for instance, from 1806 to

1808 imported 500 tons of limestone per year from Ulverston together with 4,000–9,000 quarters of oats from Ulverston, Kirkcudbright, Dumfries, Wigtown, Whitehaven, and Liverpool. Coal came in from Preston, and in return Poulton exported cheese to these places.

There is, of course, a limit to the area which a river can serve profitably, and beyond it the road must be used. It is the purpose of this book to show how these factors have operated in western Lancashire. While enjoying the pleasure of an imaginary journey along the old and forgotten westerly route, there will be opportunity for a survey of the growth of the seaside towns and of the decay of old ports. These matters, and many others, will provide the setting for our travels through western Lancashire.

B

II

THE GROWTH OF LIVERPOOL

LIVERPOOL did not become the focus of ferry crossings over the Mersey until the town grew to importance during the seventeenth and eighteenth centuries. Before that time there was a variety of crossings available further upstream. From the direction of Chester it is apparent that the northerly Lancashire route would be served admirably by the Hall ferry, the way thence by Kirkby ('Kirk' being a clue word which occurs later in Kirkham and Ormskirk on this same route), thus avoiding the lower marshy valley of the Alt. Before the area was drained the easy flooding of this valley frequently rendered it necessary for the hay to be brought in by floating it on barn doors and for parishioners to go to church by boat. The Church House, now a farm, was specially fitted up so that churchgoers could have their meals there and dry their clothes, the church providing all necessaries for the day.

To-day this is rich farming land, but it is only kept so by pumping. In winter time it is easy enough to flood the flats around Sefton for skating. The name of Altcar is best remembered for its annual Derby Day of the greyhounds, the Waterloo Cup, founded in 1836 by the proprietor of the Waterloo Hotel. This is a combined agricultural show, dog show, hunt, and race meeting. Here in February come two hundred beaters with yellow flags, bookies, tipsters, and of course crowds of people, in every type of conveyance on wheels. Before the blue riband of the greyhound world has been won more than a hundred and twenty hares will have been sacrificed. Greyhounds, in fancy woollen coats, swallow raw eggs like pills. With all their selected feeding on eggs, milk, and raw steak they still look like iron railings. But once the hare is on the course they shoot away like coiled springs. The hare will have fifty yards start, but the greyhounds will be on top of it in ten seconds.

To-day it is impossible to travel in these parts without feeling the influence of Liverpool, but in the early days of Lancashire's history there was no Liverpool. Many of the more ancient ports on the Lancashire coast were rendered useless not only by the swirl of sand and tide but by the change from sail to steam, the increasing tonnage of shipping requiring deeper anchorage, the need for warehouses, offices, and workshops due to the growth in trade—all part of the clamorous demands of

South Lancs. Coast 1598.

(from a Harlaeian Mss.)

Lerpoole Haven

Mersey Sea

Kirkdale

Lerpole

Bank Hall

Crosby
Crosby M.

Formby

Alker Ch.

Lidiate

The Moss

Meoles

Kirkby

Simonswood
Forest

the expanding Industrial Revolution. Manchester urgently required an outlet to the sea to send her textiles all over the world. The hardwares of Birmingham, and the chemical industries based on Cheshire salt, clamoured for an exit. The growth of Liverpool was the only answer.

With this end of the story we are now familiar. Was Liverpool ready to play its part in this industrial expansion? Indeed it was, and its earlier development had an important influence on its eventual greatness.

King John granted charters to the Lancashire ports of Lancaster, Preston, and Liverpool with the idea of creating seaports from which he could engage Ireland either in war or trade. Liverpool was then (1207) but a tiny fishing village, completely overshadowed by ancient Chester. For the next three hundred years there were only five or six streets—Castle Street, Dale Street, Water Street, Jugelar Street, and Chapel

Street. The oldest of these was Chapel Street. Markets were held at High Cross where Castle Street is intersected by Water Street and Dale Street. It was a long established custom that all persons attending the market were free from arrest within a specified area round the cross, marked by boundary stones, and it is interesting to note that the streets of Liverpool were first lit in 1654 when it was ordered that 'two lanthorns, with two candles burning every night in the dark moon, be set out at the High Cross and the White Cross, and places prepared to set them in, every night until eight of the clock.'

To Liverpool as a fishing village 'nature had given her what is her fortune to-day,' writes C. E. Montague in *The Right Place.* 'But it came in the form of a post-dated cheque; having it all the time in her pocket, she could not cash it before the age of the large modern steamship.' He was referring to that bottle-neck in the river between Liverpool and Birkenhead through which the tide races, scouring the channel and feeding the inner pool which moderates its rise and fall. It was too swift and dangerous for the unloading of small ships on a quay, but it evoked the inventiveness of Thomas Steers who, in 1715, designed the wet dock where ships could load and unload within safe and calm water.

Liverpool, like Blackpool, received the last part of its name from a natural creek or, as it was locally termed, 'pool.' The pool entered the Mersey where the Custom House stood before the blitz in the last war, and ran inland along Paradise Street and Whitechapel to the old Haymarket. This area saw the first development of Liverpool as a port. The Custom House, for instance, was built on the site of that first eighteenth-century dock (filled up in 1826–7) which had closed the mouth of the pool.

In 1227 Henry III confirmed Liverpool's existing charter and added the right to form a Hanse, or mercantile trading body, to govern, direct, and protect the trade of the port. King John's charter had attracted to Liverpool the Irish trade which had always had a considerable influence along the shores of the Irish Sea, for the Irish were traders before the Lancashire coast had felt the foot of the first settlers. So it is not surprising to read (Coram Rege Roll 254), that 'Adam, son of Richard, son of Adam de Lyverpol broke into the house of Richard de

Ruyton at Lyverpol and stole a falcon priced 20*s.* which belonged to John de Gloucestre, *an Irish merchant,* about Nativity St. John Bap. 14th yr. [24 June 1321].' And Leland in the reign of Henry VIII reported that 'hither Irish merchants then resorted much, as to a good haven where there was small custom paid,' bringing Irish yarn for sale to the Manchester men. In the reign of Queen Elizabeth Camden spoke of Liverpool as 'the most frequented passage to Ireland and as a place more noted for its elegance and its populousness than for its antiquity.'

Across the Mersey channel Birkenhead Priory was influential in local policy. For instance, in the matter of ferries, the monks and 'their successors for ever' were in 1330 granted the right to ferry 'men, horses, and other things whatsoever' across the channel into Lancashire. Their successor to-day is the Birkenhead Corporation which still controls the ferries. That is why passengers pay their fares on the Cheshire side of the river, for the prior of Birkenhead was granted the right to ferry to the opposite shore but not from it. Liverpool had that privilege but has allowed it to lapse. The old clause which says that the service shall operate night and day without a break is to-day effected with the modern aid of radar, and symbolized by the crown finials on the ferry gangposts.

The Irish trade was still predominant in Queen Elizabeth's reign. There is a record, for instance, of twenty-seven vessels entering and leaving the port in three months, bringing Irish yarn for Manchester, sheep and deer skins, tanned and salted hides and tallow. To Ireland went the famous Yorkshire broadcloths, Manchester cottons, Chester cups, Kendal dyed cottons, Sheffield cutlery, coarse stockings, blankets, and sailcloth. The import of Irish cattle did not begin until 1665. By that time Ireland was taking thousands of tons of coal, thousands of bushels of salt, as well as tobacco and sugar. In 1670 one hundred and ten vessels were trading from Liverpool against thirty from Chester and five from other ports on the Lancashire coast.

The mention of tobacco and sugar introduces the next great step in Liverpool's history as a port. With the discovery of the American continent and the formation of the colonies there, a new era of trade developed. Until that time British trade had been with and through the continent of Europe, and this led to the development of ports in the south of the country.   The new colonization brought trade to Bristol and the Lancashire ports on the west coast.   Britain as an outpost of the Old World was placed by the discovery of America in a position of geographical advantage with the New World, and the ports of the west coast, Bristol, Liverpool, and Lancaster, became avid beneficiaries of this profitable link.   But the new colonies wanted English supplies in exchange for their products, and of these ports it was Liverpool alone which stood with the industrial area conveniently situated on her back doorstep.

So Blome was able to write in his *Britannia* that Liverpool was a place 'in which there were divers eminent merchants and tradesmen whose trade and traffic, especially to the West Indies, have made it famous . . . the situation affords in great plenty, and at more reasonable rates than most places in England, imported commodities from the West Indies, as likewise a quick return for such commodities, by reason of the sugar bakers and great manufacturers of cotton in adjacent parts.'

Sugar-refining began in 1665 as a result of the West Indian trade when Sir Edward Moore let a croft in Dale Street, which was subsequently called Sugar House Close, to a London sugar baker called Smith.   But the greatest trade in any single import was that in tobacco.   By 1702, writes Edward Baines, Liverpool had a hundred and two vessels averaging 85 tons and 1,101 seamen—figures comparable with Bristol's hundred and sixty-five vessels averaging 105 tons and 2,389 seamen, and London's five hundred and sixty vessels, averaging 105 tons with 10,065 seamen.

Virginia was the first colonial foundation, in 1606.   New England followed in 1620 and the Barbadoes in 1625.   Then the great plague of London caused an exodus of merchants, many of whom went to Liverpool to begin anew, taking their money and experience to foster trade with the American markets.   Gentlemen's sons were apprenticed to the trading houses and built their fortunes in commerce.   French Protestants and German refugees, fleeing before the ruthless Louis XIV, settled in Lancashire and laid the foundations of such trades as silk and paper-making.

From England small sailing ships returned to America laden

with religious emigrants: to Virginia if they were for the monarchy and established church, to New England if they were Puritans and Protestant nonconformists, to Maryland if they were Roman Catholics, and to Pennsylvania if they were Quakers. It was all sound British stock which created yet more trade for west of England ports, and particularly for Liverpool.

It was not until 1699 that the town became a separate parish. Before then it had been in the parish of Walton-on-the-Hill and had had to be content with a chapel of ease. In the Liverpool vestry books is a record of the case put forward at the time in favour of the separation:

'Leverpool was formerly a small fishing town; but many people coming from London, in the time of the sickness and after the fire, several ingenious men settled in Liverpool; which encouraged them to trade to the plantations and other places; which occasioned sundry other tradesmen to come and settle there; which hath so enlarged their trade, that from scarce paying the sallary of the Officers of the Customs, it is now the third part of the trade of England, and pays upwards of £50,000 per annum to the King. And by reason of such increase of inhabitants many new streets are built, and still in building; and many gentlemen's sons of the counties of Lancaster, Yorkshire, Derbyshire, Staffordshire, Cheshire, and North Wales, are put apprentices in the town. And there being but one Chapel, which doth not contain one half of our inhabitants in the summer, upon pretence of going to the Parish Church, which is two long miles, and there being a village in the way, they drink in the said village; by which, and otherwise, many youth and sundry families are ruined. Therefore it is hoped the Bill may pass, being to promote the service of God.'

In 1708, when Liverpool had an estimated population of between eight and ten thousand, powers were obtained to construct the first wet dock. It was completed in 1719 by Thomas Steers, at that time one of the foremost builders of Lancashire's public works.

Travel then was still quaintly primitive, regarded by twentieth-century eyes. For instance, in the diary of Nicholas Blundell we read:

'15 August 1702. I went to Leverpl with Coz. Edmund

Butler.   We hailed ye Mary with a hankerchaf but she answered not; he went on board ye Harington for Dublin.

'2 May 1708.   Mr. Wareing told us his Son was in danger to lose his Passage for Ireland, ye ship being gone and he was forced to ride after her on Shore and so get on Borde if he could.'

There were yet more aces waiting to be played in Liverpool's favour, yet the sequence was a natural one.   In 1562–7 Sir John Hawkins was making voyages to West Africa, collecting Negroes and selling them to the Spanish colonies as slaves. The early English chartered companies formed for the African trade overlooked this trade and dealt mainly in gold, until about the year 1663 when they began a regular slaving business with the granting of a monopoly in the trade to 'The Company of Royal Adventurers of England trading with Africa.'   When the monopoly was abolished in 1697 and free trade to Africa established, provided that merchants paid ten per cent to the company on all goods imported to or exported from Africa for the maintenance of forts, about five thousand slaves a year were carried in English ships.

At the Peace of Utrecht in 1713 England received the large slave trader *Asiento* and soon took the lead over all other sea powers.   By 1753 Liverpool had seventy-two slave ships, averaging just under 105 tons.   Eleven years later the number had risen to one hundred and thirty-four, carrying 303,737 slaves to the West Indies valued at over £15,000,000.   A selection of five average voyages shows a profit of £21 19s. 8d. per slave, or almost £40,000 net profit.   In 1770 half of the total world trade in slaves was carried by some one hundred and ninety-two British slave ships with cargo space for 50,000 slaves. Even after the loss of the American colonies in 1787 the figure stood for some time at 38,000.   The French came next with 20,000–30,000 and the Portuguese with about 10,000.   Of the total British slave trade Liverpool had more than half in 1770 and six-sevenths of the total by the end of the century.   The remaining seventh was shared between Bristol and London.

In those days St George's dock at Liverpool came close to the Goree Piazzas, the spars of the sailing ships overhanging the narrow roadway between.   There is a local tradition that slaves were chained in the arcade of the Goree Piazzas awaiting sale. Most of this historic building was destroyed during World War

II, but five arches still stand. It is scheduled for demolition, so there is little time left in which to stand beneath the massive sandstone arches, see the iron rings in the wall, and let the imagination paint the rest of the bygone scene.

It is estimated that the Liverpool Corporation spent £10,000 in combating the abolition of slavery. The corporation and their supporters maintained that slaves were an economic necessity in the development of colonial trade and that the ships engaged provided a training ground for sailors for the British Navy. Behind the trade was a large and powerful vested interest, supported by the wealth of commerce. It has been called 'the most lucrative trade the world has ever seen.' On that wealth rose the power of modern Liverpool.

'The principal exports of Leverpoole,' wrote Samuel Derrick in 1760, 'are all kinds of woollen and worsted goods, with other manufacturers of Manchester and Yorkshire, Sheffield and Birmingham wares etc. These they barter on the coast of Guinea for slaves, gold dust, and elephants' teeth. These slaves they dispose of at Jamaica, Barbadoes, and other West India islands for rum and sugar, for which they are sure of a quick sale at home.'

To-day it is hard to realize that this was considered a legitimate business, and that one John Newton by name, the captain of a slave ship, was a composer of hymns, among them the well-known 'How sweet the name of Jesus sounds.'

All these developments gave the town the lead in the Industrial Revolution which was to make it the greatest exporting port in the kingdom. The fast slaving ships brought to Liverpool the cotton on which Lancashire was to build the country up to its high-water mark of industrialism. Both Manchester, and Lancashire's factory system, were still in their infancy when Arthur Young made a detour especially to see Liverpool—'too famous in the trading world to allow me to pass it without viewing.' In 1635 Liverpool was so insignificant as to warrant the collection of only £15 in Stafford's ship-money tax, whereas £100 was collected from Chester and £2,000 from Bristol, but by the beginning of the nineteenth century the wealth accruing from the slave trade supplied the capital which put Lancashire's Industrial Revolution on its feet. Meanwhile the conquest of Canada was in progress and Clive was bringing India under the

British flag, events which were to create a tremendous demand for north-country manufactured goods with their outlet through Liverpool.

In 1825 the completion of the Erie Canal brought the Great Lakes into easy touch with New York and the foundations were laid for 'the greatest highway of the world's commerce—New York to Liverpool.'

In January 1851 gold was discovered in Australia by Edward Hargreaves. There was a rush to emigrate to the goldfields and Liverpool shipowners provided the fastest ships. John Pilkington and Henry Threlfall Wilson were sailing the 'White Star line of Boston packets' in 1849. In 1852 they met the new demand with the 'White Star line of Australian packets' which, together with the Eagle Line, Golden Line, Mersey Line, and the Black Ball Line among others, made Liverpool the chief emigration port of the British Isles, their fastest ships reaching Melbourne in around seventy days.

By 1867 Thomas Baines could write in his *History of Lancashire and Cheshire* that Liverpool 'is now the greatest port in the world, in point of trade, having a larger commerce even than London and New York ... one half of all the British manufactures exported to other countries are shipped at the port of Liverpool.'

There have been fewer opportunities to be grasped in the last hundred years, but enough has been done in Liverpool during that time to show that the spirit of enterprise within the city is still very strong. Hitler's war found the port ready to handle record cargoes and still defy the blitz. Our peep into history has shown how, from the charters of King John in the thirteenth century, the chief ports of Lancashire all had equal opportunities, but it was Liverpool, the poorest of them all, which was able to take full advantage of them and to make herself into a leading port of the nation even *before* the export trade of the Industrial Revolution, which, because of Liverpool's position, would inevitably have been her special prerogative.

III

PEAT MOSS AND SAND-DUNES

I F we return to the old route across the Alt valley we find there is a secondary ridge which is followed by the road from Liverpool to Southport by way of Scarisbrick. Before the marsh was drained the road ended at Scaris- brick, for beyond it and to seawards was the great un- drained marsh of Martin Mere. The villages hereabouts looked inland for what they required, while the coastal villages, only four miles away at the nearest point, used the sea.

As you pass through Lydiate on the way to Halsall you may notice by the roadside the Scottish Piper Inn which claims to be the oldest inn in Lancashire, and indeed looks it. The crooked brown beams twist from room to room a few feet above the head, and through the narrow oaken door is a glimpse of barrels in a Rembrandtesque light.

Halsall is a sprawling community but the church corner still retains a village look. Because the church stands on the edge of the moss the bells used to be rung after darkness had fallen as a guide to belated travellers. There are two other points about the church which are interesting. The lectern is placed in an open stone recess extending above and below the Bible stand, so that the vicar as he reads appears to be standing in a stone coffin. And outside the church the clock is illumined by electric light, while inside the congregation have to manage vespers by candle light and the vicar times his sermon by an hour glass. If the village has a modern claim to fame it is that the first sod of the Leeds–Liverpool canal was cut here in 1760.

Before we travel further over Lancashire's plain a considera- tion of its origin, its natural features, and their later treatment by mankind, will give us a keener, more observant eye for the pleasures of the journey, and as we are approaching the coast- line we may begin with a discursive account of its peculiarities and vagaries throughout its length.

On this deposit of boulder-clay and shifting sand civilization has built up a fascinating history. I am no geologist, but I would say that the Parbold Hills represent Lancashire's oldest coastline. Stand on these terminal heights at the edge of the Lancashire Plain, and if the power of imagination is yours you can see the glacial deposits of mud and drift pushing their way round the hills and into the shallow sea to form a new coastline where now stands Crosby, Ormskirk, Preston, and Garstang, with away to the south the islands of Halsall, Hilbre, West Kirby, and Wallasey. Geologists, indeed, tell us that the bedrock here lies from six to eighty feet below the glacial drift on an inclined plane. Boulder clay from the drift is made into bricks at Croston, Hesketh, Preston, and Blackpool, and the worn, ice-scratched and rounded stones have long been used for roads in the Fylde. Even in this age of cement and macadam, cobblestones can still be seen in village backwaters, in old houses, and even in the side streets of Preston.

The drift deposit lay confusedly across the former natural river drainage of the Pennine Hills to the sea. Water collected in the drift hollows, forming shallow lakes, many of them with areas as large as those we see in northern Lancashire, Cumberland, and Westmorland to-day. Vegetation grew in the water, spreading from edge to centre, until the compilation of decayed matter became peat, swelling and growing quickly under such favourable conditions to become a boggy morass, feared by travellers, invaders, and marching armies. On the slightly higher ridges of boulder clay which edged the bogs grew the trees which formed forest lines from Cumberland to North Wales. These became the ridgeways along which the earliest travellers in Lancashire set their course, and where the first settlers made their clearings and established our first villages of the Lancashire Plain.

Some nineteenth-century authors, seeking to understand how so much water came to lie behind the coastline, assert that at some time the sea must have inundated the land, and that the sea water, affecting the trees, caused them to rot and fall down into the marsh where they were found when the land was drained. They also suggest that the force of the inundation was so great that whole forests were flung to the ground, because the trees found lying in the ooze were all pointing to the east.

John Gerarde in *The Herball, or General Historie of Plantes* (1597) writes quaintly:

'I have seen these trees growing in Cheshire, Staffordshire, and Lancashire, where they grow in great plentie, as is reported, before Noah's Floud; but then being overturned and over-whelmed have lien since in the mosses and waterie moorish grounds very fresh and found untill this day . . . so full of a resinous substance, that they burne like a Torch or Linke, and the inhabitants of those counties do call it Fir-wood and Fire-wood unto this day.'

To which let us add this passage from Elizabethan William Harrison:

'People go unto this day into their fens and marshes with long spits, which they dash here and there up to the very crouge into the ground. In which practice (a thing commonly done in winter), if they happen to smite upon any fir trees which lie at their whole lengths, or other blocks, they note the place, and about harvest time (when the ground is at the driest) they come again and get them up . . . some of them foolishly say the same have lien there since Noah's flood.'

Chat Moss lay between the Glazebrook and Irwell rivers, and Trafford Moss between the Mersey and the Irwell. Between Red Brook and Mersey was Carrington Moss, and between Red Brook and Bollin was Warburton Moss. Glazebrook Moss continued along the middle Mersey, with Risley Moss and Woolston Moss to the west of Cadishead.

The River Ribble was likewise bordered by a moss which also extended down the coast from Penwortham to the River Alt near Liverpool. These mosses stretched, in fact, along the whole Lancashire coast into Furness wherever a low plain separated the mountains from the sea. Even Oliver Cromwell had to admit defeat by these natural conditions when he wrote after the battles of Preston and Wigan: '. . . and prosecuted them home to Warrington Town; where they possessed the bridge, which had a strong barricade and a work upon it, formerly made very defensive. . . . Considering the strength of the pass, and that I could not go over the River Mersey within ten miles of Warrington with the army, I gave him these terms . . .' And in the next century, when a messenger came from the north to report that the Jacobite forces were at

Lancaster the dismantling of the centre portion of Warrington Bridge was begun.

As Celia Fiennes journeyed through Lancashire she was puzzled by the height of the bridges over streams and rivers, since there was only shallow water beneath them. She was informed that after heavy rain the rivulets swelled to a great height and that then it was usual to go by boat from bridge to bridge—in fact that in winter it was more usual to travel in this manner than to go by foot or horse. One of these high bridges may be seen in Croston.

Those who make a study of such things tell us that the west coast of Lancashire has been sinking slowly for some four thousand years and give evidence of a change in levels of 60 feet in that period, so that a fairly true picture of Lancashire's coastline at the end of the glacial drift period can be constructed by following the 10-fathom line on the map.

The Mawson report on Amounderness for the Fylde Regional Town Planning Committee (1937) suggests that in the Fleet-wood-Stalmine area the sinking may be due to brine pumping from the local deposits, that sewage works' excavations at different points have reached underground water which is tidal, and that this percolation may be more common along this coast than is at present supposed. So it is not surprising to read of our inshore fishermen fouling their nets in submerged oak forests and bringing peat to the surface, and we become more credulous of the tales and legends we hear of the villages once on this coastline being swept into the sea in a single night of gale.

Now, for the first time, let us add the sand-dunes to our picture. All is not lost to the sea. In compensation a westerly wind blows the loose sand into drifts which become a defence against further erosion and are able to raise the level of the sand surface to seaward of them at a prodigious rate. A man must live with the sap and swirl of the tides on his doorstep to sense fully the beauty and the terrible destructiveness of sand. An excursion ticket to Southport will not show him the picture.

Going inland from the coast we see a geological pattern of sand, peat moss, triassic rocks (Burscough), coal measures (Wigan), and millstone grit (from Parbold to the Pennine massif). Any walk on the Pennine Hills will show you some rivulet collection of 'silver sand' that the youngster would like

to take home for his aquarium and his father for potting
chrysanthemums, but go higher, to the foot of the living rock,
and you will see the origin of the sand on Lancashire's shoreline.

Continual weathering has produced an enormous amount of
finely powdered millstone grit which the heavy moorland rains
wash gradually down to the rivers. The wear and tear of
movement in the mountain torrents produces an even finer
sand, until Mersey, Ribble, and their tributaries drop the
sediment on harbour bars. River dredges scoop it up to keep
the channels clear and unload it further out to sea. But
Lancashire's prevailing winds come from the south-west and
west, and as they drive behind the incoming tide on the shallow
land shelf below the sea's surface, the sand pours out of the sea
before the raging wind.

The unit of all this sand is a tiny grain of quartz, set free from
the living rock of Britain's largest mass of millstone grit.
Delivered from the sea again with its fellows it rushes before
the wind with a noise like steam escaping under pressure, and
uncannily climbs up the barrier of the sand-dunes. Before
your eyes the sand-dunes appear to be moving, like locusts over
a pasture. The roots of star-grass are bared as you watch,
yet it is only they which hold back any portion of this writhing,
climbing mass of sand. It is uncanny because you know it is
dead stuff, yet it moves upwards, fills hollows, spreads down the
leeward side of the dunes like quicksilver, moving like lava
over the grass and thyme that has grown in the protection of the
sand, and that now the sands destroy. There is a wild sym-
phony of storm wrack, a shrieking gale of wind, blowing out
of purple-black skies. Always, creeping nearer and nearer,
sounds the muffled thud of rollers on soft sand. At last they
crash among the dunes. At once every hollow is a bowl
of sizzling frothy-brown, animated scum. Thud-d-d. More
sand falls into the hollows. Soon, surely, the power of the sea
must sweep away the fragile sand.

But it is not so. Come the following morning to view the
damage! Nothing could be more beautiful or peaceful than
this warm sun in a cloudless sky. The sea has disappeared
almost, over the horizon. The dunes show no sign of damage,
even though their shape has vastly changed and men are digging
to clear the railway tracks and the road beyond.

That is all, but such action repeated over thousands of years has taken its toll and coloured the history of Lancashire, as we shall see. William Ashton in *The Battle of Land and Sea* states that records kept over thirty-five years in the late nineteenth century showed a gain of 9,090 acres, chiefly between Bootle and Southport, and gain is still in progress.

The sand is not all composed of millstone grit, although this comprises a very large percentage not common to other parts of the British coastline. There is also seaborne erosion from the Cheshire and neighbouring coasts and long-distance tidal-borne material, but as there is a larger water-drainage area on this coast than in any other similar coastal stretch in Great Britain, the results of denudation in the mountainous inland regions must account for the greater part of the sand. I have seen an estimate of the River Mersey deposit outside the bar as $11\frac{1}{2}$ million cubic yards every year. To this must be added the dumpings of the Mersey dredgers.

The wide stretches of coastal sand dry quickly in the sun, and very quickly begin to move before the wind. In 1742 an Act of Parliament, applying particularly to the problem of this coastline, made the uprooting of star-grass a criminal offence. While star-grass prevents the sand from blowing inland, it builds sand-dunes. William Ashton has noted the sand-dunes which have arisen on the Southport-Birkdale boundary since the building of the Birkdale promenade in 1885. In the following twenty-four years the sand grew 20–27 feet high on a maximum width of 190 yards, that is 8 yards per year or 800 yards every century. In two hundred years, therefore, the sand-dunes would be a mile in depth. As the Lancashire sand-dunes are $1-1\frac{1}{2}$ miles in depth Mr Ashton estimates that we can consider that two hundred and fifty years have gone to their formation, or in other words, that they date from the planting of star-grass.

While the west coast of Walney Island is being washed away at the rate of some three feet every year, the northern end is growing in sand. In the south a lighthouse built on the shore two hundred years ago is now well inland.

Churchtown, within Southport, was once by the sea and it is still said that Sugar Hillock received its name from a vessel wrecked here in 1565 with a cargo of sugar—to be exact on the site of 18 Sunny Road. But more significantly we find that

Devastation by sand; planting of star grass.   Formby

H. Milne

Meols Hall behind the village is built on sand-hills, that an old wooden landing-quay was found in delving by the drive gates, and that sea shells are found in St Cuthbert's churchyard. To-day there are an arterial road, a nineteenth-century growth of town, a twentieth-century housing estate, and a reach of sand to be traversed before the first lap of sea water can be found. William Ashton writes that Bankfield Road, in the same district, was once on the shore between Crossens and Churchtown.

In the particular case of Southport it must be borne in mind that the Ribble channel followed the coast hereabouts and that it was convex three hundred years ago and could take small boats until recent times. A member of the local yacht club who joined in 1919 told me that in those days the channel always bore water and their headquarters was on the lower stage of the pier over the water. The lifeboat was also stationed there, continually afloat. Then the channel dried up but reappeared, much shallower, and nearer the shore. This did not last long, and now the yacht club use an artificial marine lake with specially constructed boats.

When the Ribble Navigation built retaining walls, conducting the river water well out to sea, this coastline lost its supply of river water to the inshore channel which filled with sand. At the same time the Mersey Docks and Harbour Board have continually dumped in the sea sand from their dredgers, but this is carried back inland by wind and water to produce a concave shoreline which is still growing. For the first time in our history of seaside resorts, Southport has the opportunity and responsibility of preparing its future development on this gift of firm sand: may it tell a warning from the examples of irresponsible coastal architecture around Britain!

Further south, at Formby, the Church Mere has disappeared in the sand. In *The Transactions of the Historic Society of Lancashire and Cheshire* (1866) Mr Hulme gave a summary of the changes which led to this as follows: Firstly, the moss, shown on maps, 1588–1610; secondly, the building of the small town; thirdly, the encroaching sand which eventually buried everything, between 1750 and 1850; fourthly, a Mr Fresh laid soil on the sand and produced land suitable for cultivation; fifthly, the building of a suburb on the cultivated land (which is called Freshfield after the cultivation). And, as we shall see in detail

c

later, the Formby family, by careful use of tree plantations and star-grass, reclaimed the rest of the land lost to the sea in the eighteenth century.

But there remained always the responsibility of sudden treachery by the sea, which could destroy in a single storm what had taken centuries of patient human endeavour to create. The years of the most severe and damaging storms were 1532, 1553, 1555, 1720, 1771, 1796, 1833, 1863, 1896, and 1927.

Heralds Map 1565.

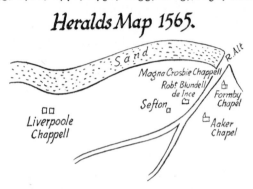

In 1553 the inhabitants of certain Furness coastal villages wrote in a petition of the 'great tempestuous rages, surges and high springes of the sea.' At that time the village of Fordebottle—which is mentioned in the Domesday survey—was washed away by the sea.

The 1833 incursion reflooded Marton Marsh and aroused the population of the new town of Fleetwood to undertake coastal protection. In 1863 these defences were swept away, as again in 1896. In 1927 Fleetwood lower town was flooded, with great damage to property and life. Even in November 1951 the concrete sea wall between Fleetwood and Rossall was broken for 60 feet in a gale and only a change in wind direction saved an evacuation of some of its inhabitants.

In Morecambe Bay, until recently, large areas have been alternately land and sea. The train journey from Carnforth over the sands will show you the scene. Tidal mudflats bear a close, fine turf of almost pure fescue. As the tide creeps in it quickly covers the grass for an hour or so, though neap tides may fall short. On the grass you will see sheep in excellent condition and men cutting turfs which are used all over the country for the best golf-courses, bowling-greens, and cricket pitches.

Now let us turn to the autobiography of William Stout, the Quaker grocer of Lancaster, 1665–1752 (as edited by J. Harland). 'My mother and father,' he writes in a quarto vellum-covered volume of coarse paper, 'were very industrious in their children's infancy, and in a few years had improved their estate to double what it was when they were married; the lands thereabout being much more valuable then, by the benefit of a large marsh or common, which maintained many thousand sheep; the marsh then extending westward from our house to Prestceare, and from Bare in the south, round about the Know End in Lindeth to Arnsid-well, except a narrow inlet for the tide in kear, but not sufficient to receive any boat or barque of burthen.   My father then could have kept 100 sheep all summer on that marsh, and about the seventh month yearly the high tides brought the sheep's dung and sea tangle to the side, which was gathered by the inhabitants;—every house at the sand's side knowing how far their liberties, for gathering, extended; and I remember ours and our then neighbour Thomas Yeates' liberties extended from the Pasture Lane yeat north, to our field called the Street South Gate, and from thence to the north end of Hest Strand, so far and Boulton liberties extended, belonged to Samuel Hutton's estate, about half or more of which was purchased by Samuel West, and the rest of it by my mother; so that if the marsh grow again, our proportion of the benefit of that should belong to our part of the estate, which was very considerable, made those estates about one-third more of value than now, when the marsh is washed away . . .   It was about 1677 . . . when the sea began to break into our marsh at the south end, next Bare, the River Kent then running very nigh Presceare on the west and south side, and came upon the marsh with a breast, five or six yards deep, and undermined the marsh some yards, so that when the tide came, it fell in many yards backwards, with the noise of a cannon, at least 10 or 15 yards in compass, and so deep as to the sold skears which in the memory of man had not been seen, but there were net stakes and poles at the bottom, which might be seven yards or more than the surface of the marsh; by which it was evident that the marsh had been gathered in about 100 years before that.   About this time all the marsh washed away from the south end of our bank to the Bare, which used to be pastured by Slyne and Hest, which used to summer many hundred sheep and some horses. . . . But for some years this breach was confined to the south of Priestsceare (Priest's Skear) and our bank, till the River Kent got about Priestsceare and then gradually broke away all the marsh ; and so our marsh washed away, there rose a marsh of some hundred acres at Winder Moor, at the south and west of Cartmel.'

Not far away is another area of marsh, from Humphrey Head to Cowpren Point which once formed part of the common land of Cartmel parish. It was enclosed in 1798 by James Stockdale of Carke Hall and a Mr Robinson of Ulverston. Nine years later they built an embankment three miles long and from 10 to 15 feet high, made of sea-sand covered with sods. It enclosed three hundred acres of land, which in three years had its farmhouses, barns, thorn hedges, and wind-break plantations, the reclaimed ground producing oats, wheat, and barley of superior quality.

In 1819 the embankment suffered from the tides but was reinforced. The River Leven, however, was changing its course and gradually undermining the sand-banks on which the embankment rested. As long as could be remembered the Leven channel had been on the Bardsea side of the Ulverston estuary. Now it came close inshore by Winder Low marsh and in a three-mile arc across the sands of Morecambe Bay it cut a new channel 20 feet deep. The incoming tide undermined the edges of the channel and the sand fell into the channel with a terrible roar. In two months it had washed away the embankment and flooded the reclaimed farmland. The one and a half miles of thirty-foot trees in the plantation fell into the water and showed only their heads. So quickly vanished thirty-eight fields, or two hundred acres of a model and prosperous estate!

The Lonely Plough, a novel by Constance Holme, uses a similar incident on this portion of coastline where the county of Lancashire is broken into two parts by a narrow neck of Westmorland coming down to the sea. There is constant tension on an embankment which may not be safe. 'Whether the full moon brought the fierce thrust of a heavy swell, or the west wind, riding a wracked sky, hurried the shock of racing billows, the bank held off the one and flung back the other, steadily throwing the tread of the tide to the further and higher side of the bay.   To-day with never a trickle of water at its base it looked like a mighty serpent on the uncovered sand winding its slow and writhing length lazily to the sea, purposeless, abnormal, monstrous in the unnatural light and leashed quiet. The sands themselves were dangerous—dangerous to walk and sad with their deep, shifting banks, unknown quicksands, and tidal bore.   The whole place had the terrible fascination of lurking ill, yet on all hands the farms lay peaceful and content, like trustful women sleeping in a tiger's cage.'

Further south, near Cockerham, stands the lonely chapter-house of Cockersand Abbey not a hundred yards from the crumbling cliffs which edge the sea.   In the grass lie the faint foundations of buildings which came almost as near to destruction by the sea as by the decrees of Henry VIII, and the monks who lived there have told us how they were 'daily exposed to perils and destruction by the sea.'   In the abbey's charters and lawsuits are place-names between North Meols and Formby of which no trace can be found to-day, names such as Argarmeols, Meandale, Romsdale, Anoldisdall, Sheephow, Winscarth-lithe, Melcaurehow, Atefield, Quitemeledrale, Alserhow, Birkedene, Ravenskils, Oddasargh, Scatherwolmer, and so on.

Of Argarmeles there is further evidence from Sir Henry Halsall, lord of the manor of Halsall, Birkdale, and Argarmeles who, when sued for king's rent in 1503, said that 'the said Argarmelys and all the lands and tenements in the same area and were at the decease of Hugh Halsall, and long before . . . within the hegh see and drowned and adnichilate with the sayd see, and oute off the lawgh water marke, and also oute of the bodye of the sayd Countye.'

As early as 1346 a Cockersand Abbey deed reads: '. . . Otto de Halsall for fourth part of one knight's fee in Argarmeles, which is now annihilate by the sea, and there is no habitation.' And in 1553, when Sir Henry Halsall's son was plaintiff, he produced evidence that there was a certain town in time past called Ayresdale, which said town, time out of mind, has been and still is overflowed with the sea, so that there remains no remembrance thereof.

The threat to other places was always present in the minds

of the inhabitants. A seventeenth-century commissioners' report on Stalmine said that 'certain Parishens and Tenants on an Iland complayn that thei oftyms have their freynes dye without Rights of the Churche, becaus thei be oftyms inclosed in with the see that no man come to them, and therefore thei desyre that where the Viccer doth fyne a Priest to syng at the Chapell within the said Iland every Sonday and Haliday that the said Priest might contynually abyde among them, and thei wold to thei Power, bere a ley towards his Salary if my Lady and the Viccar would bere some charge with them.'

Where now is the Isle of Hertye in the county of Lancaster, whose needy poor received a bequest of £10 in a will proved in London in 1387. West in his *Antiquities of Furness* mentions the ruins of a village visible in the middle of the eighteenth century at low water near Aldingham. To-day the village church is protected from the menace of the sea by a retaining wall and is all that remains of the village.

Perhaps these places disappeared in the great storm already mentioned, of December 1553, for it was at this time that the inhabitants of the Furness coast complained to the chancellor of the Duchy of Lancaster about 'great tempestuous rages, surges and high springes of the sea' which had surrounded them on 6th December, and that they had been submerged by sea and sand. Commissions were appointed by the queen and reported that the sea was continually flowing, and that no defence could be made against the rage thereof.

The coast of Fleetwood and Blackpool has always been subject to erosion. The Rossall peninsula has suffered severely. At Cleveleys the protective sea walls erected by Sir Peter Thomas Fleetwood have disappeared and the new defence line is constantly under surveillance by the local corporation while the higher cliff defences at Blackpool have been turned into promenade walks at various levels.

The rhythmic swirl of the tides carries the rock and sand which it has robbed from this area, particularly from the soft nose of the Blackpool cliffs, to build up, from South Shore to Lytham, those 'stanners' or shingle banks, on which Fairhaven and St Anne's promenades have been built, and indeed part of Lytham town. It has been estimated that a stanner completes itself in about a hundred years. To-day we see Lytham pier well out of the run of the channel tide, although when it was built its head foundations were in the waters. On such a continually changing coastline it is not surprising to learn from a pleading of 1532 that Kilgrymoles churchyard at Lytham 'was worn in-to the sea two or three miles,' and 'two miles of fair pasture had been worn into the sea.' Moreover there is a tradition in Lytham that the original church is buried beneath the sand, and that its bells are heard on Christmas Eve by people blessed with the mystic inner ear.

While Blackpool seeks to protect its friable (and amenable) cliffs with concrete bastions, thus reducing the stanner build-up on the more southerly coast where the tidal currents meet the Ribble flux, that river adds another problem to the Lytham-St Anne's area, which is similar to that of Southport in its relation to the River Mersey. Law Rawstorne, in his report on the state of Lancashire's agriculture in the nineteenth century, was able to say that 'the property near Lytham is in a fair way of being much increased in value by the works carried on in the River Ribble. The channel was formerly constantly shifting its course and in such different winding directions that it was extremely bad for navigation, and of great injury to the land adjoining it by the frequent inroad it made.' Rawstorne tells us that a Mr Stephenson at Edinburgh supervised the building of two parallel walls stretching from Preston quay down the river and out to sea with a hundred yards between them for a total distance of six miles. This construction gave a greater scouring action, and with the additional help of dredging operations vessels of considerable burthen could then reach Preston, while the sands were then collecting on each side to such a height that in a few years there was every prospect of a large tract of valuable land being reclaimed.

The writer could not have realized that this process would be carried to such an extent that vessels of 10,000 tons would be able to reach Preston docks, and that the continual dredging and consequent dumping of 3,000,000 tons of sand every year outside the bar would produce a sand build-up on the coastline north of the estuary which is a delight to children but a headache for a town council which depends upon the sea as a permanent attraction for visitors. Look at the Saxton (1577) and Speed (1611) maps of this coast and it will be seen that the land from South Shore, Blackpool, almost to Lytham did not then exist, and that St Anne's is built in what was a sea area four hundred years ago. That these early cartographers were right is borne out by the records of Lytham Priory and the Clifton family. Not only has ground been gained seaward, but the sand-dune accretion has produced a coastline higher than its hinterland. To-day there is a road from Scarisbrick into Southport across the one time undrained marshland. It provides a route by which to visit this portion of Lancashire coastline and to examine not only the growth of seaside towns but the constant battle which is being fought against wind and sand.

IV

THE BIRTH OF SOUTHPORT

NORTH MEOLS became Churchtown, and Churchtown becomes Southport. That may not be strictly correct but it illustrates the historical background of the modern town. Let us go back to A.D. 687, when St Cuthbert died on Lindisfarne. Some two hundred years later the Danes landed there and the monks fled, taking with them the remains of the saint. These remains were precious, for they were said to perform miracles. Their journey to sanctuary took seven years, and its course is marked by many halting-places where a church has arisen on a site dedicated to St Cuthbert. At last the monks came to Lytham and crossed the Ribble sands—a regular route until recent times—to rest at North Meols.

The Chapel of Mele is mentioned in William the Conqueror's time and from Domesday the name changed perceptibly into its present form (1113, Chapel of Meoles; 1189–99, Normoles; 1199–1216, Nortmelis; 1203, Northmelis; 1224, Melys; 1305, Northmeles; 1311, Mels; 1550, Northmeales; 1725, North Meales). And what else is a meol but the old Norse *melr* for a sand-dune? The meols of the Cheshire coast are called 'mels,' and of the Lancashire coasts 'meels.' North Meols came to be distinguished from South Meols, which was not so fortunate in its historical importance and therefore passes almost unnoticed.

In 1113 there was enough fishing in the district for one quarter to be granted to Evesham Abbey, and in 1224 Robert de Coudray granted the right of a market at Melys. This is one of many examples where trade and population followed the cross.

There was another 'Meols' in this district called Argarmeles and it appears in certain records such as that in which, at the turn of the thirteenth century, Robert Parre granted the manors of Halsall, Downholland, Argarmeles, and Birkdale to Gilbert

33

Halsall for life.   But Argarmeles has since been washed away by the action of the restless sea on an ever-changing coastline.

When the abbey estates were broken up by the Dissolution North Meols became a separate parish.   During the sixteenth-century Catholic persecutions the Hesketh family left their main residence at Aughton and came to Meols Hall.   The reason for this is plain when we realize that Aughton was on the high road running through Liverpool, Formby, Aughton, Ormskirk (skirting Martin Mere), and Rufford Hall, and that in those days travellers kept to the high road, particularly near Martin Mere 'which hath separated many a man and his mare,' as the old saying goes.   This move of the Hesketh family was in 1577, and only four years later Campion confessed on the torture rack that he had been at Meols Hall in 1580.   Even so Mrs Hesketh made no secret of her faith, and was eventually removed to the dreaded New Fleet at Manchester.

The eighteenth-century historian Peck wrote of the North Meols district in this period, or just a few years later, as 'this bank, a long, shelving and sandy flat. . . .   The beach is plain, open and level and at this time (18th century) is much used for sea bathing, though in Elizabeth's reign there was hardly a house to be seen. . . .   The coast, as it retires inland, consists of a chain of barren sand-hills, which are holden together by the sea-matweed, and were probably then used as a rabbit warren.'

We know from a study of racial movements, place-names, and surnames that the few inhabitants were of Viking descent. Local records give a picture of these people living in homes scattered around the church of St Cuthbert, where also stood the manor house as it does to-day, the lord's corn-mill, the inns, and where also the ancient market was held.   They passed their time and fed themselves by small-scale farming, fishing, shrimping, fowling, smuggling, and wrecking, with profitable sea journeys to the Isle of Man and Liverpool.   As long as the Earl of Derby maintained his island kingdom, and goods could be landed there duty free, it was a worthwhile port of call even for the later East India clippers before making Liverpool where duty became chargeable.   Small boats had then no difficulty in smuggling goods on the barren Lancashire and Scottish shores, much to the profit of all the local inhabitants from farm labourer to parson and lord of the manor.

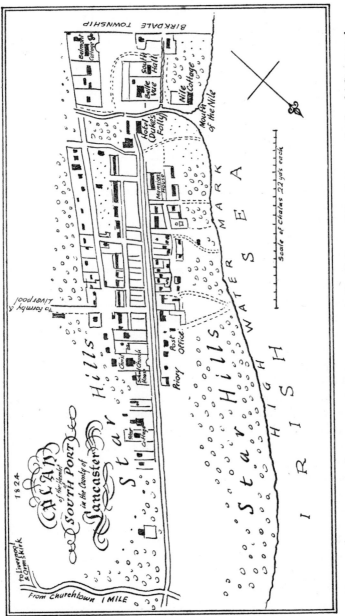

A simplification of a plan dated 1824 showing the early development of Southport on the Lords' Street and finishing at the Duke's Folly Hotel

At this time the parish registers show a growing number of births and deaths in the district between the Birkdale boundary and 'London,' known as South Hawes.   This is the area from which modern Southport grew, as will be seen when we come to consider the bathing era.   It is interesting as having a more probable bearing on the later naming of the new town of Southport than the tale we are told of the christening of the new port in Duke Sutton's hotel.   Nor would it appear from the evidence of these parish registers that the famous Duke Sutton, 'founder of modern Southport,' was the first inhabitant of this area as is sometimes supposed.   Both the local historians Banks and Bland remind us of the existence of at least one fisher-man called Peter Hodges who, in 1709, had a cottage where St Paul's Church now stands.   But this matter does not detract from the important part played by 'Duke' Sutton in the foun-dation of modern Southport.

The sea-bathing era was now to reach the Lancashire coast, and with it came the first events in the modern history of the town.   The sea-bathers who came to this area in the late eighteenth century found that the best beach for their purpose was two miles south of their accommodation at Churchtown. This fact provides the explanation for the development of Lord Street.   Between these two places the land to seaward was a saltmarsh with sand-dunes on the landward side, and a later development of sand-dunes up to the sea, thus leaving a long marshy valley between.   The fishermen of Churchtown took their visitors along this valley to the bathing place at South Hawes beach, and back again in the evening.   One of these men was called 'Duke' Sutton and he conceived the idea of building accommodation close to the beach.   So the Original Hotel, built in 1792 of driftwood, arose, and around it grew the first villas of the new South Port.

The Original Hotel was close to the Birkdale boundary and marked the limit of procurable building sites that way, so development was to the north and east, and as the marshy valley from Churchtown was not suitable for building, the new houses stood well back into the sand-hills.   Owing to its marshy state this road between the dunes had to be paved for the use of carts, and in this manner the lay-out of the future Lord Street, the pride of Southport, was produced.   It was called Lords' Street,

by the way, because it passed over ground owned by the two
lords of the manor, and the name was generally adopted and
corrupted to Lord Street around 1830.

The paved road ran on the westerly edge of the valley.
When the valley was drained the lords of the manor insisted that
the tenants of the houses on the easterly side, who had built in
the sand-hills, should continue their gardens across the valley to
the roadway.   It was this garden area that the corporation
bought and which has transformed an ordinary street into a
Parisian boulevard.   Shops took over the only remaining area
on this main thoroughfare, the westerly side, and the plan
remains to-day, the straight intersecting streets on either side of
Lord Street having been built to follow the straight boundaries
of those early house gardens.

There was another difference between the growth of Southport and that of other Lancashire bathing resorts.   The lords
of the manor were absentee landlords.   The Heskeths moved to
Rossall Hall in 1735, the Bold family lived near Warrington,
and the neighbouring Birkdale was owned by the Blundells of
Ince Blundell near Liverpool.   There was no 'society' enter-
tained at the local manor houses.   Instead, on the local
traditional Rushbearing Sunday which became known as 'Big
Bathing Sunday,' the miners of Wigan with their sweethearts
and wives donned their holiday finery and travelled in carts to
the seaside.   The construction of the Leeds–Liverpool canal in
1770 had brought the chief access route within four miles of the
place and so many more plebeians within easy reach of the
coast.   It was not difficult to arrange a variety of horse-drawn
transport to meet the barges and race to the sea.

Until 1792 the various parts of North Meols were Churchtown, Crossens, Banks, South Hawes, Hawes Side, Little
London, High and Lower Blowick, Hawes Houses, Trap Lane,
Snuttering Lane, and Birkdale.   The district around the
Original Hotel, which became known as South Port, lay between
Birkdale and London Street, a district which in 1809 had
thirty-eight and a hundred inhabitants.   The tale I have
referred to about the naming of the new district is supposed to
have originated in the Original Hotel where a Dr Barton
christened the place by breaking a bottle of champagne in true
naval fashion, and in naming the place South Port he may have

had in mind a combination of the district name of South Hawes and the creek in the shore opposite the hotel where bathers congregated, and which was the only anchorage in the district.

The early driftwood hotel was replaced later by a stone building, the Duke's Folly, which brought Duke Sutton into debt and Lancaster jail in 1803. He eventually died in poverty in Churchtown where he had been born, but his foresight had laid the foundations of a new town. The Duke's Folly was eventually let and renamed the South Port Hotel.

Duke Sutton was also a stone-mason, and those with a seeing eye can detect his work by his mark in St Cuthbert's graveyard. He earned the nickname 'Duke' because he was so fond of telling the story, time and time again, of how the Duke of York once passed through Churchtown on his way to Scotland. One day I went on pilgrimage to find the site of his Folly. The nearest approach to the actual site lies where Duke Street joins Lord Street at the end of the boulevard. At least his nickname is perpetuated in a street name. There, built into the concrete wall at the end of the gardens, are three stone tablets which tell their own story:

> These tablets formed part of a monument which stood from 1860–1912 about 24 yards west of this spot on the site of the Original Hotel or 'Duke's Folly.'

> The Year of our Lord 179(7).

> This house was built in memory of D. W. Sutton of North Meols who was the First Founder and Executor of South Port, which was call'd his Folly for many Years and it proved that his foresight was his Wisdom which should be remembered with gratitude by the Lords of this Manor and the Inhabitants of this Place also.

> This column was erected A.D. 1860 by the Improvement Commissioners as a tribute of respect to the late William Sutton, commonly known as the 'Old Duke,' the Founder of Southport. He was born at Churchtown, North Meols A.D. 1752, and died there May 22. 1840. He erected almost upon this spot A.D. 1792 the First House in what is now the flourishing Town of Southport, then a wilderness of sandhills, the house originally called 'Duke's

Folly' was afterwards known as the Original Hotel.
A Memorial Tablet, taken from its walls, has been
placed on the N.E. side of this column, and this
street has received the name of Duke Street in
remembrance of the old Duke.

Erected in present setting 1928

The first use which has been handed down to us of the new
name of Southport occurs in a lease granted to a Miss Bold in
1805 of a site 'adjoining in the east to enclosed land belonging
to Wm. Sutton called South Port.'   In 1808 an observer writes
of the place as 'the Meols' and in the following year as South
Port.   The parish register accepts the name in 1912 and maps
in 1818.

Meanwhile the lords of the manor became aware that they
would have to restrict excesses in order to preserve dignity and
amenities.   They were very particular as to who was granted
building sites near the beach.   Industrialism was prohibited
and the new cotton manufacture in particular.   Hand-loom
weaving alone was exempted as being in the nature of a craft.
It was introduced into Churchtown around 1800 by a Mr
Hooton of Patricroft.   In 1809 a return gives 159 inhabitants as
hand-loom weavers and 508 engaged in agriculture.   In 1842
the hand-loom weavers were suffering from the cotton famine,
and in the 1858 depression weaving disappeared altogether
from the district.

From the beginning of the nineteenth century we see from
year to year the gradual rise of the district as a centre of sea
bathing, and the deterioration of old customs and rural life,
although bull baiting continued at Churchtown and Crossens
until 1835 and at Easter they had a 'dorval'—dancing,
drinking, and eating fig pies—while Birkdale still continued the
Rushbearing.

Washing, as an act of cleanliness next to godliness, and
bathing for pleasure are new ideas, somehow linked with our
general advancement in civilization.   In the eighteenth
century, throughout the country, sea bathing received the
blessing of the doctors but only in the accepted idea of spas—
as a curative.   To drink the fluid as a *mineral* water had all the
attendant ritual of pill swallowing—twice a day before meals—

or whatever the formula.   Many a cart used to leave the sea-side, homeward bound with sea-bathing patients and with, hanging from the axle, a load of carefully corked bottles carrying the precious medicinal sea water.   There was a profitable trade in bottled sea water for supply to the sick who could not get to the seaside.   It appears, however, that the public soon sickened of drinking the wretched stuff and the next recommendation was to bathe in sea water as a cure for all ills.   Scarborough, Blackpool, and Brighthelmstone (later to be called Brighton) were among the places to attract the first bathers.

At the turn of the century the *Liverpool Courier* reported: 'Southport, North Meols, nine miles from Ormskirk, hitherto scarcely known, promises to become in a few years the most favoured spot of fashionable resort in the bathing season . . . and the mildness of the air, which is here remarkable, is unquestionably very congenial to weak and relaxed habits. . . . The tide flows so high up the bank that it is immaterial whether you go there at spring or ebb tides . . . fish is very plentiful, and the lovers of good eating may abundantly gratify their appetites with turbot, salmon, sole, oysters, shrimps, and sometimes with the john dory.'

Glazebrook, writing at the same period, puts the low-water mark at two miles' distance, but there were a pleasure boat and thirteen trawlers operating from the creek and from Crossens, while the lords of the manor were busily engaged in building a sea embankment.

They also drew up the following code of rules for bathers, much on the lines of those in other bathing resorts.

Rules and regulations to be observed on the shore of Southport.

1st. There shall be a vacant space of one hundred yards between the bathing ground appointed for ladies, and that appointed for gentlemen.

2nd. Any owner of a machine going out of the line opposite the front and back posts, to be fined five shillings each time he goes beyond the bounds.

3rd. Any pleasure boat, or other boat, coming within thirty yards of any machine, out of which any person or persons are bathing, the owner of such boat to be fined five shillings for every offence.

Croston

H. Milne

4th. If any fisherman throws out of his boat any entrails of fish, or any dead fish, or leaves them on the shore without burying them in the sand, to be fined five shillings for every offence.

5th. Any person or persons undressing on the beach, or in the hills, or crossing the shore naked, within one hundred yards from the two outside posts, will be dealt with as the law directs for the punishment of such offences.

6th. No person or persons on the charity will be allowed to bathe any where betwixt the two outside posts on pain of being dismissed.

7th. If any owner of a machine takes any person or persons on the charity within the two outside posts to bathe, he will be fined five shillings for every offence.

Richard Rimmer, pilot, and Richard Ball are appointed to see the above rules and regulations put in force, and to receive the fines. By order of the lords of the manor John Linaker and Samuel Maddock, stewards.

The story behind these regulations affords an amusing side-light on social manners. In all bathing places men, and some-times women, had at first sprung naked into the water. Then various 'modesty' bathing machines and umbrellas were invented. A Southport observer in 1823 'was shocked to perceive that at the height of the tide every machine was in motion, carrying indiscriminately occupants of either sex, at no unsociable distance from each other, not provided even with screens, which are common to all Continental bathing places, but left to the uninterrupted gaze of the passing crowd.' Miss Weeton declared in 1824 that the bathing here had become 'sadly exposing . . . and the modest complain much, gentle-men's and ladies' machines standing promiscuously in the water'. . . . The bustle, hurry, and confusion are most extremely disagreeable; the only comfort is that amongst such a crowd one may pass unnoticed perhaps.'

This kind of spectacle reached its height on the first Sunday after the 20th August—Big Bathing Sunday—when as many as 40,000 visitors arrived by any and every means of convey-ance—a day of donkey carts and gingerbreads and bathing machines. I remember part of a jingle of the time which goes something like this:

> . . . at noon behold a band
> Of lovely damsels troop along the sands,

D

With eager haste approach the water side,
To give a welcome to the flowing tide—
Y'clad in flannel dress of blue and red,
An oil case cap as covering for their head:
When like to the Naiads, as we read at school,
They quick descend and trouble well the pool;
Heedless of being seen by vulgar men,
They dash and splash, and dash and splash again . . .

The first breakwater was erected from the foot of Coronation Walk towards Birkdale in 1821.   During the August of that year lodgings were full to capacity and haylofts were let at a shilling per head for sleeping, only horse-cloths and straw being provided.   A temporary wooden theatre was erected as a first attempt to provide an alternative attraction to the sea.   This was the beginning of the period in which Southport was known for its 'sunsets, spices, sands, spinsters, and shrimps.'

In 1835 the first promenade was made.   The work was undertaken by a company formed by Peter Hesketh Fleetwood, who thereby made money through letting building sites on the foreshore.   Later another company extended the work northwards, but before this could be done, and as a reason for doing it, there had to be a clearance of the alarming growth of sand-dunes on the seaward side of Lord Street.   When the wind blew strongly the loose sand piled high against the houses, blocking out daylight from lower rooms and overwhelming small cottages so that they had to be abandoned.

Peter Hesketh Fleetwood was a lord of the manor, but he is best remembered as the creator of the town of Fleetwood, an enterprise which ruined him financially so that he had to sell his North Meols estate in 1842 and the Rossall estate in 1844.

As will be found in the study of the growth of any one of Lancashire's seaside towns, it was the advent of the railway which produced a mushroom growth.   What is interesting to observe is, that given the same factors for development, each town neverthleless developed a different character.

The railway came to Southport from Liverpool in 1850. The line from Manchester was not completed until 1855.   Until 1846 the area had had a rural character and was ruled by an ill-co-ordinated parish council, magistrates' bench, and manor court.   In that year a Board of Improvement Commissioners was elected and began the tasks of sewerage, paving, and lighting. The first effort of street lighting was the erection of thirty-four naphtha lamps. The railway arrived at an appropriate time, but it also brought a rather sour gentleman, the American consul at Liverpool, who happened to be a well-known and respected author—Nathaniel Hawthorne. His 'English Notebooks' show no love of the English scene. It can only be imagined that he was homesick for his native heath. Even so the picture he presents of Southport is interesting if only for providing a necessary balance to the laudatory remarks of other writers who extolled and exaggerated its virtues.

Nathaniel Hawthorne lived in Southport for ten months between 1856 and 1857. He came there to provide Mrs Hawthorne with sea air at this much-praised bathing town. He describes it thus:

'It is a large village, or rather more than a village, which seems to be almost entirely made up of lodging houses, and, at any rate, has been built up by the influx of summer visitors; a sandy soil, level, and laid out with well-paved streets, the principal of which are laid out with bazaars, markets, shops, hotels of various degrees, and a showy vivacity of aspect. There are a great many donkey carriages—large vehicles drawn by a pair of donkeys; bath-chairs with invalid ladies; refreshment rooms in great numbers—a place where everybody seems to be a transitory guest, nobody at home. The main street leads directly down to the seashore along which there is an elevated embankment, with a promenade on the top, and seats and the toll of a penny . . . people riding on donkeys, children digging with little wooden spades and donkey carriages far out on the sands—a pleasant and breezy drive.'

He notices the 'brown, weather-hardened donkey woman' and 'a Town Crier with a doleful tone,' organ grinders and their monkeys performing under windows, the wail of a Highland bagpipe 'squealing out a tangled skein of discord,' 'and a Highland maid who dances a hornpipe.' He notes the Punch and Judy shows, wandering minstrels, and military bands—'in a word, we have specimens of all manner of vagrancy that infests England.'

The new town was now growing quickly. In 1801 the population of the whole parish was 1,790. Sixty years later it was

15,947. It is interesting to compare figures with those for Blackpool:

1871, Blackpool: population 6,100, visitors 1,500 to 2000.

1871, Southport: population 18,076, visitors 8,000 to 10,000.

In 1880 the *Southport Visitor* claimed Southport as the third of watering-places in population statistics, the first two places being claimed by Brighton and Great Yarmouth. Blackpool's population figure did not outstrip Southport's until the present century.

Southport was able to attract some of the best nineteenth-century architects and engineers to achieve its development. J. Brunlees, for instance, had just completed the difficult task of building a railway across the quicksands of Morecambe Bay to Barrow, when he came to Southport to build a pier on sand by the selfsame method of sinking iron piles. To this day only South-end has a longer pier. In 1868 Paxton designed and created Hesketh Park out of an area of sand-hills. Go there to-day and the feat seems incredible. It was all part of Southport's undefined policy to create a garden city. The early steps may be plainly seen—the building of Duke Sutton's hotel and the beginning of Lord Street when the lords of the manor insisted on gardens down to the road; the creation of the Lord Street gardens, renowned in 1842, to replace individual efforts; the formation of the Boulevard Committee in 1864, on the inspiration of a local dentist, to ensure tree-lined streets. It was a 'garden city' long before the term came into general use, and it was the admiration of all visitors. The famous annual Southport flower show indicates what appears to me to have been a subconscious desire to supplement thus the rather dreary vista of miles and acres of sand without a fertile background for compensation and balance, and I am led to expect that any future development plans will transform many more acres of foreshore into gardens and lessen the bleak prospect of sands without sea.

Meanwhile I advise a visit to Ainsdale beach, while there is yet time, if you wish to see sand-dunes such as once faced Duke Sutton and the early pioneers. I can remember it before it was such a mecca as now for the week-ender, and when there was at least an acre of sand-dunes per person in which to change into a bathing suit (as it was then called) and afterwards to lie in the sun and listen to the birds in the sea matt grass, or watch the changing skies overhead, a glorious way of using a five-shilling day-excursion ticket to escape for a few hours from sooty industrialization.

Birkdale, by the action of its lord of the manor, remained undeveloped until the coming of the Liverpool–Southport railway in 1850, and then it became focused on Liverpool rather than to Southport. Its quietness and undisturbed natural beauty attracted the Manchester and Liverpool merchants who built their houses to well-designed plans. There had to be a fashionable bathing parade, for that was the custom of the age, so this was made by an extension of the Southport promenade and was called Rotten Row. There was no doubt that eventually Birkdale would be merged into the greater Southport, if only on a basis of developed amenities, and this indeed happened when Birkdale's sewage disposal into the sea threatened bathing.

Southport is now an attractive residential town, whether for retirement or as a dormitory for Manchester and Liverpool business men. Every evening the 'business men' trains rush from the cities to the coast. Every morning they reverse the direction. Those with less income take smaller and puffier trains to the country dormitory areas spread over the old Martin Mere area, such as Croston village. It is all part of the restless activity in which we live to-day and which we pay for in physical and nervous exhaustion.

Excursionists and holiday-makers came to Southport attracted by the sea and sands, but they all know mile-long Lord Street which, even in the rain, could well be a mile-long Parisian boulevard. Looked at through British eyes it has a continental atmosphere, proving that we can achieve the care-free yet dignified character if we try. Southport has tried. Even if what is seen to-day is the outcome of a certain combination of events, the last link in the chain, the corporation could easily have destroyed the work of the past and instituted a new phase. To have done so would have been disastrous, and one feels grateful that the temptation to be like other holiday resorts, putting the casual visitor's amusement requirements first, has been resisted.

The covered arcades to the shops, acres of glass and ornate Victorian ironwork, the long line of centre gardens where crowds can sit down and enjoy the green, sunflecked shade of the trees, the band, the large and gaily coloured umbrellas in open-air cafés, the setting for a war memorial, the gaiety of trees festooned with coloured fairy lamps in the evening, a ceaseless burr of traffic, including gay buses open to sun and air, a background curtain of well-designed buildings—this is the Lord Street we remember with pleasure when the holiday is over.

But there is another Southport that only a small minority know. It begins at Churchtown. When you find this place you will see an old world village, surrounded by the red rash of modern brick development, yet holding fast to ancient village traditions, the idea being fostered by a lord of the manor who protects property and tenants from new world intrusion. The old cottages remain thatched, their whitewashed walls sparkling in the sunlight. Blue-jerseyed fishermen sit on benches or tend their small plots, still remembering North Meols, Churchtown, and wrecks in the days when Southport was a young stripling rising from the sand-dunes.

If you talk to natives of this coastline, and even far inland, you may always learn of some local tradition, told to you firmly as gospel truth, that once upon a time the sea came to this spot. 'That's called Sugar Hillock,' said one old salt, puffing at his clay pipe and pointing to higher ground through the trees. 'A coaster ladened wi' sugar was wrecked theer. That's 'ow it wur named.'

Be that as it may, the words fit in with the continual variations of coastline in the days before embankments, and express the rooted idea that such things *could* happen. Indeed the forefathers of these blue-jerseyed men did build their wooden ships and moor them to a wooden wharf where now you see the entrance gates to Meols Hall.

Bull's-eye windows, Georgian bays, thatched roofs, and crudely bulging walls covered with whitewash—the eye appreciates the skip back down the centuries as one walks down the street to the church. I like the Georgian church towers of this coastline. Maybe there is not a great deal of visible history to be seen in most of them owing to rebuilding in the last two hundred years, but they have a homely quality. I like to think of Duke Sutton chiselling gravestones between the bathing seasons, and signing his handiwork with a skull and crossbones, and of Churchtown's fishermen going down to the sea with a glance at the old sundial in their church tower.

From one of the thatched cottages a middle-aged man happened to step on one occasion as I was looking that way. We went together into the wood at the edge of Meols Hall and entered into another world. Through the trees we saw the hall and a prize herd of Jersey cattle lying peacefully in the evening sunlight. Southport town seemed far away, although we both knew, as we leaned on the railing, gazing across the meadow, that behind the woods were lines of motor coaches taking home their loads of day-trippers. But they did not intrude upon this quiet backwater. As we smoked our pipes my acquaintance told me of his boyhood days when there was laughter of children in the woods. A tree which, rotten at the base, he remembered pushing over as a child still lay there before us, a mouldering memory of happy days he had spent climbing for pears. He told, too, tales of witches and spectres which had taken hold on his youthful credulity. Is there not a bloodstain on the stairway of Meols Hall which, no matter how it is scrubbed, never loses the mark? The laughter went from his voice and the kind light from his eye as he spoke of it. Is there not a certain grave in St Cuthbert's churchyard from which, if you went round it twenty times, a figure would rise from the dead? Good Lord, man, was it true!—how can we ever be sure when the most daring child would only make nineteen perambulations!

Of such things dreams are made, but there is a tenacity in legend and folklore which will not be gainsaid, even if the facts are doubted in this remarkable twentieth century of ours.

Now, as the sun has left the warm brick of Meols Hall and sunk below the level of the distant sea, I will take you to another Southport which is known only by the people of the moss. For this we have to walk eastwards along Brookside and behind Woodvale, away from the town and its six communicating roads, away from the street lamps and into the country beyond, where no light glimmers and the constantly moaning wind creates an eerie atmosphere. We have to keep to the

trackways because of the drainage ditches. In day-time the
heron and kingfisher may be seen hereabouts, the pheasant in
the copse, and the buzzard overhead. Mile after mile of eight-
foot wide ditch, full of water, is barrier enough to stop one's
progress if one leaves the track. The men who used to work
on the marsh had leaping poles to cross these ditches, but we
must be content with the trackway, keeping an eye on the
banks of white mist which hang above the watercourses.

Here you will be sure to recall Kipling's lines:

> Who hath heard the noises of the night . . .

This is a land of lost lakes—of White Otter Mere and Gettern
Mere. Even now a bittern calls eerily and the sound is drawn
out on the wind; a plover wails, and is answered by an echoing
sadness. There is a gurgle of water in the low ditch. You
are below sea level, walking where, not two hundred years ago,
a flood of rushy marsh water reflected the stars. Our generation may have forgotten this but the remaining wild life still
remembers. Let the pumps but cease to function and the water
level would surely rise again and the wild fowl nest once more
by the edge of the meres.

This is as close as I can take you to an appreciation of that
older Lancashire of marsh and mere. Only in the night hours
can one sense it, and it is too much for the average townsman.
Quickly he turns away to the comfortable gregariousness of
Lord Street, the coloured fairy lights, and the crash of brass and
timpani from the bandstand—to another dream world which
he can better understand.

Early one Sunday morning I had cycled in from Halsall
with the spring sun. The gay, bright-lighted Lord Street of the
night before was then a deserted mile. Waste paper lay forlorn
in the gutter; an old man walked slowly across the street to buy
a newspaper; a middle-aged woman strode under the trees,
having all dignity pulled out of her by two mastiffs straining at
the leash.

Nothing else.

The sun was shining gloriously but a strong wind from the
south-west made progress difficult as I cycled through Birkdale,
along a road lined with the mansions of successful business men.
To-morrow these men would be on the trains to Liverpool and

Manchester. Later to-day they would be enjoying the sunshine on the neighbouring golf-course, built on the miles of sand-dunes which hide the sea from the road. The road is more than a mile from the foreshore. This is the Argemeles area which was important enough to be rated for Danegeld, but dwindled in the thirteenth and fourteenth centuries before the action of sea and sand until it was considered lost.

Perhaps you have noticed along this coastal strip the constantly recurring 'hawes' and 'heys' of each village. The common land lying between the enclosures and the sea was termed 'hawes,' the hinterland moss, 'heys,' and beyond Ainsdale the first plantations appear which grow more profuse as they approach the Formby sand-hills.

Formby remembers the year 1739 for the gale which severed the last link between the old and the new. It is a familiar story of the Lancashire coastline. The sea sweeps away and destroys; the sand builds up and destroys.

The new church of St Peter was built at Freshfield in 1746, far enough inland to be safe from either sea or sand. Some of the stone-work was taken from the wreck of the sea on Formby Point, but the manner of building was Georgian—modern.

After the ravages of the sea, however, came the building up of the sand-dunes, fostered by the local Formby family, for Formby leases contained a clause concerning the planting of star-grass to bind the sand and stay its movement. On that land, so gradually reclaimed from the sea, we now have acres of dark pine woods, sunlit glades among deciduous trees, and undergrowth protecting rare flowering plants—a perfect bird sanctuary by the edge of the sea.

As the land came again the people built another church as close to the foundations of the old church as they could go. It was completed in 1856 and dedicated to St Luke. But there is no village clustering round its roots. It stands alone among the century-old trees. But the story might have been otherwise as we shall see.

The wanderer with an eye for the historical scene will not find it hard to imagine the place as it used to be when the monks of Burscough Abbey brought their grain this way to the ship in the creek, waiting to take it to the Pope in Italy in a time of famine; or to envisage the earls of Derby and their household troops tramping to the end of this road to take boat for their island kingdom of Man.

The decline of Formby as a port dates from around 1705 when the channel began to silt up. ('Port' is used in the old sense of creek or small inlet, these being so rare on a shallow, sandy coastline that any indent was used by boats.) Mr John Formby of Formby Hall, an authority on this area, records that there was a hamlet here in 1711 whose few inhabitants were fishermen and their families. A pier stood about six hundred yards north-west of St Luke's Church, and he remembers being told of troops embarking here for Scotland to quell the 1715 rebellion. It was between 1730 and 1740 that old Formby village was overwhelmed by the encroaching sand which had already silted up the channel.

On Bowen's map of 1720 is marked the only east-to-west road in this part of Lancashire, coming from Bolton (and further east) to Wigan and through Ormskirk to the port of Formby. It was easy for the Stanleys of Lathom to join this road and use the port for their journeys to the Isle of Man. And indeed we know that travellers from the east of the country on their way to Liverpool came this way, for it was the only road to avoid the moss. Eventually the sand-hills were tamed and turned into woodland so that the sea lapped the wooded shore, but further conversational reminiscences collected by Mr John Formby from the early nineteenth century knew nothing of any sand-hills at Formby nor of the way to Southport, which then ran over the present-day golf-links at Freshfield and on to the road along the shore.

A visitor to Formby Hall in the nineteenth century said: 'Why, Formby, you have the heather for your inheritance and the uppermost parts of the earth for your possession!' a remark which emphasizes the complete loneliness and isolation of this part of Lancashire until recent times. The hall and parsonage stood alone—the only habitations of the gentry in all that wide area of moss and sand, and the visitor had had to traverse the miles of sandy cart-tracks which separated the hall from the nearest paved road.

The life there was rustic and manorial. It was not even recognized by the post office, and all letters were dispatched and received by private mail once a week, being given for posting to the carter who went to town for provisions on Friday evenings and brought back for delivery on his return the following day. The three to four miles of sandy track joining this area to the paved road were heavy going, and the cart departed in the evening in order to make an early start on the highway and to cover the twenty miles to Liverpool and back the following day.

The dark-haired peasantry had been native to this land for generations. They moved with a heaving gait acquired on their sandy roads, and they paid an unquestioning allegiance to the hall, there being none to dispute it. They grew wheat, potatoes, and rye, for such a soil could never produce the grass crops to fatten cattle.

The sand lanes were wide enough to show three and four lines of cart-tracks, between which was a struggling green growth. They had hedgerows which served to trap a goodly portion of drifting sand, and in this they offered a marked contrast to the moss lanes, which travelled naked over the dark, peaty soil. In wet weather the sand lanes remained dry, but the moss lanes were often impassable under flowing water. The villagers cut the peat for fuel, but in summer when the lanes were dry the gentry had their annual supply of coal delivered. It came by canal barge to Burscough Bridge and was carted from there by the tenant farmers, as legally arranged in their leases. The first team of horses to arrive was decorated with ribbons, and when the last load was safely gathered in the men were taken to the laundry in Formby Hall, less for a wash than for a feed worthy of this gala occasion.

For a long time asparagus has been profitably cultivated here amid the pine woods and within sound of the sea. I remember how one Sunday morning a man wearing a cloth cap and Wellington boots emerged from the woodland on to the road near the church of St Luke, just as I was passing by. As we walked down the sun-flecked lane he fell to talking of the old days and of how his grandfather saw the bones and the skulls and the rottenness of graves burst open by the sea, and the crumbling of the church. But now, he said, he must go, for he had to ring the church bell, and he was late because he had been cutting asparagus. The church bell duly rang, and from the sunlit woods came the strains of the church organ and the voices of the tenants singing *Venite, exultemus domino*, while down the lane came the laughter and chatter of children, families from the poorer streets of Liverpool with their parcels of food, prams, and ginger pop, as they trudged the long road from the station to the sand-hills, where the Mersey ends and where still stands the deserted lifeboat house, last used in 1919 when the lifeboat was called the *Henrietta*.   Out to sea are the lines of channel buoys, and merchant ships sail into Liverpool on the tide.   Beyond the sea and the ships lie the long blue hills of North Wales, and everywhere shines a sparkling brilliant light.

Nathaniel Hawthorne dismissed the natural vegetation on this coast as 'coarse grass,' but it is naturally a sea reed or sedge, a specimen of its genus unique in this country which is specially cultivated because its far-stretching roots bind the loose sand and so protect the pasture and arable land from the drifts.

A hundred and fifty years ago there was only sand and sea from Formby lighthouse to Southport and a human being was a rare sight.   Rabbits played without interruption on the Bronc, and sand flowers spangled the dunes.   The *Manchester Guardian* reported at a later date that 'the ordinary traveller who journeys by the Lancashire and Yorkshire railway will be surprised at the poetry which mere sand-hills can inspire.'

Year by year the Formby family have won the ground between the church and the sea by planting first brushwood, then the pine woods, until the area has become a natural sanctuary of bird life and wild flowers.   Many unique speci-mens of the latter have been accredited to the sweepings brought here by the tide from grain ships berthing in Liverpool. There you will find, for instance, the *Epipactus dunensis*, or Helleborine, the Bee Orchid, the Pyramid Orchid, and Traveller's-joy; also perhaps the striped Natterjack Toad. Since 1914, however, the work has not been progressive, and in that time about a hundred yards round the point has been reclaimed by the sea.

In the churchyard are the stocks and a lead-covered oaken cross on which is a brass plate inscribed: 'This ancient market Cross and pedestal, removed from the original site on Formby Village Green, was re-erected here by Richard Formby Junior of Shorrocks Hill, Formby Point, A.D. 1879.'

One Richard Formby, an armour-bearer to Henry IV, was buried in York Minster. But when Mad Martin's great fire occurred there in 1840 the gravestone was cracked and broken, so it came to St Luke's Church, to be replaced in York Minster by a facsimile.

Woodland lanes serve mysterious lonely houses, hidden from sight, and as I walked along them scaring away the rabbits I wondered what the scene would have been now if the dreams of the Formby sisters of just over a hundred years ago had materialized. These ladies looked at nearby Southport, steadily expanding with the sea-bathing boom, and they looked again at Formby and saw the possibilities of a large, increasing commercial town on their land. They pictured the promenade along the Bronc and the rows of villas at Raven Meols. They thought of the church which might rise again in the deserted churchyard. The matter was the subject of mealtime discussion. The younger members of the family playfully denounced schemes which would invade their beautiful, unworldly sanctuary; the woodlands would be destroyed, the heronry disband, the rabbits and wild flowers disappear before the invasion. Eventually Mary Formby rebuilt the church, but that was all. Whether the family decided against the sale of their birthright, or other causes intervened, I know not. But the region of Christ's Croft has remained untouched by the concrete devastation of a holiday town.

> When all of England is aloste
> Where so safe as in Chryste's Crofte?
> Where do you think that Chryste's Crofte be
> But between Ribble and Mersey.

It is pleasant to cycle along the woodland tracks to Raven Meols. Although there is much modern building there these days an observant eye can piece together the old scene from the lie of the lanes and the thatched cottages sandwiched between modern semi-detached houses.

It is strange to think that the seashore was once hereabouts and that the lighthouse in the field when it was built was close to the coast.

The River Alt flows by the side of it and meanders through the loose sand as far as Blundellsands off Great Crosby. Maps drawn before 1700 show 'moss' from Altmouth to Churchtown (which you remember is now in Southport), but 'sand' below Altmouth in the other direction.   The reason for the change to the landscape we see to-day is that the sand from the Mersey took many centuries to cross the obstacle of the River Alt, for it had not only to cross it but to fill the estuary and completely cover it, but once this was accomplished it took only about two hundred and fifty years to build up the sand-dunes on the north of the Alt to their present dimensions.

Until the beginning of the eighteenth century the River Alt had a wide funnel-shaped mouth.   Even little more than a hundred years ago fishing-boats could manage to sail a mile or more upstream to reach the cottages.   Near the mouth stood the Grange, built by the monks of Cockersand Abbey about 1290 to store the grain gathered on their lands in this locality. Altmouth village (or Moorhouse) appeared on maps until 1789, after which date there is no record.   The village name, Ince Blundell (Blundell's Island), now so far inland, points significantly to the change, and as you walk southwards into Liverpool the low tides will show you the remains of a sub-merged forest smothered by the wet sand.

Coming to Waterloo by the coast you can see the retaining wall of Taylor's Bank revetment which controls the outgoing tide and helps to keep the Liverpool channel clear of sand.   It is still being extended out to sea.   A similar wall is built on the Burbo Bank on the other side of the Crosby channel.   Can it be possible that this work played such an important part in the changes of the adjacent coastline?

V

THE DRAINING OF MARTIN MERE

AS a route back to the main ridge from the Mersey crossing I would suggest the inclusion of Aughton, not, however, by way of the new arterial road with its dual carriage ways and cycle tracks, but by the old lanes.

During renovations of Aughton church an Anglo-Saxon cross and some Norman work were found, and a Norman doorway blocked by a later buttress is a feature of the south wall. Cromwell fought a battle on Aughton Moor, a fact which reminds us of the use of this ridge as an established road and that our English battles were always fought on lines of communication. The irregularity of Aughton church has its appeal. It has a gawky, unplanned look resulting from mixed period additions without any thought of the composite whole, but it is yet very pleasing in its lack of convention. The old stone-work has mellowed into a variety of yellow-browns and greys which, set against the trees and shafts of sunlight, must have provided a subject for many an artist.

Aughton should never be short of bell-ringers. The bell ropes come down into the church among the congregation, and surely many a boy who sits in his pew watching the rhythmic swing and pull must look forward to the day when he can take his place alongside Old Tom and Old Joe.

The churchwarden's accounts are, as usual, rewarding in a quiet way, for it is interesting to note that visiting parsons received a shilling, but killers of foxes were rewarded with half a crown. There is mention of 'Ale to the Gossips at the Christening' which reminds us that a gossip was originally a sponsor—'God-sib' (sib meaning kin) and through the christening ceremony the sponsors became 'akin in God.' The meaning of the word has degenerated from spiritual affinity to mere familiarity, and thus to trivial talk, or gossip.

In 1780 the constables were paid for repairing the ducking stool (1740). A sum was paid for the 'Bonefire' at the 'Church Style,' for Powder on Guy Fawkes Day and, in 1742, twelve shillings to the Window Peepers.

From the churchyard there is a ridge view over a large part of Lancashire and the mountains of Wales which is out of all proportion to the promise of the contour markings, underlining the place's importance as a route factor. The road then drops steeply and so up again on the further side of old Aughton Moss to Ormskirk, a town built solidly into its native sandstone.

The personal element in place-names in western Lancashire is stronger than anywhere else I know. 'The Church of Orm' marks on this ridgeway the nucleus of a main route settlement, which has developed into a market town for the district, fostered first by the many great landowners of the district, and secondly by becoming the centre of a large agricultural area that resulted from the draining of the surrounding marshes. One of the finest brasses in the country is to be found in the church. It is a representation of Henry de Scarisbrick who fought at Agincourt and was killed at the siege of Sens in 1420. The earls of Derby were originally buried at Burscough Priory close by, but after the Dissolution they brought their exhumed dead along the ridge road to Ormskirk to be buried in the Derby Chapel which they built there. The first Thomas Stanley, Earl of Derby, to be thus buried twice, was the man who picked up the crown of the fallen Richard III on Bosworth Field and placed it on the head of Henry, Earl of Richmond, and called him Henry VII, an incident that marked the end of the Wars of the Roses, installed the Tudors on the throne of England, and laid the foundation for the mixed fortunes of the Derby family. Later the earl married Henry's widowed mother, and Henry VII came to visit his mother and, of course, her husband. He got a royal welcome, marked by the erection of the first stone bridge over the River Mersey at Warrington, to facilitate the king's passage. It is strange to think that only a short time previously he had beheaded Earl Derby's brother.

The unusual feature of Ormskirk church is the juxtaposition of a spire and a tower. Two other churches in England have both spire and tower, but only Ormskirk has them side by side. The smaller steeple is the older, for the massive tower was built

Rufford Old Hall (National Trust)

after the Dissolution to receive the bells from Burscough Priory. It is pointed out that the masons' marks on the remaining priory stones and on this church tower are the same, a fact which probably solves the riddle of the whereabouts of some of the priory stone, for the actual site of the latter is almost bare.

You will be charmed by the narrow main street of Orm, the Georgian houses, the tiny courts seen through archways, and the view of the church seen across the water in the park, all growing old in a beautiful way.

Beyond, the road winds down from the top of the ridge to pursue a quiet way past Burscough and by the edge of Martin Mere to Rufford.

Robert FitzHenry, son of Siward and Lord of Lathom, endowed Burscough Priory about 1189 and gave it for the use of a group of Austin Canons. We cannot quote the whole of the foundation charter, but excerpts reveal that there are some interesting lost, or changed, names, roads, and fords: '. . . along the boundary of the land of Stephen the Bold unto Egacres between the high road of Wirplesmos and the stream of Egacres unto the boundary between Ormeschirche and Brackenes-thweit. . . . Scarth, Westheft, Scakeresdalehefd . . . and so by the brook unto the ford which leads from Alton to Urlton . . . and the whole underwood of Grittebei with the riddings which lie around it, to wit, the land of Robert the Carpenter. . . . I have also given them the whole town of Merton. . . . I have also given them the church of Orms-chirche, the church of Huton, and the church of Flixton . . . my mill of Lathum and all the mills of my demesne lands.' The canons also had the essential fishing rights on Martin Mere, which would be within two miles of the priory. In 1295 Henry de Lacy granted them a place called Ruddegate in return for looking after a leper from the de Lacy fee at Widnes: when he died another leper was to be admitted to replace him.

When the first Earl of Derby died his will (dated 28th July 1504) was read, beginning: 'I, Thomas Erle of Derb' and Lord Stanley, Lord of Man and Great Constable of England bequeth my body to be buryed in the middest of the Chapell in the North Ile of the Church of the Priory of Burscough in the Co. Lanc. . . .' The Scarisbrick family were also buried here, marking their interest in the priory by the erection of a line of

E

crosses between the hall and the priory.   Edward I granted the canons a weekly market at Ormskirk (28th April 1286) and an annual fair.   In 1534 there was a prior, five religious, and forty servants.   Speed's valuation gives the revenue as £129 1s. 10d. It cannot be counted among the great priories, but it had great importance on account of its position at the hub of a wheel of landed estates and its situation alongside an indispensable thoroughfare.   We know now that each hall was linked to the thoroughfare by its private drive, and its relation to the surrounding countryside no longer appears haphazard.

Burscough Priory, therefore, had a very favoured position and the town of Ormskirk developed as part of its local economy.   The same pattern was repeated all over England— local landowners' houses—endowed religious house—market town.   Here the pattern lasted three hundred and fifty years. The continued importance of Ormskirk as a market town is due to the growth of a local agricultural economy (dependent mainly on potato cultivation), which has benefited from the industrial expansion to the east and the proximity and growth of Liverpool.   The great families have had their changes of fortune and the story of the great Derby family can be read elsewhere.   Burscough Priory, however, disappeared with the Dissolution, having served the district and the road faithfully and uneventfully.   Now a railway runs close to its site, a few cottages stand close by the green mounds which mark its walls, hen pens are built in the chancel, and hens strut between the two remaining thirteenth-century piers which once supported the arch between the crossing and the north transept.

The road proceeds to Rufford, where the 'ford' was the outlet of the famous Martin Mere that once drained into the River Douglas close by.   But the mere also has drainage into the sea at Crossens, perhaps simultaneously, for it was once a large sheet of water in the flood season.   It is still receiving the drainage of Leyland Hundred, which in turn is fed from the Pennine Hills further east.   But before the era of the steam pumping engine the drainage settled into this bowl between the hills and the sea to form a swampy lake, which varied in size, but was frequently eighteen miles in circumference.   Where the first drains collect the first runlets partridge and coot find cover between the crops.   At Mereside is an old windmill and there the last remains of the moss show browny-green against the brilliant emerald of the surrounding cultivated ground where cattle feed luxuriously.

The route we are following runs on the eastern rim of the bowl. Only the slight ridgeway at this point has stayed the marsh from expanding eastwards. Celia Fiennes, in her journey over the Mersey, went through Prescot and east of Knowsley to Wigan where she joined the north road at the edge of the Pennine foot-hills. She gives her reasons: 'Not going through Ormskerk I avoided going by the famous Mer call'd Martin's Mer, that as the proverb sayes has parted many a man and his mare indeed; it being evening and not getting a Guide I was a little afraid to go that way it being very hazardous for Strangers to pass by it.'

If we look at the present-day map it will be seen that this ridge route, and the great halls around, are built upon lines of boulder clay which carry the tree line above the marsh— Scarisbrick, Shirdley Hill, Plex Moss, Hightown, and so into Cheshire. Swelling bogs pulled down some of the trees, for that there were trees growing at a lower level before the marsh expanded is obvious to-day. Once, when I was cycling over the area which was formerly Martin Mere, I saw a farmer tugging with a tractor, swearing and sweating at the terrible toughness of a giant bog oak which had worked its way to near the surface, and would have to be removed by dynamite if necessary before he could continue with the plough.

The mere took a hundred and fifty years to drain, from 1692 to 1849 when pumps were handling 17,000 gallons a minute to keep the land clear. To-day Martin Hall lies among the fertile fields, but there was a time when a light in an upstairs window guided boats across the water, and its isolated position provided a hiding-place for Roman Catholic priests and rebel alike, among them Robert Scarisbrick in the 1715 rebellion.

Leland described the mere as four miles in length and three miles in breadth and the greatest mere in Lancashire. It remained a marshy lake until the stimulus provided by the necessity of feeding the growing industrial population of south-east Lancashire and the port of Liverpool had made local land-owners turn their ploughs into every possible portion of their estates to take advantage of the rich harvest at their door.

Then the high price of wheat caused by the Napoleonic wars, which cut off European imports, gave Parliament the opportunity to foster home production as a precautionary measure, and foreign imports of corn were forbidden as long as English wheat did not exceed eighty shillings a quarter.

This was the climax of a growing attention to agriculture which necessitated a preliminary drive to drain the land.   In Lancashire the meres, lakes, and marshes gradually disappeared as the land drainers got to work.   The most notable attempt to drain the mere was made in 1781 by Mr Thomas Eccleston of Scarisbrick Hall (a noted agriculturist of his day).   In the *Transactions of the Society of Arts, Manufacture and Commerce*, 1786, he wrote: 'Martin Meer was formerly a large pool or lake of fresh water of an irregular form, surrounded chiefly by mosses and boggy land, containing near 1717 acres, of 8 yards to the pole, which is the customary measurement of the neighbourhood (abt. 3,632 statute acres). . . .

'Abt the year 1692 Mr. Fleetwood of Bank Hall proposed to the other proprietors to drain Martin Meer on condition that a lease (for the whole) for three lives and thirty one years should be granted him, which they agreed to.'

Fleetwood planned for an outlet into the sea at the mouth of the River Ribble.   Previously the mere had drained into the River Douglas on the east side when even the mere waters were raised above their usual height by land floods.   The intermediate ground between Martin Mere and the River Douglas, lying considerably higher than the mere, occasioned stagnation and kept it full.   A canal was made 24 feet wide and lower than the mere, from the Ribble mouth through an embanked salt-marsh, and then through a bog in North Meols, about $1\frac{1}{2}$ miles in length.   To prevent sea rushing up the canal and overflowing the mere, which lies 10 feet lower than high-water mark of the spring tides, Fleetwood erected a pair of flood-gates which shut when the sea water rose higher than the canal.   But the drainage ran into loose sand in the channel and in a few years drifting sand choked the passage.   Then the spring tides brought mud and left it as sediment at the sluice-gates, so that the whole effort was wasted and the mere returned to its former state.

In 1714 Mr Fleetwood's managers raised the flood-gate sill

20 inches. This kept them free of obstructions for a little longer, but a great deal of fall was lost with the result that the pasture previously gained was seldom free of water. Later they erected new flood-gates further out in the channel and this was more successful. Mr Fleetwood's lease expired in 1750. The flood-gates were washed down in 1755 but were re-erected by their proprietors. Owing, however, to inattention to sluice cleaning, and to the fact that the flood-gates were still liable to become choked by mud, the mere continued in no better condition.

'In the year 1778,' writes Eccleston, 'I settled here; and as the most extensive and valuable wear of the Meer belonged to this estate, I had the levels taken from low-water mark, and finding a considerable fall, I had recourse to Mr Gilbert of Worsley (who had judiciously planned and happily executed the astonishing work of his Grace the Duke of Bridgewater). To his friendship and abilities I am indebted for the success of the drainage. . . .'

In the new plan there were three pairs of flood-gates in the main sluice—the sea-gates, the flushing-gates immediately behind them and opening contrariwise, and the stop-gates half a mile nearer the mere as a safety measure. In dry seasons the tide was allowed up to the stop-gates and at high water the flushing-gates were closed to keep the sea water in.

'All these three several gates have four paddles at the bottom, three feet in length, and two feet in depth, which are drawn up by screws to flush away any obstacle that may chance to impede their working. At low water the paddles of the flushing-gates are drawn up, and the retained sea water rushes out with so much violence that the sluice to low water is in a very short time cleansed from every obstruction, sand, mud, etc., that may have been brought up by the tide.'

Mr Gilbert also lowered the sill of the flood-gates 5 inches and advanced them 200 yards nearer to the outfall upon the open marsh, protecting them by large and strong banks. The greater outlet of water was in the proportion of 162 feet to 56 feet. At the same time the fall of the sluice was altered to $1\frac{1}{2}$ feet in every foot, which, in some places, made cuttings 20 feet deep.

In April 1783 the level was carried right up to the mere, then flooded higher than it had been for several years.   In five days the head of the water had been drained off.   Then the sluice was deepened nearly to sea level through the lowest part of the mere, making it five miles in length.   A hundred miles of ditches were then dug, by means of a draining or guttering plough, drawn by eight, sometimes ten, horses at the rate of eight miles per day.   In 1784 a few acres were ploughed and yielded spring corn and pasture.   Thereafter, land which had previously let at 4s. per acre yielded barley at £11 17s. 6d., and land which had brought no price at all yielded oats at £10 17s. 6d. per acre.   From lands which had given only poor pasture in the driest summers Eccleston raised Scotch cattle which fattened better than any on the best grazing ground in the district.

Mr Eccleston died in 1809.   His flood-gates stood until 1813 when the outer sea-gates and the flushing-gates were swept away by an exceptional tide.   Fortunately the stop-gates held. His son, Thomas of Scarisbrick, employed Mr Morris, the engineer and dock builder, who substituted for the flood-gates in the Ribble channel cast-iron cylinders with valve lids which, however, sometimes became choked with sand.   There remained also the difficulty of the occasional overflowing of the River Douglas with bursting of the banks.

In 1849 and 1850 Sir Thomas D. Hesketh of Rufford drained his portion of the mere by constructing a drainage reservoir into which the water flowed, and by using a steam-engine to relay the water from the reservoir to the sluice, and so into the river at Crossens, he was able to drain it effectually.

Few strangers go down the long, straight, and stony roads between the parallel fields of Martin Mere.   The farmers who dwell there, spread out as on the blueprint of a pre-planned area, live a life apart from the crowds who travel the busy roads around it.

If you go that way it is well to remember that you cannot take short cuts.   I learned this to my cost a long time ago, when I found that my lane ended at a drain too wide to jump and I longed for the stilts which were once used by the men of the mere to help them on their way.   Instead I was faced by a long detour until I came upon a recognized road of entry.

There is nothing on the mere but farms—no churches or

Sunday schools, no cinemas or inns, no clustering villages. All these are to be found on the rim of the mere. It is said, by the way, that the local surname of Rimmer in Southport (where it is as prolific as Smith in the rest of England) comes from the people who used to live on the rim of the mere.

It was on a Sunday that I once made a call upon one of these farming families. The farmhouse had a stone floor in the one living-room, in which a piped water supply was just being laid for the first time. The boys were being washed and changed for Sunday school. Father followed suit, then took them in the car to Burscough Lane where he waited until the session was over to bring them back again. The date was July and his wife had only been to town three times that year. 'Why go to town?' she said. The butcher called once every week with the meat; hams hung from the ceiling hooks, geese and turkey fattened in the orchard, and the land supplied everything else. She was the third generation of her family to live on the mere, for her grandfather came on to the land when it was being ploughed for the first time and saw the bricks carted for the farmhouse in which we were then sitting.

Newcomers to the mere do not let it absorb them so easily, but then mere life has no traditions as yet, and no lusty pastimes, so that the newcomers pine for the amenities of life. They can hardly bear to think that they are only a few miles from Southport and yet might as well be living in the Arizona desert!

Every year the mere farmers watch the February rain literally 'fill dike,' and follow the annual round of potatoes, oats, wheat, to be garnered from the richest black earth in England. The dikes are of two kinds. Water drainage from Burscough and Ormskirk hinterland flows by gravitation from a higher level than that of the dikes which carry the water from below sea level, and which is constantly pumped to Crossens on the coast and goes into the sea. The River Crossens Drainage Board charge a rate to cover the cost of this necessary labour.

The flatness of the area is relieved by tree wind-breaks. These covers are on sandy outcrops of poorer soil and are very necessary as the strong dry winds of spring are apt to move the top soil unless countered.

The presence of the marshlands, and the long years before

there came a new challenge with the machine age in industry, had left Lancashire far behind the rest of England in rural economy.   R. W. Dickson in *A General View of the Agriculture of Lancashire* (1815) wrote that 'this county has hitherto made but little progress in the introduction of new implements, or the improvement of such as have long been in use, except in the single instance of the thrashing machine.   Except the old square harrow I met with no tool of adequate power for breaking down, cleaning, and pulverizing the soil; nothing of the nature of a scarifier; scuffler, cultivator, or horse hoe, on which so much depends in modern tillage.'

He found moss ploughs, used for cultivating the newly drained mosslands, drawn by two horses wearing wooden pattens of a special type which prevented the animals from sinking in the soft, spongy bottoms of the furrows.   And when newly drained moss was burnt before tillage he saw the use of a collecting harrow for raising the pared surface materials into small heaps.

Yet he agreed that, with the exception of London, he had found no town better served with roots and vegetables than Liverpool was from her hinterland, and he writes: 'There are always some reasons for distinguished superiority; and it has been said that the French neutrals, who were brought over from Canada in the war of 1756, and who resided some years in Liverpool, required so many vegetables in their soups, etc., as to raise the market price of these articles, which excited a spirit of growing greater quantities than had before been usually raised. As a seaport the quantities of cabbage and other vegetables taken out for the use of shipping; the quantities of dried herbs carried to Africa; and onions exported may act as stimulatives.'

The district north of Liverpool has long been famous for its asparagus, and the best gooseberries had their origin in Lancashire.   This fruit, however, achieved its fame in the manufacturing area, where the work-people cultivated allotments and held competitions at which the gooseberry received special consideration.

Mr Dickson thought it unfortunate that orchards were not plentiful, 'as cider, with the assistance of honey, might be made into a vinous liquor, as strong and as palatable as Madeira. The following is reckoned the best receipt for making it.

'Take new cyder from the press, mix it with honey till it bears an egg, boil it gently for 15 minutes, but not in an iron pot; take off the scum as it rises, let it cool, then barrel it without filling the vessel too full; bottle it off in March.   In 6 weeks afterwards it will be ripe for use and strong as Madeira.   The longer it is kept afterwards the better.'

He could not hold out much hope for an improvement in Lancashire's agriculture for the following reasons: the competition of high wages for labour from the growing industrialization; short-term leases which did not give the farmer confidence to expend on improvements; farm buildings outmoded and badly planned; few green crops raised for soil improvement; stock not well selected; land not kept clean, dry, or well ploughed, and not enough attention to draining.

Jonathan Binns in *Notes on the Agriculture of Lancashire* (1851) deplored the practice of marling, as it made the ground stiff with the clay left behind.   Moreover it left innumerable pits in the fields which filled with water and were obstructions to ploughing.   Even he had to add that the land north of Liverpool was as productive as any district of the same extent in England, and that on Saturdays 1,500–2,000 carts laden with hay, straw, potatoes, turnips, onions, and other vegetables, milk, pork, and butter, passed through one toll-gate alone on their way to Liverpool market.

The canal was also used as a means of reaching both the Manchester and the Liverpool markets.   Binns reported the nursery grounds for trees and shrubs from Formby and Scarisbrick to Burscough as the most extensive in England, and their products were sent all over the country and to America.   And it was in this area, we believe, that the potato was first grown commercially, for on its introduction by Sir Water Raleigh it was but 'a curious exotic in the gardens of the Nobility.'

John Holt, who published his *General View of the Agriculture of the County of Lancaster* in 1795, asked: 'Why should a farmer near Manchester raise crops when he can get £6 for a summer's grass for horses which worked the carding engines, or £12 15s. for hay and after-grass to feed them?'

The soil was capable of producing every vegetable and grain in perfection and abundance, yet, in general, beans and peas were still sown broadcast by hand and never hoed, cabbages never grown as an arable crop, vetches only made into hay, and oats were sown perpetually on the same land, to its ruination. The poor people of the manufacturing towns seldom if ever tasted wheat, yet they were surrounded by wheat lands as good as any in the country.   There were a few gentry who succeeded in good husbandry and introduced the latest methods and tools on their lands, but the shortage of agricultural labourers was largely responsible for the generally deplorable state of agriculture.   As one writer of the times puts it : 'Who will work for 1s. 6d. or 2s. a day at a ditch when he can get 3s. 6d. or 5s. a day in a cotton work, and be drunk four days out of seven?'

Above all the countryman was incensed by the poor rates which he had to pay.   When winter came many industrial workers were unemployed and had to be supported by the parish rates.   The cotton worker, when sick or too old, was supported by taxes levied upon agriculture.   As we know, workers (many of them Irishmen) and vagrants in their many thousands had flocked to Lancashire's factories, placing a heavy burden on the sparse population of the countryside.   And the country people were not slow to see the quick rise in vice and disease among the crowded and ill-assorted industrial population.

Another point of view on the poor quality of Lancashire farming is given by Law Rawstorne in *Some Remarks on Lancashire Farming* (1833).   He noted that when the weaving of cloth was making its highest price it was introduced into farmhouses, and all other considerations gave way to it.   A good hand-loom weaver would then earn his 30s. a week or even more ; he would perhaps work one-half of the week and drink during the remainder.   The farms became subdivided, cottages were added and shops opened so that as many families as possible could be housed at the enormous rents they were able to pay from the profits of hand-loom weaving.

Wheat was selling at 120s. a quarter, owing to the Napoleonic wars, and the best farmland was sacrificed to short-term high returns.   The prices, however, fell rapidly with the return of peace.   Landlords would not reduce their rents, tenants could neither pay nor give to the land what it required, and so it was further impoverished until its fertility was exhausted.

Whatever the particular reason may be for the lack of progress in any one area the fact remains that hard-working landlords who successfully drained the marshlands (such as Martin Mere) produced the best crop, and found that their expense and trouble were well worth while, for the soil was always rich enough to produce crops of first-class quality, as may be seen on Chat Moss in the south to Furness in the north of the county.

On the main road from Burscough to Rufford there remains to-day the significant place-name 'Causeway End.' From here the road approaches the old ford which was once the outlet for Martin Mere and which names the village and the hall. There are two Rufford halls by the roadside. The mid-eighteenth-century hall on the west of the road, but hidden from sight by parklands, was much enlarged in 1798–9 when the Hesketh family, lords of the manor, abandoned the old hall on the east of the road. The latter is now National Trust property and worthy of a visit if only to see the Great Hall (fifteenth century) and the unique screen. There is a fine hammer beam roof and much richly carved timber work.

But this is not all. The curator, Mr Philip Ashcroft, must be your guide. As a local historian he is thorough and accurate. One result of his work is the development of a local folk museum in the hall, which does more than mere words can to convey what the life of these marshland villages was like through the years.

VI

CAPITAL CROSTON TO HESKETH DIKES

THE mosslands on the east of the road we have followed lead to the hill lands of the willow workers of Mawdesley. North of these, across the River Douglas and on the River Yarrow, is the mossland village of Croston. Its approach roads show traces of their origins in marsh and forest in isolated patches, the roads being raised above the surrounding land in some places. The village is dominated by the large, square tower of the church, and behind it, painted a brilliant white, is the immense rectory, the largest I have seen. Church Street, with the steps of the ancient market cross still in position, makes a perfect approach to the north doorway of the church. I remember that as I arrived one day a wedding party was coming out, laughing and shaking confetti from clothes and hair. I crossed the single-span bridge, of pack-horse type but wide enough for modern light traffic and still in use. I was looking for a good viewpoint from which to photograph the church, but instead I found a congenial Crostonian just leaving his allotment with a basket full of eggs under his arm. I asked him what people of Croston do for a living.

'Except for them at t' mill, the two brickworks, an' t' railway they go out to work,' he replied. 'There's early morning buses and trains to Preston, Liverpool, Southport, Leyland, Euxton, Chorley, and such places.'

He was himself a motor driver. The one weaving-mill at the far end of the village was extending its plant but could not find enough weavers, he said. Some people were evacuated to Croston during the war and did not want to go back to the cities. With cars, radio, and television they were in contact with outside life and found the village giving the peace they had never known in towns.

68

Two young lads on tricycles attached themselves to us and asked to have their photographs taken.

'Get away wi' ye,' said the man. 'There's enough photographing for ye on Coffee Day.'

'What is Coffee Day?'

'That's our annual church procession and field-day. 'Course, Ah'm a stranger here. Ah cum from t' next village, Bretherton, and Ah've only lived here thirty year, but it's never rained to stop Coffee Day in that time. There's a fair hired for t' day on t' rectory field and t' kids here ride on t' bobby horses. Then a couple o' brass bands play in th' evening. The previous rector used to ring a bell at a quarter-past nine to clear us out.'

'What do you do in your spare time?' I asked.

'Everybody 'as an allotment, and there's a cinema. It's over a shop up t' road. Used to be a dance hall but now they run twice nightly and seem to make a go of it.'

Then he left me and went away to see what kind of football match was on the radio.

The crocuses under the trees had extinguished their blooms and their places had been taken by a host of daffodils braving the cold wind. This is a peaceful village. I strolled under an archway through the school, which was a seventeenth-century benefaction, to the foot of the great west tower of the church. Inside this late Perpendicular building the sunlight was lighting up the stone-work. Restoration may have destroyed much of its interest for the antiquarian but not for those who search for beauty in old stone, or for one of the little boys who was still with me and seemed surprised that I could not hear the big bell where I lived, for it told everybody to go to church.

Croston, and all the district from Penwortham, was isolated until the seventeenth century. That is a fact hard to realize under modern conditions. The marshes and peat moss then still covered the ground, a geographical fact which underlies the individuality of the district and makes it distinct from the rest of south-east Lancashire. The large numbers of intersecting hedges, dikes, and enclosures affected military actions of the Civil War, and all travellers commented on the undrained ground and the lack of bridges.

Streynsham Master, rector of Croston from 1798 to 1864, was known as 'King Croston.' He founded one of the earliest savings banks in the country (1818) but is remembered also for his winter advice to the villagers before the floods came: 'Clay up the front door and put the pigs in the house.'

This village shows all the outward aspects not only of having been the parish centre for a large surrounding area, but also of having possessed an urban district council, and petty sessions were held at the Grapes Inn where cells for prisoners were situated. In fact, an examination of records of separations from old Croston parish will show what a large area it used to serve amid the marshes. Hoole broke away in 1642, Rufford in 1793, Chorley in 1793, Hesketh-cum-Becconsall in 1821, Tarleton in 1821, Bretherton in 1835, Mawdesley and Bispham in 1835.

Wakes week was the annual holiday, when a fair came to town and filled up all spare places in the winding street. Every one of the ten inns sold the local speciality, Wakes cake, and there was a great flow of ale, and dancing in the inns and streets. Twice a year, too, there were cattle auction fairs, which again filled the town and the inns, these being features of plain life which were repeated in all the main villages.

An old lady was standing outside the quaint shop called 'Yorkshire House,' a relic of the nineteenth century, as I came out of the church. She wanted to cross the road but two motor-coaches swung by and made her pause. I offered my hand and as we slowly walked over she shook her head wistfully. 'Ah suppose we were just as mad when we had three pennorth to Hell,' she said.

'I beg your pardon?' I said.

'Hey, lad, tha' doesn't remember them horse charabanc trips to Mawdesley on a Saturday neet, dosta? We went down to t' Black Bull theer. Allus known as "Hell" at Mawdesley. 'Thank thi for tha kindness, lad.'

But I *did* know about the old 'Hell poker' they kept by the fireside at the Black Bull at Mawdesley, even now that the horse charabanc has been replaced by the motor-coach on the same pleasures bent.

At the far end of the village, on a bend in the river, is an old corn-mill which still belongs to the de Trafford family who live across the road. It had all the beauty of domestic hand-made brick, and although burnt and rebuilt several times it was still grinding by water power until 19th June 1951 when the main shaft broke; it is now converted to modern machinery and power.

Two and a half miles from Rufford Old Hall along the Preston road there is a secondary lane on the left, leading to Hesketh Bank, which is our route to the north. But before leaving the Preston road it is worth while proceeding a little further to see old Tarleton church by the roadside. Built in 1719 it is now standing locked and empty with a box on the door inviting subscriptions for the upkeep of the fabric and grave-yard. The wooden forms and high box pews can be seen through some of the broken windows, but the chief interest lies in the picturesque exterior. The church is very small, built of old red brick with a stone tower at the west end no larger than a fair-sized domestic chimney, and crowned with a four-columned Georgian dome. (There is a similar design at Euxton but not so elaborate.)

As we follow the secondary road to Hesketh Bank along the edge of the ridge it soon becomes apparent that the area has been sold to ribbon development—to small holders, retired people, and those who merely sleep in the country—without any coherent building plan. By the roadside is the new church of Hesketh-and-Becconsall, built in 1926. The vicar was in the church when I opened the door. He told me that the Hesketh family had given the tower, which bears the letter H in a crest. It is crowned with a weather-vane—a golden dolphin—a reminder of the local trade of fishing, and it is interesting to note that this superstitious symbol of good fortune should have been accepted by the church. The Hesketh family no longer live in Lancashire but their name occurs frequently, for they were large landowners, and men who played a practical part in local developments. The vicar waved his arms to the four points of the compass. 'They sold all this land for £3,000,' he said.

Old Becconsall church lies off the road and down the ridge close by the ancient crossing of the River Astland or Douglas. Like Tarleton church it is closed and you are invited to subscribe to the work of preservation which has so far included the fixing of frosted glass windows so that you cannot see inside.

I had asked a man on Hesketh Lane where to find the church.

He directed me down a side lane to the old ferry. 'You'll see it right ahead of you, a barn of a place.' He looked round, then added : 'But don't say that to just anyone you meet. They think a lot about the old church in these parts.'

It is a plain enough building—just four walls of red brick, probably mid eighteenth century, but it has a lovely setting, being surrounded by trees and standing on the edge of the escarpment, which drops suddenly behind the church to the river channel and the broad flats of the marsh. Beyond is the Fylde, and nothing interrupts the view to the far away smoothly rolling Pennine Hills. The village name (1208, Bekaneshon) suggests O.E. 'beacres hoh'—'the hill of the beacon'—which would be a guide for travellers crossing the Ribble sands on the old route.

The only reminder of the one-time Astland ferry is Ferry House and the quiet cobbled lane leading down to the river. But by the side of it is a small creek and a boat-building yard where cabin cruisers lie, drawn up on the river mud or lifted bodily on to dry land. Desultory knockings came from some of the boats on my last visit. A dozen or so men were surveying their craft to see how repairs were progressing. They had an air as of men who liked to escape into a greenhouse on Sunday morning. Here was another kind of escape—a plug to be changed, some new linoleum to lay on the cabin floor, and the *camaraderie* of the sea.

I cycled back to the road of small holders and followed it into Hesketh Bank. This is an old village of grey, cobbled, fishermen's cottages, looking so perfect in their disarrangement by contrast with present-day standards of uniformity. The old inhabitants do not like the name of Hesketh Bank, looking upon it as newfangled, for they remember it as just Hesketh. Let me quote a petition of the seventeenth century which gives some age to the name, as well as showing us the importance, at that date, of this Ribble crossing :

> To the right Worshippfull the Justices of the Peace and Quorum for the Countie Pallatyne of Lancaster assembled att the Sessions of peace holden att Preston the 4th of October 1655.
>
> The humble peticion of William Tomlinson of Warton, guide over the River to Hesketh banke.

H. Milne

Fishermen making their nets

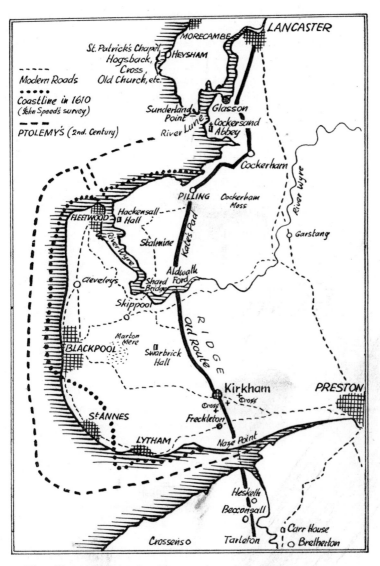

The old route follows the ridgeway through the mosses, constructs
Kate's Pad, and fords the rivers to reach Lancaster

Sheweth

.That the peticioner hath served the people of the Comon-
wealth as guide over the same River for the space of fortie
yeares and upwards and hath beene readie upon all seasonable
tymes and occasions with himself and his horse to guide and
preserve passengers from the danger of the water.   In that
tyme and service hath lost above the number of Ten horses
to his greate dammage and impoverishment, and beinge
unprovided for a servicable horse such as is requisite for that
service, though willinge to serve the countery.

His humble request is that your Worshipps would take the
premisses into serious consideracion and favourably to
grant your Order for such an allowance towards the buying
of a horse fitt for that service as in your wisedomes may
seeme meete, the same beinge the highe roade from Chester
to Lancaster and into divers other parts and therefore
necessarie, and the peticioner shalbee as hitherto readie to
attend all passengers.   And daylie pray for your worshipps
etc.

(Clerk of the Peace's note.)
Nul.

Those who visit old Becconsall churchyard may see a gravestone inscribed:

James Blundell, late of *H. Bank,* who was unfortunately drowned
on the 6th July 1844.

> Often times I have crossed the sands
> And through the Ribble deep
> But I was found in Astlan drown'd.
> It was God's will it should be so
> Some way or other all must go.

It is therefore older than the railway era, although some
would have it that it dates from then.   Rather would I place it
with all the 'Banks' along the Lancashire coast to be found
wherever there was a recognized crossing of the sands, for
example at Banks, Kents Bank, Hest Bank, and so on.

The Guide Road, which we are shortly to reach, is a relic of
the same period.   It led across the marsh and the Ribble
estuary to reach the Guide House on Lytham shore.   I have a
map published in 1850 which clearly shows the route followed.
Among the Dodsworth MSS. is a record of how this Ribble
crossing was endowed with a rest-house by Albert Bussel, who
died in 1186: 'Be it known to all present and to come, that I,

Albert Bussel, have given and granted etc., to Honkell, son of Adam, and his heirs, the whole land of Swartebonke, to wit, from Blackpool on the eastern side across to the western side of Bradelond, in pure and perpetual alms for my soul, and the soul of my wife, Lecia, and for the souls of our fathers . . . to hold of me and my heirs free and discharged of all secular service, and also for the maintenance of a certain place (ad sustinendam quandam Hospitalitatem illis qui necessitatem habebunt) for those who shall have need thereof.' There was a similar service provided by Cartmel and Conishead Priories for the Morecambe Bay crossings on this same journey.

There are many written records of the use of this route during the Civil War. In August 1644, Lord Molyneux, Sir Marmaduke Langden, Sir Thomas Tyldesley, and others of the king's supporters, retiring before Sir John Meldrum and the Parliamentarians, crossed the Ribble estuary from Freckleton to Hesketh Bank without pursuit 'so that al got over saflie and marched up to the Mealles.'

Once again the journey brings us to the edge of the escarpment whence, looking seawards, there is land as far as the eye can see. Yet stand by these cottages and you are on the edge of the old seashore line. This is also the case at Becconsall, and all around the escarpment to Hesketh Bank, and beyond to Banks, which lies close to Southport. It is still called Shore Road.

Out of the Astland river and into the Ribble a hundred years ago came the black fleet of coal vessels, 'in slow, successive train.' They came round the headland, and where you now look along the mathematically straight lines of fertile fields these colliers sailed to Liverpool.

The old seashore road to Southport carries little traffic, mainly only the throbbing tractors, farmers' cars, and labourers' bicycles. The reclamation of the sea marsh has been done in two stages, by two dikes, and if you go down the Guide Road, which cuts a straight line into the reclaimed land, you will see both of them. The road cuts through the first, now useless, dike, then travels to Marsh Farm which stands amid an array of barns and outbuildings, almost beneath the high, snaking, earthy wall which alone keeps the high tides from rushing back again to the old seashore line at Hesketh Bank. The first dike was made in 1860 and the second in 1880 to 1884, enclosing some 6,000 acres of foreshore. The marsh beyond the dikes was a rare hunting ground for wild fowl and for salmon poaching. Game was reared here and coursing events took place regularly. You can still see trespass notices which refer particularly to poaching.

Building the dikes was a hazardous business. The second one, in particular, was often broken in its three-mile stretch by high tides. Mount Farm was then called the Hesketh Arms, and to the navvies and Irishmen working on the dike was a rendezvous where pints stood drawn ready on the bar for the rush at the end of the day's work, when the fun began, ending up at closing time with numbers of rousing, bare-knuckle fights, all in progress at the same time.

With the completion of the dikes, fishing gradually died away, to be replaced by agriculture and horticulture; a score of fishermen replaced by some two thousand people spread over a wider area, and as you travel down the Guide Road to-day you will be impressed by the reclaimed fertility which supports them.

Go to the top of the furthermost dike and you will see what remains of the old marsh, stretching away to the Ribble estuary where the ships sail up to Preston. On it sheep now feed unconcernedly, while in the open drains lies the wrack of the sea, for these are the first to fill and the last to empty when high tides are running. Looking landwards, there are spread the greens, the gold, and the browns of Lancashire's plain, stretching to the blue ranges of the Pennine hills. Come here in the summer and enjoy the peace and solitude. Come in winter, and the screaming wind and heaving tide driving against this rampart of earthy sods are demons which suck away courage. That is why you may note a sense of urgency, perhaps an unconscious one, among these farmfolk when spring warms the earth. They are just released from the shackles of winter, and ahead of them is a limited time for sowing and harvest before the dead days are with them again. The newly budding green creates a wonderful sense of exhilaration.

It is worth while to walk some time along the embankment from Hesketh Bank to Crossens. The raised dike is too straight, the sea marsh too level, for those who are not used to this kind of scenery. But the loneliness! Only the eerie cries of plover and wild duck, and the ribbon of water which is the Ribble, break the silence and the continuous stretch of treacherous green morass as seen from the Crossens end. Towards Hesketh Bank the green seems continuous with the further shore. In the gathering darkness of a grey winter's evening there are queer sighs and moans from the invisible marsh which do not belong to this world. Well can one then believe the tales of the old marsh folk, who have names for those creatures of their imagination which pad along the marsh in the dark hours, their tongues hanging out like red rags and their eyes aflame. Mysterious as well as frightening are the kind which pass you in the gloaming, like Gabriel Ratchets, or like the invisible but audible hounds of the spectre huntsman. You can hear the pad of their feet and the rustle of the grass as they pass: there is nothing to see, yet your hair rises with fear of the unknown. Having travelled much in Lancashire, from seaboard to fell top, albeit in this scientific age, I can well understand the feeling of these country people when the queer noises of the night invest the loneliness with a sudden fear which drains away courage and quakes the knees with an uncontrollable ague.

But of all the fearsome things of night in these lonely places the incoming tide is the worst! To stand on this embankment in a sleeping world, to hear the gentle remorseless lap of the tide creep softly over the marsh, gurgle fanatically in the drains, then race swiftly to the wall, is indeed a frightening experience, and if it be a winter's night when the tide is running high before a following wind, one's civilized self becomes but as a dry leaf before the fury of the elements. The wind screams and tears through the grass, and whips the face with the sting of spray, while as yet the tide is but a thin, white roaring line in the distance. But its advance is unbelievably swift. It fills the drains long before it breaks over the marsh. Having been bred and born in the safety of the hills my first thought is for the security of the dike. How can it possibly withstand the onslaught of those distant breakers? Eventually, however, it is no more than a heaving, scummy cauldron that lies at one's feet. Somewhere the tide has lost the thrust and swirl with which it began, and the bank is safe. How unbelievably calm it is below the dike on the landward side! I ride my bicycle back to the road and am full of wonderment as I see the lights shining peacefully from the windows of farmhouses. I have seen the marsh on their doorsteps devoured as by a raging beast of prey, and they are not afraid.

From Hesketh Bank the road runs flat and straight towards Southport. In the early spring days, while the earth is still cold, the air is filled with the continuous trill of larks, and before we reach Hundred End it will be clear that that sense of urgency of which I have spoken is already afoot. The large glass-houses glow red with tomatoes, long rows of yellowy-green lettuce have been pricked out to the far horizon. The petrol engine has speeded the plough and, together with television and the motor-car, has brought some of the blessings of civilization to this lonely Holland-in-Lancashire. Cattle on the road are being herded from bicycles as I pass. Always, somewhere in the air, is the sound of tractors and of the wind from the sea, whose continual pressure has pushed the hawthorns until they lean heavily landwards, their trunks permanently twisted and stunted.

One day I was struggling along this road against a bitter wind when I met a man coming from the marsh. His overcoat was green with age and salt water, fastened only by a neck button. He must have been a giant of a man in his younger days but old age was pulling him down. His hair was hoary white and close cropped over a leather-brown skin. I stood to windward of him and bawled against the unearthly roar to ask him if he lived on the marsh. 'Oh, aye,' he thundered in a bass voice which rumbled around inside him before coming into the air, carrying an edge of gusto like good nature itself bubbling and frothing.

'And what is it like on the marsh to-day?'

'A bit muddy, aye, muddy it is, but it still blows cold. T' cattle are down on t' marsh, they are, but there's no grazing, not with this cold wind.'

'You'll remember the building of the dikes?'

'Oh, aye, 'appen fifty year agone it is. First they built the dike, then t' wayter gradually drained away. Ah'm living in one o' t' cottages that was built for t' workmen. There's still a mon deawn theer whose job it is to keep t' dike mended it is, and t' ditches clean.'

'Is there any trouble from the sea these days?' I asked him, and in reply he bubbled with thunderous laughter and could not keep still on his feet, for his whole body was shaking as he managed to say: 'There's no sea nowadays. It goes further an' further away. Folk blame Liverpool for it, dumping t' sand fro' dredgers. Only now and agin there's a special high tide an' it floods t' grazing a bit. Then t' cattle can't go theer 'till it's rained and washed t' salt away. There's not much o' nowt these days,' he went on. 'Used to be a lot o' wild fowl shooting on t' marsh, but not many coom neaw. Fishermen too. Oh aye, there's not so much fishing. Only shrimping in t' summer. Tha'll a seen 'em eaut wi' t' carts, shanking—that's dragging nets behind t' carts—or else spreading t' nets on stakes wi' each tide.'

'What do these men do in winter?'

'Nowt as Ah know on. They're a lazy lot o' b——s. No shooting, no fishing, an' t' wayter far enow away. We're deeing off aw reet. Might as well be deead reight neaw.'

The Hundred End is an interesting survival of the ancient division of Lancashire into hundreds. Here stood the Snotterstone by a narrow stream to mark the beginning and the end of the hundreds of West Derby and Leyland at the edge of the sea. The embankment comes inland to this spot and then retraces a parallel line on the other side of the stream before continuing to Crossens.

I never cease to glory in the quality and quantity of sky above the flat landscape whose changing patterns of cloud and shadow, colour and form, are continually creating, tearing apart, and re-creating their momentary combinations with earth and water. Look to the sky for the secret of Lancashire's coastal charm. Even at this moment, as I revelled in the early May sunshine which tempered the wind, I watched a black pall of snow and sleet roll down the fleecy cumulus, coming from the north like the marauding Scots, reducing the countryside to a sudden silence as it awaited the bitter onslaught of white hail.

Some local historians think that the Ribble estuary crossing began one mile north-east of Banks at the ford opposite the Naze, and that in the reign of Henry II there was a Guide House here marked on old maps as 'Balls,' which was later removed to Hesketh Bank. We must also remember that the actual river channel was much narrower than to-day and ran quite close to this shore and down to Southport. Until 1860 the old road was on the landward side of the present road, going behind the old rectory and through Churchtown (for there was no Southport) by Churchgate to Birkdale Common. It is at Crossens that the present-day road crosses the drainage channel and you may see there the pumping station which keeps the Martin Mere area behind Southport dry enough to farm. One Sunday I watched a mechanical dredger loading silt from the drain into a succession of lorries which then drove away through the crowds of Southport holiday-makers in Lord Street. Here too there is kept a store of pipes and some pumping apparatus. Close to the road small boats are moored in the deep channel, or lie high and dry for scraping and painting. Fishing-nets hang drying in the sun outside a wayside cottage. Yet only a few minutes' walk away lie the first houses of Southport.

From Tarleton to Preston the modern highway plays hide and seek with the old turnpike highway. Turn off down any of its curving, narrow lanes and you will be rewarded with a sight of old Lancashire villages, old inns, and forgotten smithies, even a turnpike milestone, half hidden in the overgrown hedgerows. Having crossed the River Douglas and the canal it is not long before the road from Bretherton comes in on the right, and at the junction stands Carr House, to which I will return in its proper place. Just now we will follow the old turnpike by bearing left and come to Much Hoole church, which has been isolated from the village by the later arterial road. I found the door locked so could not see its three-decker pulpit (1695) but the exterior is quaint and unusual. My first impression was as of a doll's house, a model on a small scale, for the eighteenth-century pillars on either side of the west door and the narrow tower seemed destined for a more pompous building. On walking round to the south side you will see that the stone tower is affixed to a seventeenth-century red-brick church, the oldest portion of which is at the west end. It has the genial warmth of hand-made brick and its variegated colouring.

Nine years before the body of the church was built a child was born in Toxteth, Liverpool, and christened Jeremiah Horrocks. He later went to Emmanuel College, Cambridge, but failed to take a degree, being more interested in a branch of accepted mathematical astronomical tables whose calculations

he proved to be wrong. He was at the climax of these discoveries when the curacy of the new chapel at Much Hoole was
given to him. The rest of the story appears on a tablet in
Westminster Abbey:

> In memory of Jeremiah Horrocks, Curate of Hoole, in Lanca-
> shire, who died on the 30th January 1641, in or near his 22nd
> year; Having in so short a life Detected the long inequality in
> the mean motion of Jupiter and Saturn; Discovered the Orbit
> of the Moon to be an ellipse; Determined the motion of the
> lunar apse; Suggested the physical causes of the revolution,
> And predicted from his own observations the Transit of Venus,
> which was seen by himself and his friend William Crabtree
> On Sunday, the 24th of November (o.s.) 1639. This Tablet,
> facing the Monument of Newton, was raised after the lapse of
> more than two centuries, December 9th 1874.

It is doubtful if Curate Horrocks paid much attention to his
congregation on that famous Sunday. He was naturally
anxious to prove his theories, but an autumn mist obscured the
sky. Then, at a quarter-past three in the afternoon, the mist
suddenly cleared, the sun shone out, and he saw the new spot,
of unusual size and perfectly round, on the left of the sun.
Astronomer Crabtree in Manchester was also watching, by
arrangement. They each projected the sun's image through a
telescope on to a piece of white paper in a darkened room, with
identical results. The calculations had been checked by
Gascoyne, inventor of the micrometer.

The chancel of Hoole church was extended eastwards in
1859 in memory of Jeremiah Horrocks and a window and clock
erected in the tower for the same purpose. It is said, but
without proof, that Horrocks witnessed the transit of Venus
from Carr House. The latter stands isolated from the church
and again we must remove the modern highway from our
picture as we try to recapture the eighteenth-century scene.
The house is certainly worth seeing. It, too, is a building of
hand-made brick, with two slightly projecting wings, a projecting porch, three storeys, and mullioned windows with
leaded panes. It has remained substantially untouched since
the seventeenth century when it was erected, as the stone over
the doorway testifies in beautifully carved, raised letters:
'Thomas Stones of London, haberdasher, and Andrewe Stones
of Amsterdam, merchant, hath builded this house of their owne

charges and giveath the same unto their brother John Stones, Ano Domini 1613 Lans.'

I do not know the story behind this, but it suggests one of the many concerted ventures of that period, with a liaison effected between London and the Continent for the very profitable export of English goods, particularly wool. In this case the

Carr House

business was a family concern, and whether brother John raised sheep on the marsh for his part in it or was just a poor relation I do not know. However it may have been I would not, for my own part, like to have a carved stone over my doorway telling all the world that the house had been given to me by my brothers 'of their owne charges.'

Whatever smart appearance the house had once has gone with the centuries, for it is in need of repair and the gardens need attention. But it is pleasant enough to speculate that maybe behind those walls the transit of Venus was observed for the first time.

It would be hard for a stranger to say where Longton, Walmer Bridge, and Much Hoole begin or finish, for the straggling houses form a continuous thread. Narrow lanes lead off to left and right, ending in dirty cart-tracks which serve the fields. They could be followed across country, but as they have never served the motor age they have been allowed to retain their dust and hedges.   And it is at the ends of these lanes you will find such places as Little Hoole, Much Hoole Town, and Moss Houses.

Down the old turnpike you may see the Longton Arms, one of those fast disappearing inns no bigger than a four-roomed cottage, with curtains to the tiny windows, a fire in the tap room burning red between all its five bars, and ale drawn straight from the barrel.   Longton village straggles for over a mile, showing the ribbon development of a past age, when the fields on either side of the lane belonged to the farms on the roadside and the gaps between were filled in by market gardeners, small holders, and a brewery.   A little further along the high road is Hutton.   A conveyance of some land between 1236 and 1242 refers to the 'strata ferratam' or paved road, as a boundary to the land.   It is another clue to the persistent character of our ancient route.

By turning away from the present high road you can pass through the more secluded part of Longton and strike through the fields to Old Grange, a marsh farm which lies on the edge of the River Ribble channel, protected by a dike wall from the high water.   Although it looks modern enough there are enormous outbuildings which carry the dints and scars of great age.   One barn is dated 'W. R. 1703.'   On the morning that I passed that way the sheep had been brought home from the marsh beyond the wall because it was the time of the twenty-seven-foot tides.   The farmer has a cowman, a stockman, and a marsh man to superintend the live-stock, for it requires a specialized knowledge to understand the various departments of a marsh farm.   The incoming tide creeps up the ducts and thus may cut a man off very easily if he is not alert to the danger. Sheep have to be brought home, because their fleeces become heavy with water and they would drown, but the cattle can swim home.   I saw the ewes and lambs safe in the fields beyond the marsh as I passed along the marsh lane to the Bottom of Hutton.

As I followed the narrow ribbon of macadam back to the main road the air was full of a perturbation of tractors competing

with an exultation of larks, for it was springtime and the
dry east wind had brought forth every farmer's resources to
take advantage of the first fine weather of the season.   Dogs
and children were playing in the sunshine and villagers were
gathering firewood from beneath the trees.   Over the dike wall
I saw the top only of a smoke-stack and two masts of a ship,
slowly moving up-river on the tide to Preston docks.

Every year the salmon travel the way of the ships in the
course of their journey into the Pennine Hills to spawn.   We
have many records of the ancient Ribble salmon fisheries, for
many folk were interested and zealously guarded their rights.
The riparian landowners who had fishing rights included
Sawley Abbey, Whalley Abbey, Stydd Hospital, Penwortham
Priory, the Franciscan Convent, and St Mary Magdalen's
Hospital in Preston, Lytham Priory, and the town of Preston.
That is why we have Fishergate in Preston to this day—the
fisher's road which led into the town from the river.   Even as
late as 1823 we read: 'On Tuesday the fish stones presented a
sight of not less than 116 fine salmon caught by one man's nets
and weighing 1,000 pounds.   They were sold for the Yorkshire
market at 9d. lb.'

The shape of the river has been considerably straightened
and widened, so that the old litigation maps are now useless as
guides and the originally staked areas have been lost.   Salmon
fishing in our rivers is no longer a real necessity as it was in
those days and the sportsmen prefer the higher reaches of the
river and its tributaries, so that the 15,000 salmon caught in
1867 is not comparable with the present average of around
1,000, which is, however, slightly increasing, possibly as a result
of the greater care taken to prevent unnecessary river pollution.

The main road is rejoined at Horwick Cross and leads
through Penwortham into Preston on the other side of the river.
To-day Penwortham is a residential area, and still expanding.
It is the first stride across the River Ribble from Preston, and
ancient Penwortham looks down from its fortress height, the key
to the ford.   Rather unfortunately the electricity authority
have chosen to build their works, including four huge chimneys,
across the river from Penwortham, so that the latter is on the
same eye level and the trail of blue smoke cannot be very
pleasant to its inhabitants.

But rows and avenues of identical semi-detached houses are not our concern.   Under this modern rash of red brick may still be discovered the importance of the hill outlook above the marsh, and the importance of the ford.   The hill was chosen for a Norman castle which was in existence in 1086.   It was followed by a priory, built as a cell for the great Benedictine abbey of Evesham which thereby stakes its claim at a strategic point on the Ribble, just as representatives of the other monastic orders were doing along the river banks as far as Sawley.

Excavations in the castle in 1856 revealed the site of a dwelling, possibly British or Romano-British, which further emphasizes the importance that was attached to the guarding of the ford.

The church, with decorated chancel and Perpendicular tower, has carried on the purely religious side of the priory's work since the Dissolution.

VII

AMOUNDERNESS: (1) FROM FOREST TO FYLDE

FROM the earliest days of civilization in these parts the River Ribble was the west-to-east trade route linking the traders of the Irish Sea to the other side of Britain by giving them access to the Aire Gap. This was, indeed, the only through route in this direction for Lancashire, for between Lune and Mersey was an area of forest, deteriorating into marsh because of a slow sinking of the land which continues even to this day.

When the Normans took control of England the Ribble trade route was guarded by Roger de Poictou's castle at Clitheroe, which was erected before the castle at Lancaster. Its building was shortly followed by gifts of land along the banks of the Ribble to a number of newly instituted religious bodies which wanted a share in the salmon fisheries. Preston's importance, situated on two fords of the river, was recognized immediately, and the status of this town's future in Lancashire's life firmly assured. The fords served routes across Amounderness which, including the road we are following, kept to the only ground which was free from the encumbering forest, and this ground lay on the ridgeways. For the land between Ribble and Wyre is not flat, as is often supposed, but has a series of ridges running roughly north to south. In these days of roads and railways which drive straight routes from the manufacturing towns to the newly created seaside towns, that is from east to west, we are apt to see the area between as a jumble of villages joined by hap-hazard connecting lanes, but if we remember the old conditions we can see that the ridgeways are deliberately used to link the villages. For instance, one of the old trackways followed the ridge from the vicinity of Preston through Lea, Bartle, Salwick, Treales, Mowbreck, Wesham, Bradkirk, Weeton, Preese, Great and Little Singleton, to reach the River Wyre at Aldwath ford. Another followed a more southerly route, by Lund and Dowbridge to Kirkham and still westwards to Plumpton and Weeton.

In the thirteenth century the only tree-free ground lay on the areas of higher ground; firstly on the ridgeland of Salwick, Treales, Kirkham, Westby, Weeton, Singleton, reaching the River Wyre at Aldwath ford (above the present Shard bridge which has replaced it); secondly, on the coastal cliffs from Blackpool to Rossall; thirdly, on the raised areas beyond the River Wyre from Rossall to Preesall and Stainall.

The high coastal area has as background an inland depression which is lower than the twenty-five-foot contour, so that in Blackpool the natural drainage is away from the sea inland and into the River Wyre at Skippool. This depression runs from the Wyre alongside the main drainage dike southward between Hardhorn, Singleton, Staining, and Mythop into the ancient Marton Mere, then continues between Little Marton and Plumpton, joining the general mossland until it reaches the Ribble at Lytham. Here occurs the first wave of higher land formation followed by a low trough, then another rise to the Kirkham–Wyre ridge, then another depression from the River Cocker to Freckleton Marsh which drains the eastern Fylde, and so back to Preston. It is an interesting switchback area whose ridges can lay claim to habitation from the Bronze Age by evidence of the archaeological finds made there. The village names are Celtic—Tulketh, Treales, Eccleston, Inskip, Preese—the Romans used the ridge to link their ports to the hinterland arterial routes which pushed their vigorous ways north to Scotland and across the Pennines. These ridgeways, free from forest, were the links between river and river, ford and ford, and represent our oldest thoroughfare from Chester to Scotland, and also the life-lines of those settlements above the forest and marsh which were our earliest habitations in these parts.

While the historian looks at the ridgeways the town planner looks at the drainage values of the limited area at his disposal, and calculates their effect on the distribution of population, finding them inadequate for the number of houses which would be required to house all those who wish to retire from their work and spend their last years on the coastline they have known since childhood.   Mosslands are apt to fill in bad weather, and the town planner must take no risks on the old marshes.

Marton Mere has been successfully drained.   It is first mentioned in 1120, when Theobald Walter, Baron of Amounderness, granted to the abbot of Stanlawe (on the Mersey) the right to use the mere to turn his water-mill at Staining.   Apart from this its chief use was for fishing.   Its outflow once gave power to a water-mill in Blackpool before flowing into the sea. The site was, approximately, on Waterloo Road to the east of Marton Square.   The River Spen dike, which drained Marton Moss, flowed into the nearby mill pool.   A sixteenth-century map in the County Records Office in Preston shows this with, near by, a small group of cottages called 'Pool Houses alias North Houses.'

In 1655 the flooding of the land due to the mere caused the inhabitants to send a petition to Parliament pointing out the great losses sustained in their meadow and low lands, and that they were 'many tymes in the winter debarred from the benefitt of the Marquett at Preston, at the most beneficiall and usuall tymes of comerce at the said place.'   It 'utterlie spoileth and decayeth all or mosses for digginge and gettinge or turfe, and soe anoyeth severall parts of or high waies that in the winter tyme or utmost endeavors is not sufficient to keep them passable,' they said.   In summer the passing of many carts to obtain turf 'slitcheth and sandeth up the said watercorse, And in the winter is soe soft, by reason for the said slitch and water, that it is not passable but with great danger of losse or spoilinge theire goods that have occasion to passe that way.'   There was constant trouble over the clearing of the watercourses, and it was not until 1731 that a successful drainage was made into the River Wyre.

The crossing of the River Ribble from Hesketh Bank finds two good landing places on the opposite bank ; one by the inn at Warton Brow, and the other close by at Naze Mount.   The distance between is slight.   Hennett's map of 1829 shows the track running from Guide's House, Nook, a little west of the Naze, with roads connecting to Freckleton, Kirkham, and Tarleton.   I would say that the oldest crossing is at the Naze. There is a tradition of a Roman fort at this point, now washed away, which appears to have been linked with the Roman road from Ribchester to Kirkham. The route from Freckleton to Kirkham is marked by wayside crosses. It then continues by the present A 585 road through Esprick until the latter turns to Singleton, just after Brackinsall Lodge. Beyond this point the old continuation of this route follows the first turn to the right leading to the River Wyre where stands Old Castle Farm on the right and Windy Harbour Farm on the water's edge.

There is another Windy Harbour, just north of Warton Brow, situated on a straight piece of old road which looks like a track leading through Wrea Green and along the secondary ridge to the west of the Esprick ridge, through Weeton and Great Singleton, then through the parkland to this second Windy Harbour, as if for the purpose of crossing the River Wyre. This supposition is borne out by an account of the route followed by the sixth Earl of Derby when making his last visit to Derby House at Upholland in 1651, just before the skirmish at Wigan Lane. He had come from the Isle of Man with three hundred Manx troops, 'those pore naked snakes,' and had landed at Rossall, near the future site of Fleetwood and the only civilized inhabited portion of that coastline. The same day he marched to Weeton and next morning marched 'over Ribble water to Latham House, staying supper, then after went to Holland (Upholland) and from thence took post after the King.'

Charles Philip Hampson, in a study of Fylde place-names in the Lancashire and Cheshire Antiquarian Society's *Transactions*, vol. lvii, discerns in the name of Wrea Green the Old English 'wreon,' to defend, and speculates as to whether the huge green, now famous for its cricket matches, may not conceal a *castrum*. It is interesting to note that the route we are following runs by the east side of the Green to Warton (Old English 'wearian,' to guard) and to Windy Harbour.

The parish names in Amounderness are grouped in an interesting manner. A recital of a list of the principal villages is full of the poetry of the Scandinavian and Anglo-Saxon tongues—Hardhorn with Newton; Weeton with Preese; Westby with Plumpton; Ribby with Wrea; Bryning with Warton; Medlar with Wesham; Greenhalgh with Thistleton; Little Eccleston with Larbreck; Treales, Roseacre, and Wharles; Inskip with Sowerby, and so on.

Ormskirk's relation to the road between Mersey and Ribble

G

is paralleled by Kirkham's to the road between Ribble and Wyre. Each ridge was a key position and Kirkham holds the key to more than one ridge. It is therefore no surprise to find there remains from many epochs, including the only Roman remains of any importance in the district.

A Roman road having been traced from Ribchester to Kirkham there has been much conjecture as to where the road went afterwards. The older writers seem to agree that the Romans would have aimed at the coast, and they found a lost port for them, now in the sea among the lost lands off Fleetwood and in the Wyre channel, which they called Portus Setantiorum. John Porter declares that the road was still visible at Fleetwood about 1836. My theory, on the contrary, based on a study of the road and the traveller, is that the Roman vessels would sail as far up the River Wyre as was practicable; that the Romans would use the old ridgeways as far as possible; that they built a road from Ribchester to Kirkham with the object of reaching a choice of practicable landing places on the Wyre or the Ribble; and that the choice of such places was made in accordance with the fact that their road from Ribchester to Kirkham was built to link up their new road system to the old route at the key point, beyond which they could use the old route either south to the Naze or north as the shortest way to the River Wyre. According to this line of reasoning their most likely landing place would be at the old Aldwath ford where one reminder of the past survives to-day in the name of a farm—Windy Harbour. And that, I believe, is the extent of the Roman infiltration into Amounderness. Isolated finds have been brought to light but do not link together. Field work might do much to illumine the historical past of this part of Lancashire, but for too long it has been considered as mere marsh and ignored.

Road connections from the east ended at Kirkham, for beyond it none was necessary. As we have seen, the Ribble was navigable to the Naze and Lytham was a port for the southern Fylde. In the north was the River Wyre with its port of Skippool bringing supplies and taking produce away from Poulton. The name Poulton gives us yet another 'pool village,' and 'Skippool' is the place on the pool where the River Skipton enters the pool after draining Marton Mere. Sometimes the 'pool' is disguised, as in Pilling, which keeps the Celtic 'pyll' for a pool or creek, but the pool was an important feature for shipping on a sandy coast and so became an early centre of civilization.

The development of Blackpool as a bathing resort rendered inadequate the old local arrangement of one through road linking the two ports and market towns which had served the Fylde successfully for many centuries. When William Hutton, the Birmingham bookseller, set out to discover this new bathing village for himself he got lost beyond Kirkham! Mr Sharpe France has discovered that, from some time in the seventeenth century until 1902, there actually ceased to be any direct road even between Preston and Kirkham except by the use of two miles of private road on which a toll was payable. The public highway went by way of the Plough Inn, Ashton, down Lea Road and through Lea into Deepdale Lane and past the Clifton windmill to Lund church and Scales. But the journey over the Lea Marsh was shorter, even though toll had to be paid to the Hoghton and Clifton families as lords of the manor. The existence of this Hoghton rental is clearly recorded in the following examples: 1648, 'Passage money over the Marsh £4.' 1660, 'Passage money at the Stakes £3 10s. 0d.' 1720, 'A toll for Passage over Lea Marsh sett £24.'

Until 1781 this road out of Preston ran quite close to the river south of Lea Hall and joined the present road opposite the Lea Gate Hotel. (A new housing estate makes the journey a little difficult at present but a portion of the track can still be traced to the south-east of the bridge over the Savock.)

As, however, the traffic to Blackpool increased newcomers to this countryside found the toll road under water at periods of high tides, and the public highway lengthy and ruinous. In 1781 Thomas Clifton and Sir Henry Hoghton built a new private road, the basis of the present road, in the effort to meet the needs of the ever-growing army of travellers to the coast. But in 1824 letters to the press and other condemnations of the vile state and narrowness of this twelve-foot road witness to a problem that has remained with us to this day, Blackpool having always attracted an amount of traffic out of all proportion to what has been anticipated or provided for. When the Lancashire County Council took charge of affairs in 1889 they described the road from Preston as 'by way of Ashton Lane, Lea Road, and over the now Private Road repairable by Mr Clifton and Sir H. de Hoghton through Clifton to Scales, thence through Kirkham to Ribby Hall, Wrea Green, Brown Moss Side Station, Shell Hill House, Lytham, Heyhouses, St Anne's, Blackpool.'

The religious orders which erected their crosses, and later their churches, on this ridge road at important junctions, seem to have left evidence of this in early place-names. We remember, for example, Orms*kirk*, and we arrive now at *Kirk*ham. Prior to the Norman Conquest a charter in the York registry tells us that the church was in existence and was the ecclesiastical centre of at least fifteen vills, and that the whole district was granted to the church by Athelston early in the tenth century. There is nothing to be added to the study of the history of Kirkham while the book by R. Cunliffe Shaw, *Kirkham in Amounderness* (1949), is in existence. It is a model history and a monumental work which has surely exhausted all sources. For our present purpose it is sufficient to note that Kirkham was important as a thirteenth-century borough and that until the middle eighteenth century it was the most popular and fashionable town of the Fylde.

The minute books of the 'Court Leet of frank pledge of ye foundation of Henry VIII' gave a variety of rules, fines, and regulations which show how the life of a Kirkham citizen was then regulated. These are my favourite quotations:

'30 Nov. 1728. Ordered that a Lamp should be fixed up in the middle of the borough of Kirkham in some convenient place, and that the charge of it together with oyl necessary for it be paid out of the town's stock.'

'All persons refusing to clean or cow the streets opposite their respective houses to be fined 6*d*. after notice from the sergeant with his bell.'

And we find an official notice written from this last minute as follows:

'To the Inhabitants of the Burrough of Kirkham. You are hereby required forthwith to cleanse the Streets over against your Dwelling Houses, Outhouses, and all other Buildings, together with all Frontsteads whatsoever on Penalty of Sixpence for each default. You have also hereby notice to remove all the

Dung-hills out of the Streets in a month's time or otherwise they will be removed for the use of the Burrough. Likewise all the Rubbish out of the Streets on such Penalties as the Bayliffs and Common Council shall think fit to inflict. Given over our Common Seal of the Town this first day of December 1728.'

Although it was common enough to have dunghills in the village street I feel that, in the case of Kirkham, we can see the origins as far back as the Middle Ages, when the two cross streets comprised a series of 'tofts' or 'burbages' and when every householder in the street had his farm, orchard, and garden while his arable land was to be found in strips in the town fields around the settlement. Step forward in history to, say, the year 1675, and in the marriage settlement of Margaret, daughter of William Walker, to James Lowde, we find mention of 'and one oxgang of land and the following closes belonging to it: the Barnfield, the Plumpton Roote, the little Turn-bricke' . . . etc.—all of which can be traced to-day, as R. Cunliffe Shaw points out, as lying in the original town fields, just as they were ploughed from the moss before enclosure.

The old custom of the twelfth century by which certain men from each parish were required upon oath to give aid to the twelve men elected in each hundred for assessment purposes, is common knowledge. The 'Inquisitiones Nonarum' of Edward III of 1340 calls these parish representatives 'sworn men.' They became known as the 'Four-and-Twenty Sworn Men,' though Kirkham was exceptional, having thirty. It was in this corner of Amounderness—Preston, Garstang, Goosnargh— that this old custom was preserved into the nineteenth century, and Goosnargh was the last to relinquish it in Amounderness.

The form of oath that these men swore can be read in the Goosnargh vestry book, 1678, and runs: 'You shall well and truly observe and keepe all antient lawfull and laudable Customes as heretofore in this place hath been observed and kept as far as they shall agree with the lawe of this Realme and the good and benefit of this Chappell and Chappellrye according to your power and best understanding and your own Counsell and your fellowes you shall keepe. So helpe you God.' The 'sworn men' had to be landowners in the parish, or the sons of such, and were elected for life. They appointed churchwardens, sextons, and clerks, levied rates, and attended

to all church business.   Although they had no official warrants
from the king, and therefore no authority at law, the Bishop of
Chester ruled in 1638 that 'their acts relating thereunto
[church matters] were as effectual and binding as if they had
the King's sanction.'   Their minute books, in whatever parish,
and wherever preserved, give interesting glimpses into the life
of the times, particularly that of the seventeenth and eighteenth
centuries.   At Kirkham in 1683 2s. o½d. was paid for a whip to
whip dogs out of church, and the same year £10 12s. 4d. was
paid for magpies' and sparrows' heads.   People were warned

Some examples of windmills which still enliven the Fylde landscape

and punished for selling ale during church services, and it
was a churchwarden's duty to go through the parish and warn
the people to come to church.   The schoolboys of 1653 bore a
likeness to those of to-day, for we read that the Thirty Men
agreed at that date that no 'scriffener be suffered to teach in the
church unless he procure some honest townsmen of Kirkham to
pass their word that whatsoever his scholars do, either in
breaking glass or in abusing men's seats—and that they meddle
not with the bells—he shall make good what they abuse.'
   Kirkham   had   its   manufactures,   particularly   sailcloth
making, and from this sprang about half a dozen small cotton-
mills.   In the nineteenth century the town employed a lot of
Irish immigrant labour both in the mills and in the countryside
around, and it was their liking for ale that gave Kirkham its
name of the 'snuff and porter' town.   But that phase is now
long past.   The old Roman road into the village carries a
perpetual hum of traffic to the coast, and few will try to picture
the street scene on old fair days with its stalls and booths and
cattle blocking the broad highway.   But every passer-by can

still see the fish-stones round the modern lamp and the remains of the windmill on the crest of the hill—the hill of Roman finds and a wonderful spot for a view, for across the rolling farmlands towards the sea are farms and orchards, market gardens, and acres of glass-houses among fields golden with corn and long-eared barley.

From this Fylde country came the famous Lancashire long-horn cattle, and the Lancashire pig-breeders who gave a good name to Lancashire bacon.   There was an ancient cattle fair at each of the ridge towns as 'Drunken Barnaby' had cause to remember in his capers :

> Veni Garstang, ubi nata
> Sunt armenta fronte lata,
> Veni Garstang, ubi male
> Intrans forum bestiale,
> Forte vacillando vico
> Huc et illuc cum amico,
> In juvencae dorsum rui
> Cojus cornu laesus fui.

Although Lancashire was behind the rest of the country in the application of the newly developing agricultural techniques, its horticulture, as we have noted in the Liverpool district, won nothing but praise from such eighteenth- and nineteenth-century experts as Jonathan Binns, John Holt, Dickson, and Law Rawstorne.   Many farm leases of the nineteenth century specified that only certain fields were to be ploughed, with the result that these had borne grain crops 'beyond the memory of man'; uncertainties of weather and crop failures were not taken into consideration and sometimes a clause was inserted which stated that there could be no redress either in law or equity. But horticulture was another matter.   Poulton supplied vege-tables to Lancaster, Preston, and growing Blackpool.   Bare and Heysham used the new train service to send their produce to the markets of Bolton, Manchester, Carlisle, Penrith, Kendal, and the West Riding of Yorkshire.   They found splendid markets for early potatoes and became famous for their carrots. The fishermen organized the industry, getting their women and children to help, and manuring the lands with loads of decayed shrimps and mussels.   Cockerham on the marsh had 300 acres of rich alluvial soil, covered at high tides, which bred renowned sheep, and the district also bred carriage horses and hunters. In the southernmost parts Mr Clifton owned 20,000 acres at Lytham, half of it liable to be covered by the sea, but in 6,000 acres he laid 10 miles of drains and produced 1,000 acres of turnips and excellent dairy stock.

Moss drainage was the key to Lancashire's success in intensive culture. It began in the 1770s. Much capital was sunk in the venture, but courage and foresight have since reaped good dividends. Estimates of the acreage of mossland at this time vary between 26,000 and 36,000 acres, of which the top five to seven feet was soft and spongy, flooding in bad weather, while below lay some fifteen to thirty feet of hard black peat.

In draining the land the first move was to cut large open drains, two or three feet wide and two feet deep, and these were left for twelve months. Two years later the ground was laid with smaller, covered drains, at first nine yards apart and then, as the moss consolidated, ever closer together. As this process went on further drains were laid across the others and at a lower level. Finally the land was divided for letting purposes by division ditches, with long slopes on one side which were sown with seed.

The ground was now ready for the first year's work of burning the top moss cuttings, ploughing to a depth of seven inches, harrowing, rolling, and adding soil compost, after which turnips or root crop were sown. In the second year oats would be sown. The third year saw slight ploughing and turnips again, in drills. In the fourth and fifth years the ground was ploughed for oats and after harvest a compost was spread on the stubble and the whole lot turned in for sowing of winter rye. After this treatment the ground was considered suitable, after heavy liming, for pasture for the next five to six years.

We may walk on this mossland to-day and see many a farm, fully mechanized, with light tractors, combined harvesters, grain drier, potato harvesters, cabbage planters, and so forth. Acres of peas go thence to the canning factories, potatoes go off for a three-year lay, to stop the eel-worm disease which developed seriously about twenty-five years ago, but there are plenty of vegetable crops to take their place, followed by cereals in rotation. With an average of 53 cows to 100 acres and 600 head of poultry per holding, the Fylde is both Lancashire's milk can and provider of its breakfast egg. Statistics compiled before the 1939 war showed that in the Fylde and East Lancashire there was a greater concentration of poultry than in any corresponding area—some four hundred square miles—in the world. The annual egg value reached £5,000,000, and milk £10,650,000. The wide variety of cash crops that can be grown is always ready as a quick balancer of farming economics. Pigs and the 'golden hoof,' or wintering of sheep from the hill lands, give a variety to intensive farming which places Lancashire, to the surprise of many, among the agricultural counties.

The *Preston Guardian* during 1950 reported that 'some years ago a member of the Cardwell family began to grow tomatoes under glass for commercial sale in the Marton district of Blackpool. From this beginning has grown an industry of glass-house cropping that ranks as one of the most important in Britain's food-producing policy, and Blackpool, the district where it was pioneered, remains one of the biggest areas of development. . . . The significance of Lancashire's position within the glass-house industry is further exemplified by the fact that a new research station is to be built near Kirkham.'

Glass-house after glass-house shows the bright green of winter lettuce which reaches the household table under the persuasion of soil steam to around 200° F., feeding with between 20 and 30 tons of manure per acre, and hydrated lime, plus sterilization with formaldehyde. During the season, when the lettuce crop can be grown outside, the glass-houses cope with the demand for tomatoes. There is an urgent feeling in the Fylde air which seems to say: 'We're not wasting a minute of time or a yard of space. Right enough to sing the praises of Lancashire men in industry, but we're pioneers in horticulture and don't get a word from anybody!' It seems a far cry from Jonathan Binns's words of a hundred years ago: 'The mountains of Cumberland and Westmorland . . . are often the cause of alarm when, late in spring, they exhibit their fair mantle of snow, the precursor of frost; the cold northern air being then attracted from these mountains across Lancashire, the bloom of fruit, the early potato, and other tender vegetables suffer lamentably.'

VIII

AMOUNDERNESS: (2) LYTHAM

ON certain days of the year the Fylde Road out of Preston is one of the busiest in the country, for it leads to Blackpool, and a stranger anywhere between Morecambe and Preston could easily believe that Blackpool is the only place in the Fylde. Roads of this kind offer little to explorers, but there is not much that can be done to escape from them at this juncture. Later, when we leave the coast, we may cycle all day in country lanes and not meet a dozen cars, but for the present we must just follow the macadam to Lytham.

On the way lies Marsh Farm, Clifton, where conditions are similar to those on the farms on the south bank of the river. The farmer keeps one eye on the wind and the tide-table, the other on the weather. A 27-foot 6-inch tide in summer with little wind will cause the farmer to bring in his 650 ewes and lambs from the 230 acres of out-marsh, but he will also bring them in if it happens to be a 26-foot tide with a following wind.

The road passes through Freckleton which has a water-mill. Gilbert Singleton also had one here in 1325. Nearly eighty years ago a cotton-mill here was manufacturing sailcloth, rope, and sacking, and there was a shipyard for small coasting vessels in the 'pool.'

In another three miles Lytham begins at Saltcotes, and here is a place-name which brings to mind a trade of long standing on the Lancashire coast. There is another Saltcotes near Carnforth and a Salthouses ('cote' means 'house') near Thornton. Sarah Fell in her *Household Book* mentions the purchase of 'Wyre Salt,' which would be loaded at Skippool along with other merchandise and carried to Furness by boat, whence the return journey would be made with a load of iron from the Swarthmoor furnace for the building or repairing of Skippool Bridge, for she has an entry regarding the sale of ore to John and William Bickerstaffe who were engaged on the bridge.

A charter of William de Cowdray grants to Sawley Abbey his saltpit at Crossens and land there with sufficient sand, turbary, etc. This place was also called Saltcoats. The cross erected on this property is more likely to have given Crossens its name than the 'cross sands' derivation, for Hesketh Bank claimed the crossing of the sands. The salt used to be taken up the Ribble to Sawley Abbey by boat for the winter meat and fish curing. Long Lane leads from Saltcoats inland to Sugar Stub (a guiding pole) for the moss crossing, which suggests a trade in salt from this place. The salt roads of Lancashire, and in fact of the whole country, have played a vital part in opening and keeping alive many tracks into secluded areas.

Of the getting of salt, Camden says 'that water is poured from time to time upon heaps of sand till it grows brackish and then they boil it into a white salt with a turf fire.' John Lucas in his *History of Warton*, 1710–40, tells of a visit to Saltcotes near Carnforth and gives a fuller description of the process. 'In hot weather during the neep tides they harrow with a Thorn or such like thing, the Flats that are always overflowed by the Spring Tides then skim and scrape into Ridges which they take away in Caups and preserve under cover. Then put the Sand in Troughs lined with blue clay with holes in bottom and pour fresh water on which drains the salt with it into waiting vessel containers. So long as this liquor is strong enough to bear an egg they pour on more water and as soon as the egg begins to sink they empty the sand out and refill with fresh. The drained salt water is boiled on turf fires until only salt remains. They use leaden pans for boiling.'

Salt was also made at Dungeon Point near Liverpool in the seventeenth century, but there they used a Cheshire-mined salt, eked out with sea water. (They also used coal from nearby Prescot, thereby earning a strong protest from Northwich manufacturers on the basis of unfair competition.) It provided a cargo to Cornwall for the salting of fish there, and the return journey was made with china-clay for the Liverpool potteries.

Lytham is a familiar name on old maps, lying always at the edge of the area depicted as moss. It must have been on safe

ground, for in the twelfth century a Benedictine priory was
founded here.   It became a cell of Durham Abbey, and at the
Dissolution was granted to Sir Thomas Holcroft, a noted
'trafficker' in confiscated monastic property.   He made his
profit by selling it to Sir Cuthbert Clifton and that was how the
Clifton family came to settle here, although they had held a
large number of Lancashire estates since 1258.   There is now
no trace of the religious house.   It has been thought that the
present hall is on or near the site, as monastic remains have been
found in the buildings, but the complete rebuilding in 1751–64
by John Carr of York, replacing the 1625 building by Sir
Cuthbert Clifton, seems to have destroyed any evidence there
might have remained up to that time.

The Clifton family suffered as Catholics in the Reformation.
Sir Thomas Clifton was arrested four miles away at Wrea
Green in 1594, taken to the dreaded Tower of London, and
brought to Manchester on a charge of high treason, together
with a group of other Lancashire Catholics.   Eventually he was
acquitted but he died shortly afterwards.

There are few records to give us a picture of the place as it was
before the building of the priory.   Ancient spellings of the place-
name such as Lidun and Lethum suggest a settlement, and
Edward I granted 'wreck waif and stray' of Lytham to the
Earl of Lancaster.   But a changing coastline and the disappearance of villages beneath sand or sea have mixed facts with
legend and it is difficult to be accurate when this occurs.
Kilgrimol, or Lytham Common, disappeared.   In 1601 the
Dodsworth MSS. affirm the existence of Waddum Thorpe
and that the Horsebank was a pasture for cattle.

We are on surer ground in considering Lytham as the home
of the Cliftons, as Formby was the home of the Formbys, until
the eighteenth century when the bathing-machine heralded an
invasion of this peaceful coastline.   In 1794 there were two
inns and two smaller licensed houses, together with a row of
whitewashed mud and thatched cottages, called Lizmakago,
commemorating a racehorse belonging to Sir John Clifton,
which did well at the Blackpool annual races.   He also had
his own three-and-a-quarter-mile racecourse and paddock.
An anonymous description of Lytham and its neighbourhood,
written in the early nineteenth century, tells of the recent

building of many excellent and convenient houses in the village
and on the marsh to accommodate bathing visitors, likewise two
most excellent and extensive hotels: the Wheat Sheaf, proprietor
Mr John Crookall, and the Clifton Arms, proprietor Mr
Hampson. 'Exclusive of these there are two other Public
Houses of an inferior description (equally good in their sphere)
and are usually frequented by bathers of the lower class of
society, who in the height of the bathing season literally come in
shoals during the spring tides from some of the populous
districts of the county; when males and females are seen lining
the shore in promiscuous groups, and not embarrassing themselves about appearances, but enjoying the salt water as well
internally as externally, to the no trivial amusement of numerous spectators, who usually assemble to behold the motley
scene. The generality of these people usually come for the
purpose of washing away (as they suppose) all the collected
stains and impurities of the year.'

Although this writer notes that 'vice has not erected her
standard here,' yet on Douglas Street 'a new house of confine-
ment of considerable strength has been erected containing
distinct apartments for the punishment of offenders of both
sexes.'

P. Whittle in *Marina* recollects visiting Lytham in July
1824 when Mr Lardner's troop of comedians were performing
in the 'New Theatre.' If only a regatta could be organized, he
observes, 'on the principles of that annually displayed at
Sunderland near Lancaster, it would tend to great and lasting
benefit.' He further suggests 'that some rules be formed, as at
Southport, to prevent men bathers shamefully exposing their
persons to the great annoyance of females . . . that bath
carriages are wanted to carry people to church on Sundays
and for visiting during wet weather . . . that houses require
numbers and lamps required for dark evenings.'

A letter describing life in the 1830s gives a brief glimpse of a
holiday-maker, a prominent Lancashire manufacturer in those
days. 'For twenty years or more he [the grandfather of the
writer], with one daughter or more, was regularly the tenant of
that same cottage we have both since known so much of. Each
weekday he took his regular walk on the green beach . . . and
each Sunday one of the two sole bathing-machines the place was

endowed with carried him, and one or two elderly friends taken up on the way, to the then small whitewashed church in the fields. It jolted on two wheels, with the round holes out of reach to let the light in, and the door fastened on the inside with a peg.' Porter, the Fylde historian, says there were three bathing-machines, but we will not quibble about such small numbers. This mode of transport to church, however, was sufficiently common for the pathway to be kept wide enough for their passage. The anonymous writer already quoted says that two of the machines belonged to Mr Parkinson and the third to Mr George Gillats, 'both of whom from long experience and constant practice, are declared to be particularly adroit in delicately handling the fair females out of the machines into the water.'

In 1801 there was, surprisingly, a population of 920, and there was a steady increase in the following years. Clifton Street was built and Mr Edmondson, draper, had his own Baptist Church attached to the shop premises, seating about thirty people. He was also the minister. Hugh Holmes was barber, doctor, and shopkeeper in the old tradition. A road was constructed over Freckleton Marsh to put Lytham in closer touch with civilization, and in the season two steamers brought holiday-makers down the Ribble from Preston. On Whit Monday there were annual races for farm horses on a course from the Windmill to a disused limekiln a mile towards Saltcoats. Otherwise the visitors could walk for miles (and a good distance *westwards*) on the sands, or 'to Heyhouses for bad ale.'

By 1824 there were three coaches a day to Preston in the season. One anonymous visitor has given us an account of how the local inhabitants procured a living.

'The sea here,' he writes, 'is supposed to abound with fish, but few are taken, and those principally with hook and line, the fishermen either for want of spirit in not possessing proper boats to go out to sea, or not chusing to trust themselves on such a boisterous coast. The kinds generally taken here are chiefly salmon, cod, ray or skate, and flounders. The salmon is usually taken in the river, which is brought to the tables in finest perfection. Shrimps are taken on this coast in great abundance, and in supreme excellence. The river ells are obtained in plenty during the season which are remarkably fine. Many of the natives procure their livelihood collecting shell-fish, such as cockles and "muscles" which they regularly take to Preston market every Saturday, where they meet with an immediate and ready sale for their week's labour.'

New buildings were but tardily erected before 1820 as the lord of the manor had reversion of them after only forty years. At this date, however, the time was extended to sixty years, later to ninety years, and finally to the more usual 999 years. Here again it was the coming of the railway, on 16th February 1846, which created expansion. It was a branch line of the Preston and Wyre Railway. The first train departed 'amid a volley of cheers and discharge of cannon.' If you would like to see the original station, and it is typical of the period, go to Lytham Railway Goods Depot, where it still plays its part. Since that day there has been a dignified accretion of houses. The town received its lighthouse in 1847, but it was washed from the Double Stanner Bank in 1863 and later rebuilt in the sand-hills, such are the vagaries of the sea. In this year of storm the seven and a half miles of railway to Blackpool were opened, and from that date one may say that this coastline was given over com-pletely to the holiday-maker. A small dock was made out of Lodge Pool in the mid nineteenth century as an incentive to develop a port, for Lytham, in common with most other seaside towns, swelled with importance at its unprecedented growth on the coming of the railway. Until, however, the River Ribble was dredged large vessels had to unload into lighters at Lytham or Freckleton. As we can now see, nearby Preston was well ahead of all competitors, and Lytham has had to find a special-ized trade in building for boats suitable for launching in shallow water and rivers, particularly in Africa.

The establishment of a mussel purification station at Lytham —there are only two in the country—was rendered necessary by the pollution of the river water. Mussels gathered in the Ribble, Wyre, Morecambe Bay, and as far away as Ireland are brought here for a forty-eight-hour purification course. They are tipped in concrete cleansing tanks and left to soak for two days. A dash of chlorine in the water then closes their mouths so that 'the poor man's oyster' arrives to the customer as pure as the minute it left Lytham.

The old and traditional site of the Kilgrimol (meol = sand-hill) received a new lease of life on 31st March 1875 when John Talbot Clifton cut the first sod and laid the first stone of the new town to be called St Anne's on the Sea, which was planned on a drawing-board and the land leased to a company for 1,100 years. The church was the first building to be erected and was dedicated to St Anne. The place filled a gap on the coastline between Lytham and Blackpool, and has proved to be a popular residential area, sometimes called 'Manchester by the Sea.'

IX

AMOUNDERNESS: (3) BLACKPOOL

THE ancient link between St Anne's and Blackpool was an area of 1,800 acres of common land, called Layton Hawes. It stretched from Division Lane in St Anne's to Manchester Square, Blackpool, and all that remains of the common to-day is a little parkland between Ansdell Road and Waterloo Road, and the street names of Hawes Side Lane, Common Edge Lane, and Division Lane. There was a time, as Mr R. Sharpe France points out in 'Layton Hawes and Marton Mere' (*Fylde Hist. Soc.*, vol. i, 1940), when every person from the parish of Bispham to Marton in Poulton had the right to pasture his sheep and cattle and dig his turfs from the common land of Layton Hawes. But the boundaries between common land, lord's land, and priory land were ill defined and disputes were many. During the Civil War, when Prince Rupert captured Liverpool, he appointed Colonel Clifton of Lytham to guard it. In order to find the necessary food and clothing the colonel 'caused many pore mans stocke of sheep to be taken out of that common belonging to Laton called the Hoos and also out of many mans house within Kirkham, Poulton, and Bispham parish their best bedding to be taken.' It was the early period of enclosures, and in 1649 Robert Bamber of Great Bispham granted a messuage there, together with its right of common in 'so much of Laton Hawes as hath not lately been sodded, marked out, or appointed to be enclosed by William Fleetwood of Ellinge, Co. Middlesex, deceased.'

Into this rather desolate region there came Edward Tyldesley of Myerscough who built Fox Hall about the year 1650 on the edge of Layton Hawes. Fox Hall arose because Charles II had considered the idea of rewarding his helpers by the creation of a new order of knighthood to be called the Order of the Royal Oak. There was no doubt in Edward Tyldesley's mind but that he would be one of the first knights and be granted land at Layton. He even added in stone the crest and the motto of the order to be to Fox Hall, and in his petition to King Charles he included the common land of Layton Hawes among the lands he wanted, describing the area as 1,800 acres of goose green.

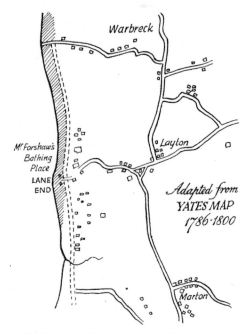

Blackpool begins with the bathing age

But Charles II never created the new order, 'from the apprehension that such an order of knighthood might create heats and animosities, and open those wounds afresh which it was thought prudent should be healed,' and Layton Hawes remained common land for another century. It had a certain fame as a racecourse patronized by the Fylde gentry, and this was remembered at the beginning of the sea-bathing craze, and has a bearing to be remembered in the story of the beginnings of Blackpool. Thomas Tyldesley, son of Edward, kept a diary in which we find under 31st May 1712: 'Went to Hays to see a race betwixt Mr Harper's mare and Sanderson's. Met a great deal of good company but spent nothing.'

Start of yacht race (Fleetwood–Isle of Man)

A Lancashire 'nobby' type is third from left, and the winner of this race

In 1767 the local landowners submitted a plan to Parliament for enclosure of Layton Hawes. Six commissioners met at John Forshaw's house on 26th May 1767 and two years later signed the award. It was the end of the common land and of its age-old rights. The commissioners ordered new roads to be made and Sunday Leach Lane has now become St Anne's Road. Sunday Leach, Goose Leach, and Black Leach were large pools which were drained by order, Sunday Leach having lain between the present Highfield Road and Watson Lane. Moss Lane was another road then made (it is now called Ansdell Road after a painter who lived here), also Common Edge Lane and Hawes Side Lane. Spen Green Lane is now Bloomfield Road extended to the sea. Cow Gap Lane is now Waterloo Road. Daggers Hole Lane has become Watson Road. (The present Daggers Hall Lane is merely a corruption of the old name.) Milkers Gate Lane is now Highfield Road, and Stoneyhill Avenue and Little Marton Lane have become Squires Gate Lane.

Our other link with the past, Fox Hall, was used as a hunting lodge until 1688. Thomas Tyldesley liked this quiet retreat and he settled there as a Catholic country squire, like his father, content with the social round and taking no part in politics. We know a great deal about Thomas Tyldesley by reason of his diary kept from 1712–14—not a long time but long enough to give an accurate picture of how he lived, of the countryside and its people, and to some extent of the Catholic underground movement. Tyldesley kept a resident priest and Fox Hall had a ready welcome to any Catholic in hiding. Significant of this lonely coast was the incident of James II's coming to Fox Hall from Ireland on his return to this country hoping to regain the crown.

Together with a few fishermen's cottages, Fox Hall and those dwellings dependent upon it represented the settlement which was to grow into Blackpool, the greatest show-place on earth. And when you see there the Fox Hall Hotel you also see the site of the home of Thomas Tyldesley. No name was given to these other houses in the midst of the marsh and no roads led there but tracks through the bogs which could only be used by those who had local knowledge of their treachery. Small wonder that a tale was told of a chained fox at the door of the hall and a secret chamber, always prepared for James II should he wish to hide from the Protestants.

Thomas Tyldesley writes in his diary:

> May 6. 17—. To the cockes at Conder Green.
> 1712. May 6. A-ffox hunting to Sullam.
> May 16. Went around the common a-ffowling, shot twelve times for one poor twewittee. To Thornton Marsh after dinner, we killed ffive or six head of fowle.
> June 26. To Roshall a-sea pye hunting.
> 1713. July 7. Made a bargen between Jo. Wadsworth, Tom Few and Jo. Twentiman ffor building a 60 tune ship att £1 -2 pro. tun.
> 1714. June 9. Won 2s. 6d. at Dr. Hesketh's cocks.

There was one natural condition which was eventually to provide a name for the new town to come. In the marsh lay a large drainage lake called Marton Mere, and from it the Spen Brook flowed into the sea, staining it with the dark-coloured peaty water. The name Spen is now only remembered on a railway signal-box.

The drainage of Marton Mere was begun in the late seventeenth century, for many lords of the manor in this country were then feeling the movement afoot for the improvement of agriculture, and reclaimed land was soon shown to provide an excellent return on the money expended. This improvement to the land was the first step in providing a passage to the sea coast. The second was the annual event of the Layton Hawes Moss horse-races. (We became familiar with the name 'Hawes' meaning sand-dunes, in the Southport area.)

It would be misleading if there was no mention at this point of the ancient settlement of Bispham further north, with its Norman church, for to-day it is included in the Blackpool township. Also on this coastline settled the Clifton family of Lytham, the Heskeths of Mains, the Rigbys of Layton, the Allens of Rossall, together with a few other Catholic families, sufficient in number to support the Layton horse-races which they organized for their own amusement. But others also became attracted as soon as tracks from outside the area were made passable.

In the early eighteenth century the first few venturesome souls arrived at Fox Hall for bathing. For fifty years, from

1735, they were catered for by Ethart à Whiteside and his wife. By 1770 there were some thirty houses for their accommodation, including four with slate roofs which were looked upon as extremely modern in comparison to the usual thatch. Eventually Ethart à Whiteside's house was bought by the local cobbler and converted into an inn, which, I think, must be the one John Porter refers to as being on the site of the present Clifton Arms Hotel. Even at this late date the houses were mere hovels surrounded by peat turfs and refuse. All luxuries and extras had to be brought from Poulton-le-Fylde.

The Gynn was there in 1770, charges 8d. a day inclusive, and Bonney's Hotel charged 10d. a day. The word Gynn is connected with 'ginnel,' a narrow passage, and should have a hard 'g' sound as ginnel is pronounced to this day among Lancashire folk. At Blackpool it denoted a narrow way from the North Cliff down to the beach and so the hotel at the upper end took the name. This area has long since been washed away and the present hotel of that name stands much further inland. John Porter tells a tale of this cleft in the rocks, that during a storm in 1833 a candle was put in a window of the Gynn to guide a ship in distress to the safety of the creek, making a reversal of the practice of a hundred years earlier when the local inhabitants made a decent living from the wrecks of the sea and the unloading of contraband whisky on the sand-dunes of the lonely South Shore, a practice in which the Tyldesleys took a fatherly interest.

By 1770 the Tyldesley family had left Fox Hall and eventually passed into obscurity. The hall became a farm. It seems a strange mixed story to a distant observer—the secret contraband at one end of the shore, the establishing of fortnightly fairs at the other for the entertainment of visitors, and the disappearance of the Tyldesleys when they should have been developing the district for the pecuniary benefit they so much needed.

In October 1788 Blackpool was visited by William Hutton, the travelling Birmingham bookseller who wrote books on the places he visited. His description of Blackpool is the earliest full account of the town. His visit coincided with the beginning of the cult of sea bathing in England and the first visitors had been noted only for 'bloated disease and silken folly.' In 1771 Emmanuel Bowen drew a map which showed a little towered house to the north of the black pool and he named it Black Pool town.   A later map shows an additional row of houses.   John Porter writes of thirty-five houses in 1788 when William Hutton arrived, and some four hundred people present at any one time in the busy season.   He found a parade, that is a grass walk on the sea bank six yards wide and two hundred yards long.   'Here is a fine display of beauty and of fashion,' he writes.   'Here the eye . . . conveys intelligence from the heart

Poulton Cross, stocks, and milking stones

of one sex to that of another. Gentle tumults arise in the breast: intercourse opens its tender language; the softer passions are called into action; Hymen approaches, kindles his torch, and cements that union which continues for life.'

Are not young people still cocking an eye at one another in Blackpool and getting wed?

In Hutton's day visitors had to travel to neighbouring Bispham to go to church and to the market town of Poulton to find a theatre.   That theatre is still standing.   It was in the tithe barn, now scheduled to be demolished to street widening.   In 1751 it was used as a temporary church during the rebuilding of the parish church across the road.   It was being used as a theatre as late as 1822, for a playbill of that date advertises it as 'up to date' and presenting 'Maria Marten—or the Murder in the Red Barn.'   Catherine Hutton wrote, in 1788: '. . . and the place is dignified with a theatre, if *that* will bear the name which during nine months of the year is only the threshing floor of a barn. . . .   Rows of benches are placed one behind another, and honoured with the name of pit and gallery, the first two shillings the other one. The house is said to hold six pounds.'

If the visitors stayed in Blackpool they could play bowls or practise archery, or even go for a short sail.   In the evening there were cards and backgammon.   Moreover, in 1786 the

Musical Society of Gentlemen in Preston arranged musical concerts in Blackpool.

Here is an advertisement of 15th June 1785:

'Laurence Bailey takes the liberty of acquainting the Public that he has completely furnished and fitted up a commodious genteel house in an elegible situation, and that he hopes by his accommodations to merit the encouragement of such ladies and gentlemen as may be pleased to favour him with their company. N.B. a bathing-machine will be kept for the use of his friends.'

A picture of this date shows a half-dozen groups of houses. There is Bailey's Bathing House, Bailey's Tavern, Forshaw's Tavern, Crooke's Post Office, Hudson's Tavern, Hull's Tavern, Bonney's Wine House, Elson's, an archery ground, a bowling-green, and a public walk on the grass verge to the seashore. I can only think that there must have been a number of lodging houses somewhere handy to make so many taverns a paying proposition. We are told that 'the bed of the sea, at low water, is a place of amusement. Here the gay make a figure, the decrepit seek for health, and the netters for shrimps; the carters gather stones to make their roads and their walls, and the curious gather shells; the builders seek for pebbles to burn into lime, and the healthy seek pleasure. Thus various descriptions of men lay a tax upon the sea; nay the very cattle snuff up the sea breeze until driven back by the tide.'

The first Manchester to Blackpool coach was at last on the road, charging 14s., single fare. The rush to Blackpool had begun. We now read of visitors who hastened into the dining-rooms, their knives and forks at the ready, and shouting for their dinner. The Padiham folk (Padjamers) wore coloured stockings and saved holiday money in weekly clubs. They swam in the sea, sailed on it, drank it in quarts, and took it home in large stone bottles hanging from their cart axles. They boarded for 3s. 4d. per day but provided their own tea, coffee, sugar, and liquors. 'These people are, in general, of a species called Boltoners,' writes Catherine Hutton, 'that is, rich, rough, honest manufacturers of the town of Bolton, whose coarseness of manners is proverbial even among their countrymen. The other houses were frequented by better company, that is, the Lancashire gentry, Liverpool merchants, and Manchester manufacturers. . . .'

The usual custom obtained here of ringing a bell when the ladies were allowed to enter the water, and any gentleman seen on the promenade during the ladies' session was fined a bottle of wine. One person at least must have been disgusted, for he describes their appearance as 'more deplorable than so many corpses in shrouds.'

Another custom was a 'Wakes' every second Sunday at Lane End, where 'the old women wished to dispose of their fruit and the young of their hearts.'

The year 1799 was always known as Pea Soup Year by old inhabitants. The story is told by Frank Hird and Allen Clark of how, in the winter following a blighted summer, the few resident villagers were faced with starvation. Then a storm broke. Thatch was blown off the cottage roofs and the sea raced inland half a mile, but it also brought with it a shipwreck and the sands were strewn with a cargo of peas. The villagers were saved by a winter's diet of peas and cockles, and ever afterwards it was referred to as Pea Soup Year.

In 1811 there were 580 residents and five years later there was a coach service from Preston. At this time we have first mention of streets—Church Street and Chapel Street with their cottages, fields, a few shops, and Bonney's Hotel.

The year 1827 is recorded as a very prosperous year when the Lancashire cotton towns as a whole began to take an interest in seaside holidays. Every bed, stable, and barn was full as far away as Poulton. The sea-walk was made into a promenade the following year—a green turf walk leading from beach to church through pleasant fields and furnished at intervals with covered seats. There is an observation by a visitor in 1830 which is interesting in view of our comparison of Lancashire coastal towns. 'The inhabitants,' he writes, 'seem to have no taste for ornamenting their doorways or windows with trellis work or verandahs, or with jessamines, hollyhocks, or woodbines, similar to those at Southport and many of the sea-bathing situations in the South.' To this day Blackpool remains bare of floral and tree decorations outside the parks.

Uncle Tom's Cabin was a wooden hut built by a Thomas Parkinson who was always known as Uncle Tom. His wooden hut became a rendezvous for visitors taking an evening stroll to the top of the 100-foot cliff on which it stood. Uncle Tom served them with toffee and ginger beer, his wooden hut became 'a place of amusement' and he sold out to a Mr Taylor for £5. There is a story told that a Negro's bust from a ship's figurehead was washed up on the shore and that Mr Taylor connected it with the book *Uncle Tom's Cabin*, then newly published and a best seller, so he put the figurehead on the wooden hut and painted the sign 'Uncle Tom's Cabin.' The chief attraction became the dancing on the grass around the hut, and this was a centre-piece of Blackpool amusement until the building of the Winter Gardens. As the cliffs were washed away the wooden building was taken down, but the name is still preserved and is a feature of Blackpool to this day.

American friends of Blackpool will be pleased to know that one of their kinsmen initiated the postal service to Blackpool at this time by collecting and delivering at Kirkham three times every week. He informed the public of the arrival of the letter-bag by chalking on a board 'The post is arrived.'

The year 1840 saw Blackpool's rise to fortune. That year the Preston and Wyre Railway was opened to Poulton, and every train was met by a motley collection of horse conveyances which raced their passengers to the seaside. Cheap day trips were an early feature of the railways which saw profit in the seaside holiday idea, from which people were held back solely by lack of transport, or lack of cheap transport. They tell a tale in Lancashire of two day-trippers undressing on the beach for a bathe. 'By gow, Bill,' says one, 'but tha's mucky.' 'Aye,' was the reply, 'tha sees, Ah missed t' cheap trip last year.' Such were the people whom the clergy sought to protect when they accused the railways of running Sunday day trips and carrying people 'swiftly and safely to Hell.'

At the 1841 census the town had 2,168 residents. The Market House was opened three years later, and Talbot Road christened by John Talbot Clifton of Lytham.

Blackpool received the railway branch from Poulton in 1846, and in 1853 a local government board was formed. It is surprising that when the Preston and Wyre Railway was planned in 1835 it was not planned to go to Fleetwood by way of Blackpool, by that time the most prosperous town in the Fylde. On the day of the opening a special train 'adorned with flags' carried shareholders and directors from Fleetwood. They had dinner at 'Miss Nickson's Clifton Arms Hotel,' while 'a good old English dinner' was given to the workmen who had laid the line at 'Mr Carter's Talbot Hotel.'

At the beginning of the century the South Shore had held no more than a gipsy encampment, where 'Gipsy Sarah' lived to be a hundred years old.   The first house was built there in 1819.   It seems fantastic that Britain's first aviation display was held here, behind the Halfway House as early as 1909!   Now it is the greatest showground on earth—a safety-valve for the high spirits of mankind, set in a scene of man-made beauty, for there *is* beauty when night falls and the stucco palaces become a stage-set lit by multi-coloured moving lights with the players taking their part in the changing scene.

At the other extreme of the town is Bispham, once a Saxon farming colony lying between the Danish settlements of Norbreck and Warbreck.   (Blackpool lies in the township of Layton-with-Warbreck.)   There is not much of the old village left but the church has Norman remains, including the carved zodiac signs on the door archway.   In the churchyard you will be reminded of the grim days of shipwrecks by the records of those who perished in the sea and were buried here.

There was a free grammar school at Bispham, established in . 1659 when Blackpool was but a bare coastline.   Even when the latter was attracting nineteenth-century holiday crowds, Bispham had its factory, manufacturing 'linsey-woolsey,' and Norbreck's first house is described as a 'marine retreat' for gentry who did not wish to mingle with the plebeian crowds further south.   Thornton Marsh was a free and open common until 1800, when it was enclosed, together with Carleton Marsh, and it has remained agricultural land until the more recent invasion of semi-detached houses and bungalows for people retiring from the workaday world of south-east Lancashire.

Blackpool makes no secret of its attractions for holiday-makers, and modern highways, improved roads, and speedier transport, bringing large numbers of motor-coaches and private cars, have added to the railway's ever-increasing totals of day visitors, but surely no other place has such great superficial attractions with so little of permanent value, as can be seen in late October when the crowds have gone, the hucksters have put up their boards, and the paintwork has peeled off the

Golden Mile. A fierce winter makes one wonder why anyone lives there at all! Then comes Easter, the new paint, the returning crowds, and Blackpool is once again the mecca of the holiday-maker who seeks all the fun of the fair and loves to be one of a crowd. Blackpool's advertising campaigns reiterate, year after year, the appeal of the biggest, the funniest, the most colossal, the most outstanding, whether it be person or thing, and the people race along the modern highways and railway tracks to see the sight. That is why the secondary roads of the Fylde are caked with cow dung and free from the fumes of petrol.

The sky-line is always changing and yet it remains the same, because the smaller features are dominated by the Tower and the Tower buildings. I miss the one-time open-air pianist and singer of Lawrence Wright songs, followed by the selling of copies of the song among the gathered listeners. What artistry it took to 'plug' a song which the whole country would sing, before the radio, the talkies, and the last war paper shortage took the lungs out of this enterprise! What a knowledge of crowd psychology in competition with the fellows lower down the promenade who always had something for nothing to offer! What a change from the days when the only entertainment was a concert by the Gentlemen of the Preston Musical Society!

It is an experience to go to Blackpool with people (and there are many of them!) who regularly spend their holidays there and treat it like a second home. They have their invariable annual formula—booking here, drinking there, a particular time for a walk on the promenade, the same hotel and café visits, and of course the same landlady. A stodgy English custom, maybe, but it offers the same pleasure as that of putting on a favourite jacket worn well past its heyday.

X

AMOUNDERNESS:
(4) THE RISE OF FLEETWOOD

THE old route which we are following north from Kirkham passes through Esprick on the ridge and makes straight for the River Wyre and Windy Harbour Farm. Singleton lies on the left on the Weeton ridge road which runs on this higher ridge land. The view inland up the green river valleys, flanked by lonely outposts of the Pennines such as Longridge Fell, Pendle Hill, and Black Combe, but running back into the vast area of Pennine and Lakeland hills behind, is something you will always remember about west Lancashire.

Singleton's chapel dates from the fourteenth century. In 1578 a visitation brought this charge against the curate of that day: 'There is not servyse done in due tyme—He kepeth no hous nor releveth the poore—He is not dyligent in visitinge the sycke—He doth not teach the catechisme—There is no sermons —He churcheth fornycatours without doinge any penaunce— He maketh a donge hill of the chapel yeard, and he hath lately kept a typlinge hous and a nowty woman in it.' This chapel eventually became an inn, and the chapel to which Thomas Tyldesley alludes in his diary was erected in 1650. In 1749 it was called 'a popish chapel,' but in 1756 it was dedicated to St Anne and became a chapel of ease to Kirkham. The Roman Catholics opened a new chapel in 1768.

One winter's day, towards dusk, a little old man was walking down the road hereabouts, ahead of me. He wore a cap and thick jacket, over his shoulder was a small bag, and he carried a small spade in one hand and used a walking-stick with the other. I thought he looked sad.

'Caught any to-day?' I asked.

His face shaped into a grin as he put a dead mole in my hand.

'It'll do to plague t' missus,' he said. 'Freetened to t' death on 'em they are.'

'Are there not so many moles these days?'

'No, perhaps not. But theer's less mole-catchers too and so Ah'm kept busy enow. Tha sees, it's a day out wi' traps, an' a day collecting. It's quite simple; just prod t' greaund until it strikes hollow, then find the line of it and set thi traps with the catch just under the surface.'

He took a trap from his pocket, a small half barrel with a wire noose at each end so that when the mole gets into the barrel it knocks out the catch. There are also the full barrel and the spring type of trap.

'That's all he gets for working hard,' said the mole-catcher philosophically, 'but he's a grand fellow. He could teach some of t' young folk to-day a good deal abeaut work. Why dosta know that. . . . What dosta say? Oh aye, a pint o' mild, please. As Ah wur saying. . . .'

The old Aldwath ford (whose name conveys a picture of its construction) across the River Wyre was served on the northern bank by Kate's Pad, a trackway of wooden logs which crossed the marsh by Hale's Hall to Pilling. The longitudinal spars can still be seen in a peat cutting to the north of Hornby's Lane, consisting of split tree trunks arranged end to end. A recent pollen examination of the peat suggests that the track is much older than the Roman period and further evidence is awaited.

The higher land lay along the coast, so that apart from Kate's Pad the only other communication with Pilling ran along the shore marsh or by sea. Pilling Hall might be reached by boat at high water. The Stalmine road was not begun until 1780 and the Garstang road was opened in 1808 after the drainage of Pilling Moss had made this possible. As has been noted elsewhere, Stalmine church once petitioned for a resident curate as the place was so often surrounded by the sea.

Yet there must have been some value in the area, for Theobald Walter granted 'the Haye of Pylin' for the building of a Premonstratensian abbey in the closing years of the twelfth century. This was never built, although a small chapel was opened and Cockersand Abbey had a grange where Pilling Hall was to stand later. The abbey grange lay on the edge of the old road at the end of the crossing of the moss on Kate's Pad, and thence the road proceeded by the edge of the sea to Cockerham, allowing a passage between tides.

Instead of crossing the River Wyre by Shard toll-bridge let us have a look at Fleetwood and afterwards rejoin the track at this point.

Blackpool's 'tram-railway' speeds along enclosed tracks to Fleetwood by the edge of the sea. The country is semi-developed on modern ribbon development lines as might be expected in such close proximity to towns which exist for entertainment and their bracing sea air. I see no beauty in this stretch of desecrated coastline and only come this way in order to visit Rossall.

Rossall was written Rushale in Domesday. In 1247 Henry III granted 'to God, the Church of St Mary, and the Abbot of Deulacres and his successors forever, the manor of Rossall with its appurtenances and with the wreck of the sea.' Much of this manor, however, has been washed away by the sea. One farm was three times moved inland and rebuilt. The site of the original hall has also disappeared into the sea, and in 'Churchyard Field' Porter tells us there were once the stone foundations of a building, perhaps the church which the Elizabethan Harrison mentions '. . . that at the Chapell of Allhallowes tenne miles from Garstone it [River Wyre] goeth into the sea.' The Allen family of Rossall Hall have their place in history by reason of Cardinal Allen. (See page 124.)

In 1843 the idea of Rossall School was conceived by the Rev. St Vincent Beechey of Thornton and Fleetwood for the education of the sons of clergy and other gentlemen, under the direct superintendence of the Church of England, and at a cheaper rate than other public schools. It was opened the following year as the Northern Church of England School in the former Rossall Grange which belonged to Peter Hesketh Fleetwood who gave it for use as a public school.

In 1836 the first buildings of Fleetwood were erected on the site of a rabbit warren as the outcome of a scheme prepared by Peter Hesketh Fleetwood—another example of a landowner developing his possessions to take advantage of the Industrial Revolution and the new age of machines. Railways, harbours, and visitors with money to spend, required buildings to cater for their needs.

N. Wolstenholme

Lowering the shrimping net, Morecambe Bay

Fleetwood's land covered the mouth of the River Wyre. Was there not a local saying: 'As safe and easy as Wyre water'? Surely this was an ideal place to construct a new port large enough to attract shipping to ply to and from the commercial centres of Lancashire, and a railway line from Preston would provide the final link. A small farmhouse stood on the south side and a warrener's hut among the sand-hills when the plough was used to mark out the future streets which all converged to a central point, a star hill, on what was to be the promenade, called the Mount. The first foundation-stone was laid at the south-west corner of Preston Street by Robert Banton of East Warren Farm. That farm was to become an inn and a brewery, and then a private house called 'Warren-hurst.' The first completed building was another inn on Church Street. As in other modern towns there is a lack of either originality or tradition in the street names which are typical of the period: London Street, Preston Street, Dock Street, Customs House Lane, Lower Queen's Terrace, Upper Queen's Terrace, etc.

Early visitors could picnic on the Mount and watch the rabbits on the warren and the nesting sea-birds. The railway arrived on 15th July 1840. An embankment reclaimed four hundred acres of marshland. Two lighthouses were built in 1841 but there were no signs of dock buildings, so that ships had to tie up in the river and cargo loading and unloading was at the mercy of the tides. Railways ran to their own daily time-tables, which were not so variable as those of the sea. A pilot boat used to come from Cowes, but as there was nothing for the crew to do they passed their time in trawl-fishing until they found work on the Irish boats, and their pilot boat was bought by some local men who hired four more hands from North Meols to form the Fleetwood Fishing Company. In a short time, however, this venture also failed. Then a boat sailed into the Wyre from Kirkcudbright and stayed to fish, and the Leadbetter family sailed in from North Meols and settled in the town. Their success attracted others until, by 1860, there were thirty-two fishing-boats operating from Fleetwood. A trade was thus added to the new town which was otherwise not prospering, for other towns had been quicker to cater for the requirements of the sea-bathers, Fleetwood had started late and its people were obliged to admit that their natural background was less attractive than that of other seaside towns.   A writer of the day says: 'In 1842 I first visited Fleetwood . . . it then presented a most gloomy aspect—a splendid modern ruin, no shipping, no steamers, no passengers for the trains.'   But in 1846 the same writer was able to report that there was now more work to do than hands could perform, that wages had been increased and railway receipts were up from £100 to £1,500 per week, and that there was a demand for more room at the quays.

In that same year the barque *Diogenes* arrived at Fleetwood with the first cargo of cotton.   It had been chartered by a Mr Evans of Chipping, a village in the Pennine foot-hills near Preston.   The coastal trade reached its zenith in 1856 chiefly owing to dock charges which were less than those of Liverpool at that period, and at least one large firm of Manchester cotton merchants took advantage of it.   The revival was sufficient to warrant an Act of Parliament in 1864 authorizing the building of a dock.   The first sod for this was cut in 1869 but then the scheme was abandoned until the Lancashire and Yorkshire Railway Company completed it about eight years later.

The following years witnessed the rise of Fleetwood, not on any previously planned schemes but on the private trade of its fishermen.   Peter Hesketh Fleetwood's failure was taken over by the railway company as the most interested party.   The fishing trade was prospering within its natural limitations.

A localized inshore fishing industry pertained to the whole of the Lancashire coast, the mussel and cockle fisheries of Morecambe Bay and of other places as far as the Welsh coast being probably more productive than any other area in the British Isles.   Shrimps are also caught in these parts in huge quantities.   Before 1890 the trade had been a village industry all along the coast, but Fleetwood had gradually been attracting the boats while Liverpool, for example, preoccupied with bigger commercial interests, hardly realized that it was losing its fishermen.   In 1867 Liverpool had fifty trawlers and Fleetwood 'more than twenty.'   The Liverpool boats worked as far as the Isle of Man and the North Welsh coast.   There was a smaller class of trawlers working from New Brighton, and the fishing villages around the Mersey river mouth fished the Mersey and Dee estuaries for soles and flounders. There were a hundred and fifty boats in Morecambe Bay which concentrated on shrimps, and these reckoned 30 quarts each tide per boat a good catch. Baines calculates a rough total of 1,000 trawlers out of some 9,300 boats of all sizes worked by 37,416 men and 5,530 boys. Calculating on shell-fish, the chief catch, Baines gives these figures.

	MORECAMBE BAY	FLEETWOOD
1862	2,482 tons	670 tons
1863	2,274 ,,	886 ,,
1864	2,056 ,,	1,003 ,,

which shows a gradual decrease for Morecambe Bay balanced by a gradual increase by Fleetwood boats.

When steam trawling came in the nineties Fleetwood was first to develop the trade, beginning on the shallow, sandy bottom of the Irish Sea. The town had the required dock facilities, the railway, and the capital. In 1914 between 200 and 300 trawlers used the port which was one of the best organized for fishing in the British Isles. Subsidiary industries arose, such as ice making, box making, fish preserving and curing, oil and manure manufactures. The L.M.S. railway removed the small Irish passenger service to take advantage of the better harbour and river navigation for larger boats which had been created at Heysham. Fleetwood's trawlers, however, continued to go further and to bring back larger catches until now it is the third largest fishing port in England and Wales. It would seem, therefore, that the natural advantages of the River Wyre have found a suitable use without the expense of creating deep-water channels for larger boats. Fleetwood could hardly have competed with Liverpool, which has the advantage of being closer to manufacturing areas.

Throughout these years there remained a nucleus of holiday visitors, and to-day these are catered for by an ever-widening range of amenities.

I

XI

ROMAN CATHOLICISM IN AMOUNDERNESS

IT is impossible to build up a picture of Amounderness without reference to its Roman Catholic inhabitants. Lancashire history in these parts is indeed largely their history, for it was once possible to walk from Lune to Mersey without leaving Catholic-owned acres. Wherever you go to-day in the west so you will eventually find that some knowledge of earlier Roman Catholicism will be helpful.

Roman Catholics in Amounderness to-day can be classified in two main divisions. Firstly, there are those who are descendants of long-established families which did not accept the new doctrines of the Reformation and which will be found in what was the 'hiding' country of the seventeenth century—around Stonyhurst in the Hodder valley, in the Fylde, and in the area behind Liverpool and Southport. These are usually of pure Lancashire breed. Secondly, there are the descendants of those who came here to escape from political persecution elsewhere, for Lancashire was a good retreat, and also of many Irishmen who came in the eighteenth and nineteenth centuries to find work in the district's expanding agriculture, in the factories of the Industrial Revolution, or in trading connections. We have already noted that there has been an Irish influence on this coast as long as the two areas have been inhabited. In the Salisbury MSS. there is a letter to Cecil suggesting the danger to Protestantism in such Irish trading and hinting at control or prevention of this intercourse.

It is not, therefore, surprising to learn that the Roman Catholic diocese of Liverpool, for example, contains more members than any other of comparative size in the country and that it has embarked on the colossal task of building the world's largest cathedral. In Preston and Lancaster also the Roman Catholic Church is heavily represented.

In 1950 Catholics celebrated the centenary of the hierarchy of the work begun in a house in Great Eccleston, now the presbytery of St Mary's Church, when, at a meeting of high Catholic clergy, Bishops Wiseman and Sharples were delegated to go to Rome to urge the restoration of the hierarchy as the most efficient means of governing the Catholics in this country. This plan was carried through on 30th September 1850, and so ended two hundred and sixty-five years of Catholic oppression, persecution, or mere toleration.

In these last hundred years the Catholic population of England and Wales has grown from 1,000,000 to 2,850,000, the number of priests from 862 to 6,643, of churches from 597 to 2,868, of religious houses from 70 to 1,547, and of schools from 200 to 2,328. This expansion received its main stimulus from the coastal district of Lancashire which had held so strongly to the faith throughout the years of persecution.

All this invites the question as to *why* the Reformation never broke down the Catholic faith in Lancashire? Despite hostile laws and persecutions Roman Catholics actually increased their numbers in Lancashire during this period. There were a number of factors working in their favour, among which must never be forgotten the conservatism and tenacity of the pure Lancashire character which were brought to their strongest manifestation on so important a matter as religion; a conservatism, especially, strengthened by lack of contact with the outside world. And again it must be stressed how difficult and all but impassable was this countryside, so that villages were seldom visited by the queen's search-parties, priests could be hidden, and mass celebrated continuously throughout the period of oppression. Nor did Bishop Downham of Chester show great zeal in carrying out his orders from the queen, whatever may have been his reason. Nor did the Earl of Derby show any wish to prosecute the influential Catholic gentry, who were his neighbours and his friends.

The peasants for their part were very dependent on the great Catholic landowners, the Molyneux of Sefton, the Blundells of Crosby, the Hesketh Fleetwoods, Asshetons, Allens, and so on, with most prominent of all the houses of Lathom and Stanley, later united in marriage to lay the foundations of the future greatness of the house of Stanley.

From this family came the lords lieutenant of the county during the Tudor and Stuart periods, as well as leadership in local government. When they had to choose between changing their religion or losing power, they chose the former, but by reason of their power and lack of religious conviction they were able to interpret orders from the throne in a manner which seemed to them best for the county. Loyalty to the Derby family excluded the risings and plots which were a strong feature in other parts of the country. The Stanleys were able to stop the Roman Catholics of south-west Lancashire from taking part in a threatened revolt against Elizabeth and in a suspected plot against James, and on the other hand they applied the recusancy laws only when it was impossible not to apply them, and then only half-heartedly.

Meanwhile a missionary zeal for the spread of Catholicism was fostered by such men as Arrowsmith, Barlow, Finch, and Vaux, employing something like the commando technique of working singly or in small groups in difficult country, protected by peasant and landlord from a common Protestant enemy.

Cardinal Allen was a son of Rossall Grange. He became principal of St Mary's Hall, Oxford, and later went to Louvain to live with exiled Catholics, but he felt a call to return to Lancashire and there moved from one house to another of the Catholic gentry, strengthening their faith and asking them to work harder for the cause. On the continent he established training centres, particularly at Douai, where he trained men to become priests to replace those who were being killed in England. Lancashire gave more men to this cause than all the rest of England, and the Fylde gave more than all the rest of Lancashire. In one area of fifteen by ten miles there are fifteen Catholic churches representing sites or chapels which have been in existence for over two hundred years. No other district can boast so many pre-Reformation vestments and so much altar furniture. There were villages here such as Little Crosby where no Protestant had ever been known to live and towns such as Wigan where only a few traders were not of the faith. T. O. Blundell in his *Old Catholic Lancashire* reports an incident in 1610 when the Sefton parson refused to bury a Catholic woman as she was excommunicated. Her friends buried her in the road outside the church. Some pigs dug up the corpse and partly

devoured it.   Then William Blundell of Little Crosby heard of
the incident and enclosed some of his land as a burial ground for
Catholics; for which act he had to pay a fine of £2,000 and to
endure many years of persecution.

Cardinal Allen was followed by Edmund Campion—scholar,
priest, and eventually martyr—who travelled from Douai to
Tyburn gallows by way of Lancashire (1581).   He was very
well liked by the people and did much damage to the government cause, particularly by the distribution of leaflets from a
hidden printing press.   It is said that the people were so eager
to hear him preach that even the gentry would spend a night in
some nearby barn in order to be early at the preaching place
next day.   He was seized in Berkshire when returning to
Lancashire after passing some proofs at his press.

The facts that the arm of the government was weak here
and the Lancashire Fylde a difficult terrain must be borne
continually in mind as we study this history.   Even as late as
1718 the commissioners appointed to inquire into the estates of
certain traitors, and to sell them for public use, 'and also of
Papists and Popish Recusants,' show 469 'Lancashire Landed
Papists,' out of a total of 2,679 in the rest of England; of these
only three other counties slightly exceeded a hundred.   Two
government documents published in the 1590s show obvious
public sympathy here for the Catholic struggle and an equal
scorn for attempts to suppress or convert.   'A Summary of the
Conditions of Lancashire and Cheshire' surveys the reasons for
a decline in convictions of recusants, and for a low state of public
morality, and concludes that the ecclesiastical commission
was not keen on its job, that churches were empty on Sundays
and holy days, that there was a multitude of bastards and an
abundance of drunkards, that even Justices of the Peace and
ecclesiastical commissioners were present at cock fights on
Sundays during the time of divine service and had not been to
communion for years.   Nobody stopped Jesuit priests from
initiating public discussions.   They solemnized marriages and
christenings illegally 'in corners,' and nobody tried to inform
against them.   Even among J.P.s and ecclesiastical commissioners were some who took upon themselves gifts, or grants,
of the goods and lands of recusants, so that the recusants had
legally nothing to forfeit when they were fined in the courts.

The recusants retained the use of their goods but gave up the title to them by a legal fiction.   Only long-standing friendship could carry through such undertakings and they provide the best evidence of the utter failure of Catholic suppression in these parts.

The second document, 'The State, Civil and Ecclesiastical, of Lancaster,' described the Lancashire people's stubbornness against the new laws to fear of losing some of their old-established pastimes and merriment connected with the passing Catholic order, and inveighs against the wickedness, slothfulness, and vice in Lancashire which refused to take account of the new order, or to attempt to stamp out the old.

Even in 1585 a Catholic priest could go abroad dressed in a very conspicuous manner as the following description shows:

'The said Holford is a tall, black, fat, strong man, the crown of his head bald, his beard marguezated; his apparel was a black cloke with Murrey lace, open at the shoulders; a straw coloured fustian doublet laid on with red lace, the buttons red, cut and laid under with red taffeta, ash coloured hose, laid on with byllient lace, cut and laid under with black taffeta; a little black hat lined with velvet in the brims, a falling band and yellow knit stock.'   And the following is an inventory of things found hidden on the person of a captured priest: 'An alb, a girdle of thread, a stole, a corpus, a supalter, three little pewter boxes in a leather case for oil and chrism, a cruet, a surplice, a vestment, a "phannell," a chalice of tin, two little pewter bottles for wine, two little boxes for singing bread, three crucifixes, one Agnus Dei, a Mass Book.'

Because of a certain amount of Catholic participation in plots and suspected revolts against the throne, it has been wrongly concluded that these people were all antagonistic to the regime, a point which Burghley skilfully used at the time of the Spanish Armada, naming Catholics as in conspiracy with the common enemy but not choosing to note that the Catholic gentry had placed their vessels at Drake's command and directed their men to Tilbury to meet invasion.   Stanley Leatherbarrow points out that the Elizabethan Catholic martyrs died first and foremost for their religion.   It seemed that these men were ahead of their time in believing it to be possible to be loyal to the throne as well as to a separate spiritual ideal.   But the government would not support toleration when a rich minority to persecute offered a valuable source of profit (even as late as 1718 the estates of the remaining 2,679 Roman Catholics were valued at £375,284 15s. 2½d.).

By the 1580s the government began to realize that persecution was not going to produce in Lancashire the results anticipated and that a reasoned case must be put forward to support the new Protestant religion. As Hastings wrote to Bishop Chadderton of Chester: 'Good, my Lord, be careful to Preston and other places in your Fylde country. Surely the want of diligent and faithful preaching doth wonderfully hinder the building of our church. . . .'

It was after Elizabeth's reign that a small band of Queen's Preachers and true-hearted Protestant parsons found their work bearing its reward. They gradually built up on their side an imposing list of personalities which captured the imagination of the populace, and left the hard core of Catholics so isolated that pioneering work in this corner of Lancashire made little further progress.

The Catholic cause had thriven in part on lack of opposition, on empty Anglican churches, and priests who never visited their livings, or if they did were more than probably like that Singleton curate who made a dunghill of the chapel yard and kept a tippling house with a 'nowty woman' in it.

The Queen's Preachers largely changed this situation. Moreover another forty years of heavy fines had worn away the weaker edges of the Catholics' solid core. Arrears of fines, for example, could be remitted if the person would conform to the new religion. We know, too, of the results of Cecil's well-devised use of the Gunpowder Plot incident. The public now became imbued with a horror of scheming, plotting Catholics, a horror which, as manifested by 5th November bonfires, has been a long time a-dying.

Later the newly rich merchants of Manchester used their surplus capital to loan money to the impoverished Catholic gentry or to buy land from them. The increasing industrial population and the trade connections of Manchester with London created a growing stronghold of Protestantism in neighbouring south-east Lancashire. The collegiate church at Manchester became a well-known centre of Puritanism and its clergy took the lead in opposition to Catholicism. A minor social revolution was an aspect of the turning of the tables brought about by the Industrial Revolution. The Catholic influence which we see to-day has been built and is being built up again from what remained after that crushing avalanche. Even so there still persists among some Protestants the hatred and fear of Catholics which was born during the early Reformation years.

XII

FROM PILLING MOSS TO GLASSON DOCK

THERE is a busy ferry which crosses the River Wyre near the mouth to Knott End—busy because the nearest bridge across the river is Shard Bridge (Shard is from the Norse, meaning 'shallow,' and when Morecambe Bay fishermen feel the boat going over a shallow place they say it is 'shaarding'). It is seven miles upstream at the spot where Thomas Tyldesley of Fox Hall paid sixpence to be ferried over in 1713 and 'saw ye ferry man carry out of ye boat a Scot and his pack, a sight I never saw before, being 56 years of age.'

While waiting for the ferry you may be lucky enough to see the trawlers sail out on the tide, with a billowing of black smoke from the ungainly stacks which lies heavily on the wind for many a mile, while the crews are busily coiling ropes and getting ready for their long and arduous voyage off the coast of Iceland. Or maybe they are coming into harbour, with their red and green lights twinkling from afar; with in this case no bustle but rather the grim silhouette of patiently waiting craft against the night sky.

The ferry journey is short, but it involves a battle against the fast-moving current. It seems strangely still and quiet at Knott End after the streets of Fleetwood, and this quietness has eventually silenced the railway, for it was closed in November 1950, unable to compete with motor-bus services. It held many memories, however, for Fylde travellers, including that of one old lady who opened the gates at Hackensall Road for forty-two years, and of the guard on the first train out of Knot End (as it was then spelt) who latterly became stationmaster there, and is still alive to recount vivid memories of this one-time essential part of the local coastal life. The line has been

closed from Knott End to Pilling, being part of a branch line
from Garstang. For some time there had been only one freight
train daily and everyone knew it as the 'Pilling Pig.' The line
was opened from Garstang to Pilling in 1870 and the remaining
four and a half miles were not completed until 1908.

Once past the cafés and ice-cream stalls there is a deserted
beach, and at Cocker Houses, if you keep to the shore, there is
only an unfenced road on to Fluke Hall. Alternatively you
might follow a footpath at the edge of the sand all the way from
Knott End. The road proper begins again at Fluke Hall and
leads on to Pilling.

This village, on the turn of the coast, marks the beginning of a
type of scenery which has no equal on the Lancashire coast,
nor do I believe it can be paralleled in any other place, yet it is
strangely deserted and even difficult of access. From now on
we need to watch the road ahead and the warning notices,
for when the incoming tide covers certain marked stakes by the
side of the road it is to be considered impassable. Until the
drainage of these twenty-five miles of moss, Pilling was isolated
in history. The monks of Cockersand Abbey had a grange
on the land above sea and moss, and were doubtless responsible
for the first chapel, of which now so little remains as to be
scarcely worth an antiquarian's study. The new chapel was
erected in 1717 and produced one of the many pugilistic parsons
of the Fylde, Parson Potter, who is said to have fought thrice
and preached twice on one Sunday. Another kind of fighter is
mentioned in the famous ballad of Flodden Field:

> From Pemberton and Pilling Dikes,
> For battle billmen bold were bent. . . .

The construction of dikes was the only way to keep out the
water when it was in a fierce mood:

> First a forest,
> Then a sea,
> Now a moss
> And ever to be.

That old saying and another one, 'God's grace and Pilling
Moss are endless,' do more than I can to convey a picture of the
unrewarding situation of this tiny corner of land which, because
it was just high enough to escape the sea and the moss, provided

a livelihood from the soil, the moss, and the sea. What did it matter if one was cut off from the rest of the world when it was possible to be self-supporting? But we must remember that while the village was growing the old route was still in use to link it to other civilized communities.

As this is true moss country it is worth while to take note of the

Peat-cutting spade and hedging and ditching tools with a 'robin' peat stack in the background

long, deep, and straight drains lying well below the level of the fields, and the roads like causeways standing above the fields. If you leave the road and walk on to the moss by one of the farm lanes you may see a harvest of golden oats growing on the rich black earth, or if not oats, a crop of potatoes. On the ordnance map a portion of the original moss is marked as surrounding Cockerham Great Tarn, but that farmer who has just stopped his tractor at the end of the field has heard of the pool only from his grandfather's talk. It has not existed since his day. Only a small portion of the original marsh remains and that only because at one time the grey top soil was cut away for peat turfs, and without this soil the land is not fit for cultivation.

Along the ditches which edge the fields are stacks of these peat turfs, turning from black to chocolate brown as they dry in the wind and sun. The men who cut the turfs are a race

apart, who 'delve' in spring, then pick potatoes, and finish the
year cleaning ditches.   They cut the turfs with a narrow peat
spade, slightly wider at the bottom than the top, with a
V-shaped cutting edge and polished to a silvery brightness.
The handle is short.   The first stage of cutting is called
'delving.'   To dry quickly and evenly the turfs are laid flat
on the ground.   At the right time they are turned end up, and
this process is called 'plucking.'   Next they are set on their
opposite ends, and this is called 'bullernecking.'   Now they can
be stacked in dozens a step known as 'memoing.'   Finally they
are stacked in long rows known as 'windrowing,' or alternatively the peat cutters have the choice of building round
stacks called 'robins' or 'arks.'   The wide space between each
turf and its neighbour gives free access to air, but continuously
wet weather allows grass to grow round the robins and so
creates a creeping dampness in the stacks which defeats their
purpose.

The strip of macadam beyond Pilling divides the marsh from
the moss, and after a high tide a stranger could be pardoned for
wondering where to find the line of division.   Yet even in such
close proximity to the uncertain sea there are some cottages on
the edge of the marsh.   One of them bears high on its wall a
stone which is marked to show a particularly high tide in
December 1855.   The cottages are banked sufficiently to turn
the average high tides away from their doors, and grouped close
to a spring which used to supply them with water, but nowadays
a pipeline is provided by the Fylde Waterboard.   Like other
outlying places on this coast their inhabitants have always had
their rations delivered between tides, and consider that in this
they have an advantage over townsfolk, having heard dreadful
tales of queues.   As to their battles with winter weather and the
vagaries of the tide, well, one becomes accustomed to such
things!

On the landward side of the road lie the farms which are
above tidal level, and where the road leaves the marsh there is
a change of husbandry.   To the south of it, as far as Liverpool,
lie the hen-cotes and market gardens of the small holders.
To the north of it are the potato and wheat fields of an older
husbandry.

Above all, however, it is a visual memory which the visitor

will carry home with him.   Seaward lies an expanse of marsh grass, shading from yellow green to misty purple.   Behind him is the deeper brown of the sand, the estuary of the Lune, Sunderland Point, and the further shores and blue hills of Furness.   Looking backwards he sees the spire of Pilling Church rising out of the plain on its tree-clothed hillock.   Inland is the vast amphitheatre of the Pennine Hills—a cloth of gold, heather purple, or dun green according to the season.   And in his ears will be the constant sough of the endless wind from the sea, the long shrill call of the plovers, wheeling and circling, and the plaintive bleating of the sheep on the marsh.

For centuries sheep have fed on the marsh, and for a very good reason.   Eighteenth-century John Lucas tells us why: 'These Salt Marshes bear a short Grass which is very valuable for its Excellency in recovering, preserving, and feeding Sheep, and their being of a fat and unctious Soil, as is generally agreed by the Philosophers, may perhaps be the Reason that they abound so in the choicest Mushrooms, which are very much valued by the neighbouring Gentry, who frequently cause a Piece of Marsh to be swept in the Evening and have Abundance, like Truffles, sprung up in the Morning.'

The road rises from the marsh to Cockerham village.   If it were not for this one road (A 588, the only 'first-class' road between the coast and the main north road through Garstang to Lancaster) then Cockerham would be an ideally peaceful village.   Tall trees surround the extremely large vicarage; there is a village inn, joiner's shop, smithy, and old cottages clustered round the centre of the village.   Only the church, a modern one, lies bleak and bare, standing alone in a field.   It calls sadly for trees and clustering homesteads.   'It's a true community,' said the rector.   'The really remarkable thing about Cockerham is not fancy.   It's something rather rare and precious.   Although it is a huge area, from the hills and woods of Forton down to the marsh, the moss, and the sands, it is still a community, with one centre, the village.   In it is the one church, the one school, one parish hall, one pub, and one vicarage.'

But the smithy is closing down.   'There are no horses and no carts,' said the smith, as we glanced at the old tools lying idle on the walls.   'Everything goes on rubber tyres.   It's easy for t' trade to go to Lancaster nowadays.' Another old man, leaning on the wall and smoking a pipe in the peace of the afternoon, seemed to have the same outlook. 'Tractors are nooan so good as horses for t' fields,' he said; 'they compress the earth same as, and don't drop ony muck. You mark my words, farming's ruined wi' tractors. T' fields is already showing results.'

The rector of Cockerham receives the ancient and uncom-muted tithe of the salmon caught in the Lune channel baulk on the early morning tide every fortnight in the season, and any fish left in the trap at the first tide after each new moon and full moon. It is known as 'the Vicar's Tide.' When Cocker-sand Abbey was dissolved it passed into the Thurnham estate and now belongs to a Rawcliffe farmer. The baulk is fished and repaired for him, I was told by the rector, by one Richard Raby who, at eighty-four, still cycles down Thurnham Moss against the terribly strong gales and walks out to the baulk twice a day, from 1st April to the end of August. In the winter he will still go out occasionally to do necessary repairs. 'We generally go down at half-past four in the morning,' said the rector. 'It is pretty cool but even if you catch nothing you see the sun rise over the hills, and the fishermen of Overton and Glasson going down in their boats, or standing in the water with their eaves nets.' These men will stand for hours in the water, which may have occasioned the old Lancashire saying:

He that will fish for a Lancashire man, at any time or tide,
Must baite his hooke with a good Eg-pie, or an apple with a red side.

Cockerham is a tithe village, like so many of the country districts of the old parish of Lancaster. The rector's income still comes in large part from the townships of Ellel, Forton, and Cleveley. The old parish of Cockerham extended right up the River Wyre to Dolphinholme, and in the time of the plague its victims were brought all the way to Cockerham to be buried. 'On the other hand,' said the rector, 'we have a township called Holleth, in the middle of my parish, which belongs, nominally, to the parish of Garstang.' He confessed that the place had an irresistible fascination in its position and atmosphere. 'The Fylde is not far away, but it is not Fylde. It is the first parish in South Lonsdale and the village is stone built, but it is not of the Lune folk. Wyresdale is near enough, but neither is it of the Pennines. Rather does it look towards the marsh and the moss and the sands for its character and livelihood.'

In this area you learn to distinguish between turf-cutters who handle peat and sod-cutters who handle sea turf. Sod-cutters are wet-weather workers. If they were to cut the turfs in dry weather they would be in poor condition when they arrived at some far distant bowling-green. The sod-cutters go out on to the sea marsh and cut the sods of almost pure fescue, a remarkably close, fine turf. The sites are submerged for an hour or two at the top of the tide. The rolled turfs are sent all over the country for lawns, golf-courses, and bowling-greens. There are three firms here employing sod-cutters at the moment, but the pre-war trade has not returned, owing mainly to the high cost, for the work is all hand labour. They still pay manorial dues for what they take away. It does not seem likely that Cockerham will revive the annual Sod-cutters Ball.

The road next passes Ashton Park and crosses the ill-starred Lancaster Canal. The latter was promoted in 1792 with John Rennie as the engineer. It was to have joined Kendal to Wigan by way of Preston and Lancaster, but there were constructional and financial difficulties which prevented its completion, and the sections were joined by a tram-road until 1857, when it was abandoned. The northern end was connected to the sea by a branch to Glasson Dock. The canal had an extremely long level of forty-three miles between Tewitfield and Preston and a very fine aqueduct over the River Lune, completed in June 1796.

In 1839 a certain John Fox wrote in his diary: 'From here to Preston. . . . Heard of a passage boat (at Preston) by Lancaster Canal to Kendal. . . . And now I made the most delightful journey that I ever made in my life, starting at about half past one in the afternoon. . . . The boat was 72 feet long and just wide enough for two people to sit opposite each other. It will hold about 70. Unladen it draws, I think, 3 inches of water. The head comes to the sharpest point from which 10 feet downwards, open, covered with tarpaulin, is the luggage; then 8 feet open for a boatman and about 6 passengers can sit in the open air. From this point the boat is covered with a hood-shaped covering, watertight, and divided into 3 compartments—

the first, fare 6s.—the middle, a sort of steward's room—the aft cabin fare 4s. The thing looked like a canoe. It ran into a covered dock. The passengers from the north disembarked and we entered. I took a seat in the open and at the head . . . and the manner in which we went along the water was for beauty of motion unequalled. Our boat rushed along at the rate of 9 mls. per hour with a smoothness incredible. . . . Two horses, one before the other, towed us in an unceasing canter. They were changed every four miles, not half a minute being taken to change . . . we were in Kendal before 9 o'clock.'

Each boat made a round trip each day and covered the fifty-seven miles between Preston and Kendal in seven hours.

The canal, like all other routes in this region, is focused on Lancaster, which may be seen in the bowl of the valley, standing firmly astride the old ford. As the routes are drawn into Lancaster, so they fan out again on the other side of the narrow neck, into Furness, to Scotland, and into the northern Pennines. Whatever the town may have lost by the changing fortunes of the past it can still command the west coast routes to the north.

China Lane was once called Keln Lane and was so narrow that it could only be used by horse traffic. But it was the highway through the town which served the long-distance routes. In its lower section it is called Bridge Lane, for it led to the old bridge for the crossing of the River Lune.

This is our route to Sunderland Point, bearing left on to the Morecambe road for a short distance to a point whence there is a secondary road, again on the left, bearing a warning notice to the effect that it is impassable at high tide. By walking up the Lancaster Road for a mile and taking the by-lane to Bank End at Hill House you can reach the remains of Cockersand Abbey. The lane becomes a mere footpath on the edge of the shallow, crumbling headland, for the abbey is far enough away from the amenities of the twentieth century. Leland noted that it was 'standing veri blekely an object to al Wynddes' and the monks were afraid that the sea would engulf them. The Dissolution, however (in 1539 at Cockersand), did more damage than the sea, and nothing remains to-day but the chapter-house which was preserved by a local family as a private vault. Since then it has provided shelter for cattle. To-day the entrances are boarded up but it is possible to see the thirteenth-century

vaulted roof and supporting column.   Some abbey stones jut
out from the concrete surfacing of a nearby farmhouse.   The
fourteenth-century choir stalls are in Lancaster parish church.
Other remains have been distributed far and wide.

To-day it is difficult to realize that the buildings once
covered about an acre of ground and that in influence it ranked
third among Lancashire's monastic houses.   We find its origin
in the cell of one Hugh Garth, 'an heremyt of great perfeccon,'
who found this lonely spot and was humble before the elements.
William Lancaster, however, granted him in 1180 Ashelcross
and Cook, with the Lune fishery, as the foundation of a hospital
for aged and infirm monks.   Ten years later a charter was
issued to give the hospital the status of an abbey.   This was
confirmed by Richard I and John, and we see vast and a quickly
accumulating series of rights and privileges added to the abbey
—the pasturage of Pilling, the patronage of Garstang church—
until by 1292 the abbot was able to count his well-knit connections and riches in nearly two hundred townships.   With all
their wealth, however, the monks of St Mary of the Marsh
of the Cocker Sand came to look upon their position as a
purgatory, for in petitioning Richard II to confirm their
charters did they not call themselves 'the King's poor Chap-
lains,' who were daily exposed to perils and destruction by the
sea?

Then came the Dissolution and the visitation of the king's
officers.   Where now are the 'suits of Red Damask' and the
'High Aulter of Imagerye,' the lectern 'of wodde with an egle
upon the same'?   The list reads like an auctioneer's catalogue.
The beds of the monks were noted, each with mattress, two
blankets, and two coverlets.   In the kitchen were 'two furnaces
of Brasse to boil in, twenty-four plates of pewter, eighteen
pewter dishes, fifteen saltcellars, a brazen mortar with a pestle
of iron, a pair of mustard querns, and three barrels of verjuice.'
The king's men walked into the next room with their note-books
—altar cloths, twelve copes, suits of red silk and green silk and
great candlesticks of brass—altogether a long and fascinating
list, now all dissipated, broken, lost, destroyed, forgotten.
Where the buildings stood there is now but the keen edge of a
wind from the sea and a few stunted hawthorns which have been
twisted by the weather so that their heads are touching the

K

ground.   The tide roars on the shingle and little by little more
soft earth falls on the shore.

To-day we find a footpath along the headland with a bracing
wind to raise the spirits as we stride past the century-old lighthouse to Crook Farm, and then slightly inland to reach Old
Glasson and so down to the harbour at the entrance to the
River Lune.

One day I arrived at lunch-time.   A small group of workmen
and women came between the docks from the woodyard.   Two
men, who had been painting buoys a bright red on the quayside,
dropped their brushes and sat on a log of old timber to eat and
smoke.   A fisherman in sea-boots which covered half his person
came up the shingle and anxiously scanned the houses on the
other side of the dock.   His mate was late, he said.   They were
due to sail up to Lancaster on the tide before the ebb.   He
would have to be quick.   Indeed the tide was racing fast
through the broken jetty and swallowing the sand-banks.
They were going to Lancaster to take samples of river water
which were to be tested for pollution.   On this tide and with
this wind the journey should be accomplished in twenty
minutes.

'I heard you made a catch of salmon this morning.'

'Aye, I was lucky enough.'   Still he scanned the far shore,
his cigarette hanging, wind-eaten, from his lips.

All the boats were now floating and drawing at their anchors.
Then we saw a man come from a cottage near the harbour-
master's house.   He was heavy with waterproofs and carried
sandwiches and a flask as he ran clumsily towards the shore.
The fisherman set off also.   They reached the boat together,
pushed off, hoisted the red sail, and in less than a minute they
were in the main current and speeding up-river.

And that was the only activity I saw in Glasson.

I went to an old waterwise inn and ordered salmon sandwiches, for this coast has a pride in salmon fishing and the
salmon was fresh from the sea.   From the outside the building
spoke loudly of waterfront days when freighters were coming in
on every tide with full cargoes.   The sight of it conjured up
images of singing crews, straining blocks, and the heady scent of
seasoned baulks of timber being cut at the saw-mills.   There
was riggers' tar on the air, oil from the tanning of the brown

sails, and the smell of crusted salt on glistening waterproofs. But inside I saw that the old walls were being ripped out and that modern fire-places were replacing the blackened hobs. Quite suddenly it had become just an ordinary public-house.

A young fisherman, tall and blond, was telling how thirty salmon had been caught the day before. He went on to talk about his travels in America. He came back to Glasson for rabbit shooting. 'There's allus plenty of rabbit to shoot, and duck in their season.' He showed me the double-barrelled gun he used for rabbits and the fowler's piece he took in the duck boat, which was lying outside the inn. He told me how he fired a blank cartridge in the air to rouse the duck, then let fly with the long-stemmed gun resting along the prow.

The sun was shining on smoke-stacks topping the woodyard. They belonged to small coasters tied up in the higher dock. To my left was the old Customs House, still bearing the title in peeling black paint, but to-day its weather-worn stones prop up the nets of salmon fishers. One of the lolling painters nodded to me. 'Going to be a drap o' rain,' he said casually.

'What makes you say that? It's a lovely day.'

'Look at Black Combe yon, capped wi' cloud. If she'd bin clear then Ah'd agreed with you. Fine weather would be a certainty. Now sithee, looking this way, if we could a sin t' Welsh hills Ah'd 'ave said for sure a sou'west gale was on the way. An' if Ah could 'ave y'eard Rossall's wife churning Ah'd 'ave said for sure it was a sou'west gale before morning.'

'And who is Rossall's wife?'

'That's surf breaking on Rossall Point. Tha only y'ears it when the air is still enough to y'ear a pin drop. Same as when we con y'ear railway engines hooting at Lancaster we're in for a spell o' easterlies, fine and cool i' summer, frosty cold and fine i' winter.'

The dry dock alongside carried a small coaster from Workington which was being repaired and overhauled in the workshop by the edge of the dock. In the lower dock plenty of private yachts and motor-boats were at anchor. This dock makes a good open-air swimming-pool and is alive with crabs. A cackle of children were busily and noisily fishing them out and putting them in jam-jars. Every child is a fisherman in this village, and Fishnet Point bears witness to the long association this

district has had with fishing.   Salmon fishing is tightly bound
up with 'staking claims,' and I suppose that the term as we use it
in our everyday conversation is derived from this.

When Glasson's first dock was built in 1787 it was capable of
holding twenty-five merchantmen and began to take over the
trade from Sunderland Point, which lies across the river and
where the sailing ships tied up alongside the houses according
to the state of the tide.   Glasson Dock sealed the fate of Sunderland Point as the port to Lancaster, and Glasson was in addition
capable of building the schooners which provided the lifeblood
of communications for this Lancashire coastline and its hinterland during the days when road communications were still
very bad.

In those days, before the Industrial Revolution had evolved
its mass production programme, goods were made slowly and in
small quantities.   A small ship was sufficient to move a cargo
and a small ship required only a small port.   So it was at the
small fishing ports of the Lancashire coast that skilled shipbuilders could be found—men who already knew the secrets of,
and the special conditions required for, building small ships to
work on shallow coasts.   The money came from the merchants
who were interested in the new American trade.   William Stout
of Lancaster was one of those who paid his share . . .   'I was
persuaded by some neighbours to stand a sixth part of a new
ship of about 80 tons, now building near Warton.'   She was
for the Virginian trade.

In and out of the small fishing ports passed the brigs and
brigantines, barques, ketches, and smacks.   Out of the south-
coast ports sailed fast schooners built for the China opium trade,
or to fetch home West Indian pineapples and Spanish and
Portuguese melons before they went bad.   In Lancashire the
cargoes were tobacco, rum, cotton, and mahogany.   Old-
timers will remember the schooners of Barrow owners—men
such as Ashcroft, Walters, Hunter, Fowlie, and William
Postlethwaite.   The latter's *Hodbarrow Miner* and *Hannah
Croasdall* were built at Ulverston.   James Fisher & Sons had
the largest fleet of schooners on the Lancashire coast.   The
firm grew up with the town of Barrow and the iron trade.
Local prosperity made the provision of ships a necessity, and
James Fisher was a shipping agent who rose to the occasion.

Lancashire built sailing ships
(top) *Shoal Fisher Barrow*; (centre) *William Ashburner* as an auxiliary
schooner; (bottom) *Snowflake Runcorn*

Haunters of quaysides will remember from their younger days the *Pool Fisher, Ford Fisher, Shoal Fisher,* and *Creek Fisher,* all three-masted topsail schooners. One of the last was the *British Queen,* built at Preston in 1864. The firm owned more merchant schooners than any other in the country, and when they changed over to steam some of the sailing ships were bought by a Runcorn man who was the last Lancashire man to own a fleet of sailing ships.

Many schooners were built and launched at Runcorn, Fleetwood, Barrow, and Ulverston. Smaller vessels were built at the majority of inland creeks such as Greenodd, Becconsall, and others. Schooners were able to sail well up-river to approach the Lancashire coal-fields and the Cheshire salt-fields. They brought china clay from Cornwall for the potteries. In *New Chum,* by John Masefield, there is a description of the Runcorn fleet, and of the passage down the Mersey which, I believe, after a storm, when many ships set sail together, presented one of the sights of the century.

Glasson was well known for the building of sailing ships, but Greenodd had William and Richard Ashburner. The latter built the first two steamboats for Lake Windermere and his brother went to Barrow and started the first shipbuilding yard there. Joining in partnership again they produced a wonderful line of schooners which old salts remember with pride. Many people must have seen the *William Ashburner* working in and out of Gravesend, Appledore, and many other south coast ports in recent years, although originally built in 1876. Of all the ports on this coastline I have chosen Glasson at which to recapture the old spirit of the sailing ships, for the raw materials are still there awaiting only the flux of imagination to recapture the days of spreading canvas.

But if you can paint your own canvas, if you can build up the past from centuries-old grooves in stones, or rebuild glory from decay, then look across the River Lune to Sunderland Point. Surely this village is wrapped in the tattered cloaks of eighteenth-century merchant adventurers!

H. Milne

Glasson

XIII

MORECAMBE AND HEYSHAM

YOU cannot go to Sunderland Point just when you wish. The tide tables must be considered, for the top of the tide submerges the road. To get there we must in any case move inland from Glasson, back to the main road into Lancaster.

The village lies on a peninsula between the River Lune and Morecambe Bay which has never been quite submerged by the sea. The tide has lapped over the lowest lands with monotonous regularity as far back as records can take us, but it always seemed safe enough for man to *live* on the higher land and to cultivate his fields as far into the tide as he liked to venture. Such were the ancient settlements of which we may see Saxon and Norman remains, and the more recent and quaint aspect of fields built up and protected from the tide by stone walls. We reach Sunderland Point by way of Overton. The Heysham road to Overton is the only one which is not tidal, but that way lies on the other side of the peninsula. We keep to the eastern edge of the sea marsh, and wait for the ebb, watching the muddy water running off the staked road taking with it scampering crabs and belated fishes.

The road brings us to the Golden Ball Inn, or 'Snatchems' as it is better known, the name commemorating press-gang days, tide-bound at high water and a favourite run by wagonette from Morecambe. Nothing could be more reminiscent of the last century than the sight of these old horse-drawn coaches drawn up outside the old-fashioned inn.

Our way then lies through Overton on the hill, past the Globe Hotel, and down on the other side to the small dike beyond which we once more follow a modern road through the sea. Mussel shells and mud lie on its wet macadam as it

winds its two flat miles between the mudbanks where seagulls
and wading birds feed unheeding as you pass.

On reaching Sunderland Point the road fades out gradually,
as though overwhelmed by the bank of shingle which protects
the few houses.   The village has only one lane, leading past a
house which is also a post office and continuing as a blackberry-
bordered footpath to the far side of the narrow peninsula.
There is a path above the tide-line which leads to 'Second
Terrace,' now a row of three-storeyed cottages which were once
Robert Lawson's warehouses.   The quay alongside is now
moss grown and the anchorage a mass of shingle.   A few
cottages and a barn continue the building line, which ends in
the beautiful seclusion of Sunderland Hall.

In William III's reign Robert Lawson, a Quaker merchant,
sent war transports to Ireland.   He also built warehouses and
ships for the new trade with the West Indies, and his sailing
ships tied up alongside the quay to unload rum, tobacco, wood,
and, for the first time in this country, cotton.   It is said that
the strange stuff called cotton lay twelve months in Robert
Lawson's warehouse without a buyer.   Hundreds of West
Indian planters brought their servant slaves with them when
they came over to England, and there were perhaps at one time
fourteen to fifteen thousand such slaves in this country.   One of
these was Samboo, who died at Sunderland Point in 1736.
You may find his grave if you go along the blackberry footpath,
and no doubt there will be a posy of flowers on the stone upon
which is carved:

> Full sixty years the angry Winter's Wave,
> Has thundering dashed this bleak and barren Shore
> Since SAMBOO's Head laid in this lonely GRAVE,
> Lies still and ne'er will hear their turmoil more.
>
> Full many a sandbird chirps upon the Sod
> And many a Moonlight Elfin round him trips,
> Full many a Summer's Sunbeam warms the Clod,
> And many a teeming Cloud upon him drips;
>
> But still he sleeps—till the awakening Sounds
> Of the Archangel's Trump new life impart,
> Then the GREAT JUDGE his Approbation founds
> Not on Man's COLOR, but his WORTH OF HEART.

Growing alongside the barn on the quay is an unusual tree. its white 'cottony' flowers are so un-English as to attract attention.

A lady at one of the cottages was cleaning the steps so I asked her what it was.

'That's our cotton-tree,' she said proudly.

'But cotton grows on a bush, surely.'

'Ah yes, when it's pruned back. But, you see, that was once a cotton seed from a cargo which has been left to grow natural. Some folk says it isn't a cotton-tree, but they can say what they like, they won't take our cotton-tree away from us.'

I don't know the answer, but I have read in one place that it is a kapok-tree and in another that it is a female black poplar and have heard a thousand other guesses. But as Sunderland Point has lost any prosperity it might have had, I have not the heart to dig too deeply for a correct and scientific explanation and would wish it to have a 'cotton'-tree as a reminder of the romantic past. Anyway I have brought away with me some leaves and 'cotton' to stimulate the imagination.

Next century, in 1821, when the shipping had moved across the river to Glasson, the Ship Inn possessed one bathing-machine. Once more it was ahead of local rivals, for that was more than Poulton village had acquired. Three years later the road across the sea marsh to Lancaster was being improved to attract visitors, and a carrier made the journey to Lancaster twice a week and almost, but not quite, daily in 'the season.' A newspaper referred to Sunderland in 1828 as 'much resorted to for sea bathing.' But once again fame and fortune failed to come to Sunderland. By 1834 Poulton's popularity as a bathing resort outstripped that of its rival and, as we now know, Poulton became Morecambe. To-day the few tiny cottages of Sunderland are let for the season to the few who enjoy doing just nothing, who are overjoyed to be cut off from civilization twice a day and who can feel the influence of that tattered eighteenth-century coat of romance I have mentioned. It is there if only you have within yourself a strong enough desire to find it.

As I stood examining the various types of fishing-nets and equipment lying against the wall of the barn, a young fisherman strode past and down the shingle. He picked up an eaves net and walked carefully into the river. When he was waist high in the water he placed the net in front of him at a slight angle to allow a free running net in the current, then stood perfectly still facing upstream.

Among the Chancery Rolls of the Duchy of Lancaster is an edict, dated 3rd June 1382, which has played its part for nearly six hundred years in allowing such as that lad to step down the shingle, for it declares that the Duke of Lancaster, on behalf of the poor fishermen in the duchy, has issued a precept of the sheriff to publish the king's mandate prohibiting any persons within the duchy, holding lands on the sea coast, from preventing the fishermen from setting their nets in the sea and catching fish there for their livelihood.

The eaves net consists of a long pole with a short handle in the centre at one side. The other side has two downward poles at the extremities, and the net is cunningly arranged between the poles so that when a salmon touches the net the fisherman feels the tug and at once pulls upwards to wrap the net once round the fish. Then he thrusts an arm under the water and forward, so that the net folds twice round the fish. This is a deft and quick movement. The odds against a catch are great, so the fisherman told me, as I stood and watched on the edge of the tide. 'Sometimes they're moving tail forrard and when they feel t' net they spring away. At night phosphorus on t' net keeps 'em away. It's best after a shower o' rain. Then t' fish move down-river afore t' flood watter or if they're still in't channel t' rain watter from t' streets o' Lancaster pour its muck in't river an' t' fish can't see so weel so they bump into t' net.'

'How many have you caught this week?'

'Ah've caught none for a week, an' there's only a fortneet to th' end o't season. But its bin a bad un. Salmon may be dear to buy,' he added, 'but this gear cost forty quid, a drag-net would be more than a hundred and badly torn in three weeks.'

He had planted his net in front of a deep hole in the river-bed. Here he would stand, eight hours a day from May until the end of August, with only a break for meals. As he talked he turned his head every few minutes to watch two other fishermen off Cockerham skears. When they moved he would know that the flood water had reached them.

Old quay, warehouses, and 'cotton tree' at Sunderland Point

H. Milne

Higher up-river and nearer Glasson there was a drag-net across the river. This is operated by a fisherman who goes into the river in a boat and pays out the net behind him, from its fastening to a stake on the bank where his partner stands. He then makes a semi-circular sweep and the hauling begins, the man on the shore pulling in the net. As the boat returns to shore the fish go down to the lowest part of the net and at the last haul are thrown high on the sand-bank.

That day we watched till the men off Cockerham left the water, and then the fishing sprawners came up-channel at a stiff pace, their red sails full spread. We would call them 'prawners' but the local fisherman insists on calling them 'sprawners,' trawling for *Leander serratus* or the pink shrimp. The boats are of the 'nobby' type (a point we will consider later) but are adapted to trawling on a hard bottom, the home of the shrimp. The trawl beam must not exceed 25 feet in length nor the net be longer than one and a half times the length of the beam. The foot-rope is strung with wooden bobbins to drag easily over the hard sea bottom. The belly and cod-end of the net are covered with strips of leather to prevent wear on the rough bottom.

How like yachts they look, sailing before the wind! I like the long mast or topmast with its gaff topsail, and the grace of the deckline. In Lancashire 'nobby' is hardly a century old, but has a longer history of development behind it, chiefly in the Isle of Man. It has a graceful, curving stem, a narrow counter, and a raking sternpost. It is cutter-rigged. The hull stands high from the water at the bow and low aft. It is surprisingly buoyant, keeping its stern high to sail the choppy, quick-falling waves of the Irish Sea. It is quick on the helm, working within four points of the wind. Unfortunately the introduction of motor power has altered the form and rig of the nobby; the mast has been shortened, the sail cut down, and the jib boom has practically vanished. Even so it remains a boat with beautiful lines which has earned the praise of fishermen from every coast of Britain.

On the opposite bank from Sunderland Point two men were just entering the water. The fisherman watched them and smiled.

'A couple o' part-timers,' he laughed. 'They work at

Glasson docks and make a bit o' baccy money wi' fishing. They don't know first thing about the ways o' salmon, and that place they're standing hasn't seen a catch in three and a half years.'

These part-timers are, nevertheless, a threat to the livelihood of the regular fishermen. Gradually, however, their licences were being restricted. Last year sixty licences in all were issued, this year only forty-five of which twenty were to full-time fishermen.

This lad I was talking to had gone straight from school to fishing. His father was also a fisherman and was in partnership with another man, both of whom were now standing in the channel nearer the sea.

After the salmon fishing come shrimping and musseling and a variety of inshore work which keeps the fishermen busy all the year round. There is gear to be mended and boats to be painted, and they have little enough time to cross the tidal roadway except for an occasional visit to Morecambe or Lancaster. The place has an Adult Educational Institute which feeds the fishermen's minds during the long winter months, and serves also for the farmers on this narrow peninsula. The winter weather can be very rough, and the few inhabitants are thankful for the thick walls which keep out the driving spray and the house steps which rise above the swirling tide. All rations and supplies are brought over by regular vendors. If it is necessary to walk to Overton for the bus then the Sunderland Pointers think nothing of the one and a half miles, but bear in mind the tides. When a newspaper article observed that Sunderland Point had been asleep for two hundred years they smiled—they had no time for sleep.

I had been talking too long. Already the tide was well up the channel when I set out on the one and a half miles of winding road, and lapped into the sand-dunes and covered the road behind me as I raced forward to the welcome safety of Overton. As I looked back there was nothing to see but a racing tide between the small dike and the isolated village of Sunderland Point.

Overton's lanes run up and down the fifty-foot hill between the clustering cottages. In 1650 the parliamentary commissioners reported that there were eighty families in the villages and that they were surrounded twice in the day by impassable sea. For this reason the villagers asked for their own parson. To-day land reclamation has beaten the sea between Overton and Middleton, although I noticed that men were busily cleaning the drains on which the reclaimed land depends.

The chief beauty of Overton is around the old church. It lies away from the village among the lanes and fields with a breath-taking view through the trees, over the seven miles of Lune estuary, and away to the horizon of mountains. Why, one wonders, should the village have clung to the bottom of the hill, even to lie along the road, when it could have had this view through the centuries?

Once upon a time a family born in a Lancaster ginnel moved to the industrial belt of Lancashire and became rich. They bought, among other things, the field next to Overton church, and one of the family laid it down that when he died he was to be buried in that field so that he could view at leisure the beautiful scene he had not been able fully to appreciate while he was alive and busy earning 'brass' in south Lancashire. The problem was overcome, I am told, by burying him beneath the wall, half of the coffin slab being in the churchyard and half in the field. There is not sufficient evidence to prove that any part of Overton church had an Anglo-Saxon foundation, but there is no doubt about the weather-worn doorway with its beak-head and chevron mouldings.

It is two and a half miles on to Heysham, and it is worth while taking a bus there to escape what appears as devastation to a country lover, or an industrialist's dream according to your fancy. I would otherwise have lingered at Middleton to study the reason for its position on the hill above the ancient sea level, to look at the Roof Tree Café which was once Middleton Hall, and to ponder how the building grew into its own magnificence around its well. While Britain, however, was preparing for the last war, giant industrial plant was laid down behind the Heysham harbour life-line, and to-day is still expanding to meet the present demand for chemicals and refined oil. It is well, therefore, to travel quickly by bus into Morecambe, where this slight blot on the coastline is soon out of mind.

None of the major sea-bathing towns of Lancashire can offer

such glorious scenery as Morecambe.   The bay is shapely and spacious with, as a background, the Lakeland and Pennine mountains which are close enough to play their part in providing a constantly changing pattern of light and shade according to the weather.   From the sea rises Black Combe (1,969 feet) and then, peak by peak, Haycock and Harter Fell, Seathwaite Fell, Walna Scar, Scafell, Doe Crags, Coniston Old Man, and Great Gable.   Humphrey Head stands out into the sea near Kents Bank, and behind rises Wetherlam and the Langdale Pikes.   Behind Grange lies Helvellyn, to the right is Fairfield, and as the eye sweeps eastwards and south-wards it follows the Pennine range as far as Howgill Fells.

This unique landscape, however, played no part in the early development of Morecambe which owes its existence to three circumstances: first, the eighteenth-century craze for sea bathing; second, the competition of early railway companies to provide connections and sailings to Ireland; third, the fact that it was the nearest approachable point on the coast to provide the facilities required by the other two circumstances.

Before this early nineteenth-century settlement there was no such place as Morecambe.   There were four villages in the neighbourhood—Poulton-le-Sands, Torrisholme, Bare, and Heysham.   Of these only Heysham has a past history which commands attention, and is important enough to be considered separately.

A suitable year from which to date the early history of Morecambe is 1820.   Poulton was then a small fishing village of some 360 people, administered by Lancaster three miles away, and in that year a cottage at Poulton was advertised 'To let' as a base for sea bathing.   It was called Morecambe Cottage, thus anticipating the future name of the district, though it had in fact no bearing on the naming of it.

As in the cases of Southport and Churchtown, so at More-cambe the interested visitor can search for the ancient core of the place and find it here in old Poulton-le-Sands, clustered around Poulton Square, the church, and Lord Street.   The modern town has grown up around the old village where seventeenth-century fishermen's cottages still stand, and fishermen are still bred between their cobbled walls.

There have been some changes, as you would expect.

Poulton Hall, for example, has been demolished to make room for the market, but the old gateway has been preserved and re-erected behind Morecambe town hall. It is a little-known link with George Washington, for the hall was owned, in part, during the fifteenth to sixteenth centuries by President George Washington's direct paternal ancestors, whose main residence was at Warton.

In Poulton Square a farmhouse still stands, dated 1675. Observe the manner in which the date is carved so that the figures stand out in relief. It is noticeable that from the beginning of the eighteenth century it became customary in Lancashire to incise such carvings.

The ancient cottages have been built of rounded seashore cobbles of irregular size. In their yards you may see boats brought up from the sea, nets spread out to dry, or a hand net laid against a sunlit wall. The local fisherfolk are believed to have come from Scotland a long time ago: first the Baxters and Bells, then the Armistead and Woodhouse families. To this day you can safely assume that the fisherman who offers to take you for a sail in the bay will be called Woodhouse, Willis, Baxter, or Gardner. They have profited in their profession and keep abreast of the times, and they are joined together in a local trawler co-operative sales organization which pots the shrimps and bags the mussels to send all over the country, while many a housewife earns spare-time money in shrimp picking— that is quickly separating the 'shruffs' from the fish. One of the fishermen had a retail shop on the old market and died leaving £60,000. Even as I walked across Poulton Square the other day a neat and modern motor van threaded its way through the passers-by: 'James Baxter—fish salesman' I read on its side.

Apart, however, from taking visitors occasionally for a sail round the bay, the fishermen live an existence separate from the holiday life of Morecambe. It is just possible, perhaps, to touch the fringe of it in a number of ways. If you see a funeral procession on the promenade with blue jerseyed fishermen in attendance, you will know not only that a fisherman has died but that an old tradition is being followed, and the deceased is being taken for his last look at the sea. Or, next time you are walking on Morecambe promenade, look out for the fishermen

—old and young—gathered in groups, sitting in the sun and talking shop about tides and currents, sand-banks and skears. Some are now retired and have discarded the blue jersey, but they cannot resist the pull of the only life they know, and are oblivious of the constantly passing crowds of holiday-makers. At the heads of the runways are their nets, partly painted boats, running gear, hand-nets, and the like with perhaps an old shrimp-boiler such as is used on the boats while they sail homewards with the catch. Many a time the mussels are bagged on the slipway near the town hall.

I remember seeing the south cone hoisted one evening. Dark clouds had crept inland from the sea as I hurried into the pier pavilion where, during the interval, Morecambe's own comedian Eddie Morrell, brought a group of local fishermen before the curtain and introduced them as the lifeboat crew who would now collect for the lifeboat funds. Briefly he told us that they were 'standing by,' for a trawler was aground in the bay. As he spoke there was a dramatic beating of rain on the pavilion roof, and doors clanged in the gusts of a howling wind.

The next morning was sunny and I made my way to the head of a slipway to listen to the talk of the fishermen. A young fellow in sea-boots was standing in the centre, telling how he had been out in the bay in the storm and had gone aground off Silverdale. The old men were quizzing him as to the exact position. Every sand-bank was scrutinized in memory and experience until the very place was found.

'I know it,' said one of the men triumphantly. 'Mi feyther went agreuand theer, mi grondfeyther went agreaund theer, an' Ah've bin agreaund theer.' Then they all laid down what, from their own experience, should or should not have been done in the circumstances, and so the youngster had learned another lesson.

The ancestors of these men went fishing and smuggling from this shore when at the beginning of the eighteenth century the will of Francis Borne provided that 'Whereas the Town of Poulton is at a considerable distance from any Church for Worship of Almighty God and free school for instruction of youth,' certain rents be made available for the erection of a 'Chappell.' This chapel of ease to Lancaster existed in 1745, and its reconstruction of 1841 stands on the same site in Poulton to-day.

In 1829 a coach, 'The Old Times,' was advertised to run from Lancaster to the Bull Hotel, Poulton, during the season, 'to suit the times of bathing,' and the Heysham Hotel advertised accommodation for families, baths, and bathing-machines. People of fashion and quality were attracted as at all other bathing places, but Poulton's special attraction was its regatta. Local men began to build houses along the barren seashore, and the magnificent view across the bay was, then as now, a feature of recommendation which no other resort could offer.

Five years later another coach, 'The Royal Sailor,' was added, and the regatta constantly advertised. The new steam-boat *Windermere* from Ulverston called at Poulton, Blackpool, and Liverpool in its three weekly sailings, and in 1838 the *Windermere* was berthed at Poulton and took tourists to the Lake District.

Two years later came the first approach of the extending railway system. The Preston–Lancaster Junction Railway brought London, Birmingham, Manchester, and Liverpool within three miles of Poulton. Soon it was carrying four hundred passengers a day and the working classes began to find their way to Poulton, *en masse*. 'Everybody' joined the rush to the coast. The railway whetted the appetite, and the sea-bathing fever was catching. There was no restriction on the type of vehicle used, provided it could carry the load.

In the 1841 census the Poulton population was still only seven hundred, of which a large proportion were fishermen, but in 1844 the town fathers decided to leave the fishermen to take care of themselves and to cater for the new type of holiday-maker. The Morecambe Bay Harbour and Railway Company was formed and work began on improving the town. Gradu-ally the 'Bay' slipped from the title of the company. As the town grew through the activities of the company, the company's name was heard more frequently than that of the town, and 'Morecambe' came to be the short way of referring to Poulton, and was officially adopted as the name in 1870.

The North Western Hotel was begun in 1847, and the sea wall, built to protect it in 1849, became the beginning of the promenade. The North Western Railway was responsible for

L

the venture, in anticipation of the construction of the railway which reached Morecambe in 1850, by which time a jetty—'The Little North Western' as it was affectionately called—had already been constructed, and the company immediately began to ship pig-iron from Furness.

They had their eye on two attractive businesses. On 31st December 1851 they announced a Belfast–Morecambe steamer service with direct connections to Yorkshire. The very first excursion train carried a Sunday-school outing from Clapham and Austwick in the heart of the Pennines, and this was followed by a succession of mill and factory trips from all over Lancashire and from Yorkshire, particularly the West Riding, for the railway to Morecambe was the only connection it had with the west coast. You may often, to this day, hear Morecambe called 'Bradford-by-the-Sea.' One district was actually dubbed 'Little Bradford,' boarding-houses had such names as 'Sheffield House' and 'Bingley House,' and the Yorkshire folk became firmly established before the direct railway communication with Lancashire in the 1880s brought a fresh influx from the county. To-day it is still the Yorkshire business man's home, from which he travels to work each day in the same way that Manchester men travel from Southport, St Anne's, and Black-pool.

A plan of these early years, however, shows the only buildings then to have been the railway station, the Old Terrace, rows of houses in Queen Street, Poulton Hall, and Poulton village, two cottages on the shore, the North Western Hotel, and the New Inn. The many thousands of visitors could find no accommodation, so that the publication of a petition for a resident policeman is understandable even if his efficiency must have been doubtful in a town that was growing too quickly. The fare from Morecambe to Ireland then was 3s. 9d. return, with a three times a week service. There were also daily steamers to Barrow and Furness Abbey, and a daily yacht to Grange across the bay.

There was a bewildering mixture of old and new ideas. Mr Curtis ran his omnibus to meet the trains, proudly telling his customers that Morecambe now had eighteen bathing-machines and a confectioner's shop, while the churchwardens angrily announced that they would 'vigorously prosecute all persons found bathing and sailing during the hours of divine service.' Of course, by 1861, there was the usual by-law—'That there be 50 yards between bathing-machines used by men and those used by women, pleasure craft not to approach within 50 yards of the machines.'

In the following year the promenade was opened and Morecambe's future as a fashionable watering-place seemed assured. It was about two hundred yards long, extending from the present Central Pier to the stone jetty, but only seven yards wide, paved with a mixture of grass and cobbles and running round a tiny harbour where fishing-boats were moored. Just behind it was the West View Hotel, now a multiple tailor's shop. Before the promenade was extended, the sea at high tide flooded the houses round the gas works and rushed into Poulton Square. Now the older natives ('sand grown uns' is the local name for them) feel that they are away from the sea, which is a sadness with them. I know some of them, and one old lady in particular, who find more pleasure in looking backwards to the Morecambe which was, and to them is, still a village. They can re-create a picture of West View Road, once facing the sea, where some of the old cottages remain. Then a row of better-class houses was erected in front of the cottages on the sea side of the road with their stabling and gardens stretching inland in parallel lines. Some of them are still there, now providing storage for a variety of small traders. Where West View Road curves seaward to meet the present promenade you will now find Northumberland Avenue, once gated at the seashore end, while at the other once stood the Midland Railway station, the foundations of which still exist in the adjacent car park. Opposite stands de Lacy's Café, which was in its heyday when the Midland Railway unloaded hungry trippers on its doorstep. I have referred elsewhere (in *The Roof of Lancashire*) to the all-powerful Norman de Lacy family of Clitheroe Castle, and am reminded at this point of a solicitor friend telling me of the large number of noble Norman names now borne by labourers and other plebeian members of the working class which he had come across in his work.

The old lady in her tiny dwelling behind Morecambe gas works told me of the shrimp-sellers and butterscotch vendors who used to follow the trippers back to their waiting trains, and of the women in white aprons and starched bonnets who met the incoming trains with 'Want a nice place for tea and hot water?'

'Aye,' she went on, 'there were wagonettes to Heysham, and a visit to t' Strawberry Gardens was a perfect night out for a young man and a girl.   Or to t' Summer Gardens for a change.   They had just everything.   If we wanted a doctor, though, or a bottle of medicine, we had to tramp to Lancaster and back.   That was over Moss Lane, Poulton Square, and Torrisholme on the coach road.   There wasn't much coal to burn then but an old fellow used to come from Heysham carrying peat from door to door.   "Ony turf to-day, Elizabeth," was his cry.'

In a neighbour's house I noticed a beautifully carved wooden box on the wall.

'Aye,' she told me, 'mi husband brought it home from t' breeaking-up yard.   He used to wark theer.'

There are many visitors to Morecambe who remember the ugly shipbreaking yards at the stone jetty, where many famous ships came to their last berth, including the battleship *Centurion*. The workmen took home many articles of the ship's furniture, and there was a room where visitors could buy them as souvenirs before this area was cleared to make the present open-air baths and neighbouring gardens.

'Why is it called Battery?' is a question often asked by Morecambe visitors when they see at the southern end of the promenade the Battery Hotel, which has played a part in local history.   This area was originally called the Cattle Fields, for it was here that cattle were impounded on their arrival by the Irish boats.   As Morecambe developed, the Figure Eight Park was built on the site, only to be taken over from 1867 to 1876 by the artillery for a practice range.   An indenture of 1587 refers to a windmill in this area, and an old engraving shows what remains of the structure being used as an ammunition lock-up for the artillery.   But as more and more visitors arrived the practice grounds became dangerous and they were removed to Bare.

A footpath along the shore leads to Heysham village whence, from the crest of the promontory, can be seen the steamers for Ireland in the harbour, and the answer to the question: 'What happened to the Irish service from Morecambe?'   In the early days of railway construction, during the mad competitive rush of the various companies to provide rail connections and port facilities to Ireland, the original choice of port was not always good.   In the case of Morecambe the promoters were bent on linking together various ideas to make the proposed railway a good investment.   In addition to the conveyance of holiday-makers and day-trippers there was iron ore to export, cattle to import, and the hope of providing port facilities sufficient to attract shipping with mixed cargoes for destinations in Yorkshire and Lancashire, Kendal and the north of England.   Many of these schemes were defeated by the shallow water in Morecambe harbour and the steep rise and fall of uncontrolled tides, making fixed Irish sailings, and therefore regular train services, impracticable.   The Belfast steamers transferred to Piel Pier and then to Barrow, a quickly growing town with excellent docking arrangements.

The Midland Railway had a working agreement with the Furness Railway but was determined to have a dock of its own, and found the answer close to their Morecambe base, in Heysham Lake with its deep water, enabling the building, in 1904, of the modern harbour of Heysham.   This solved the problem of the competition of the Lancashire and Yorkshire Railway, which was running an Irish service from Fleetwood. After the railway amalgamation Heysham was chosen as the port for Ireland, and Fleetwood was allowed to specialize in the trawling industry.

Historically the new industrial age had returned to an Irish trade route to Heysham Lake which had been in operation a thousand years earlier, leaving as one of its desirable memorials the chapel of St Patrick, standing in splendid isolation on the headland above Heysham church.   The story, or legend, about its foundation is that St Patrick landed here after shipwreck in the bay.   Be that as it may, the building remains of supreme interest to the archaeologist and a source of wonder to the rest of us who find it hard to grasp in imagination the fact that this single-cell chapel has stood at any rate from pre-Norman Conquest time, and is the only one of its kind in England.   The experts may argue from that point onwards as to whether it is Saxon or Irish or a bit of both.   The legend of St Patrick and the very general intercourse with the Irish along this coastline support somewhat those who adhere to the Irish claims, more especially since Heysham's natural deep-water harbour was the only one on this sandy, shallow water coastline and attracted traders from the earliest days of our civilization.

It is truly remarkable to be able to stand here in the twentieth century and feel the influence on you of this ninth-century (or even earlier) church. It is a plain rectangle 27 feet 6 inches by 9 feet with rubble walls 30 inches thick. The west wall and part of the north wall are down. The east wall is blank but on the south side are the remains of a window and a perfect semicircular headed doorway, crudely ornamented. But that is not all. The first visit always brings its reward in the finding, close by, of six graves, hewn in the living rock, which are shaped to the form of the human body. At their heads are the sockets for crosses.

I have tramped and wandered in many corners of Lancashire, but in three places only am I aware, in loneliness, of a close affinity to some previous race, of some rare Celtic quality of the atmosphere not to be denied. One of these places is in the neighbourhood of Pendle, another is by the circle of standing stones on Birk Rigg near Ulverston, and the third is by St Patrick's chapel at Heysham. Come to this chapel in late evening when the tourists have departed and the villagers are sitting in the lamp-light behind the grey stone walls of their houses. Let there be a gentle wind from the sea, with the waves lapping at the foot of the headland below the ruins. The mountain frieze will be merging into the dark velvet curtain of night. The broken walls of the chapel will stand in silhouette against the last light of day. Then you will have the perfect conditions for evoking an atmosphere which would have fallen richly and darkly from the pen of Thomas Hardy.

But we have not yet finished with the Northmen. Below in the churchyard is a 'hogback,' estimated as of late tenth-century date. It is one of those fascinating memorials of men who were becoming Christian but could not dismiss entirely their upbringing in the lands of mythical gods, so that their new Christian ideas were carved in old forms. What do we see on the Heysham hogback? The experts say that the crude figure hanging from a tree is that of Christ in the form of Odin—a very early representation of the cross of Jesus.

Rock-hewn graves at Heysham on the cliff edge high above the sea

H. Milne

The Anglo-Saxons also found Heysham worthy of their art and religion. They built their church below St Patrick's chapel, on a larger piece of ground on which a church still stands. Before going inside this church inspect the two-and-a-half-foot cross-shaft which, more than anything else there, and especially in such close proximity to the carving of the Northmen, conveys an idea of the Anglo-Saxon approach to religion. On one side is represented a seated figure below an arch, on the other is a building with three windows and in each window is a head : below is a doorway in which stands a figure, wrapped in a swathing band, which some say is perhaps the raising of Lazarus, others the resurrection of the Lord. But in either case it surely marks a stage in those developments of religion at Heysham, commemorated in order by St Patrick's chapel, the hogback, the Saxon cross, and the little Saxon church, which received decorated and Perpendicular additions through the centuries. In 1904 the church was granted to the Abbey of St Martin of Sees, in Normandy, later passing to the Abbey of Syon in Middlesex. At the Dissolution it was sold (1554) to Thomas Fleetwood. In 1844 the advowson was acquired by Clement Royds of Rochdale and has remained in a branch of his family. There is no other place where the sense of the growth of the church in its earliest period in this county so stirs my imagination as upon this quiet headland at Heysham.

If you pick out the fifty-foot contour line on this peninsula, between the River Lune and Morecambe Bay, you will be following the line of a yet more ancient civilization in these parts. The barrows at Heysham are linked with those at Torrisholme by way of the coastal ridge, or by Middleton, Moss Side, and White Lund. Middleton shows a later village formation grouped round a spring-water supply and a hall, but White Lund is a place-name reminiscent of Druidical rites; there are other similar examples in Lancashire, as, for instance, Lund in Amounderness. The fifty-foot contour must always have been valuable to all dwellers on this peninsula, for the sea covered the low-lying land between tides, as it still does in some parts. So it is that the ancient villages of Overton, Middleton, and Heysham have grown up on that land which rose safely above the sea marsh.

As on the rest of Lancashire's coastline here too the Norse

immigration brought the fisherfolk, whose descendants to this day prefer to keep themselves a race apart, and who, although their dialect is gradually dying out, still speak of *skear, craam, raap, roost, shaard*, and so on. The old families of Blacow, Curwen, Siddall, and Hadath, whom you may find in their little cottages making teas of home-made cakes, salmon, and chicken, are numerous enough to play cricket matches with one family a side.

In the summer months Heysham prepares to receive thousands of daily visitors and literally sets out its stalls, which add a picturesque quality to the short street in the old headland village. There is an oriental gaiety about this open street bazaar. The crowd surges backwards and forwards between the ice-cream vendors, the golden piles of oranges, the bewildering disorderliness of cheap toys and knick-knack mementoes, while children tilt mineral-water bottles down their throats and parents sample a Heysham speciality—nettle beer. Some walk further, past the church. The contrast between the two sides of the churchyard wall is fantastic. All about the Elizabethan hall on Heysham Head is the fun of the circus, and across the valley you may see the members of a large holiday camp enjoying themselves in organized games, but in the same glance you may also see the neolithic burial-grounds, raising huge rounded knolls above the earth's surface. Heysham loves contrasts. Best of all it clings to the horse landau. These vehicles follow one another like black beetles along Barrows Lane which, in consequence, carries a heavy scattering of stable manure, the smell of which conjures nostalgic memories of days in any town before the advent of the motor-car. But all this is the Heysham of summertime, which is false.

With the end of summer the village returns to its normal life, except for the annual stir of the New Year's Day procession. This began in 1844 with a resolution by the local freemasons that they would have a procession in full regalia, gloves, and rosettes, and that the silk-mill band should play for them. The procession then began at the school and led to the Royal Hotel, with a tremendous dinner and the famous roly-poly pudding. This has now been changed to a morning procession to church, followed by a good old dinner of roast beef and Yorkshire pudding, and Christmas pudding, followed by speeches, after which there is a further parade in the afternoon, finishing with dancing in the evening.

Yes, give me a winter's day at Heysham with the sun shining and the sea spume in the air, when the villagers have packed their stalls away and the dry leaves rustle down the empty wind-blown street. There is the thunder of surf in the air and tall trees moaning in the storm wrack. Then you can see the low-built, grey stone cottages as truly functional in their bareness, crouching against the side of the hill, whence they can laugh at the stucco 'Sea View' villa, flaunting itself to chilly death on the exposed summits. The wisdom of men who built the old village in a rocky cleft behind the headland is a wisdom to be admired.

XIV

MORECAMBE BAY

WE are now advancing into the huge semicircle of
Morecambe Bay. The name is Roman—Sinus
Moricambe—and there is another Moricambe
to be found in the Upper Solway Firth, which
still carries the Roman spelling unaltered. It
would almost seem that the name was intended to denote a sea
rather than a bay, but this is dangerous ground. Many anti-
quarians of the eighteenth century, misled by the forged
Itinerary of Charles Julius Bertram, adjusted Ptolemy's latitudes
and longitudes and put Moricambe estuary where we find the
well-known Morecambe Bay. The map-makers followed the
antiquaries, although there was still a Moricambe estuary in the
Solway estuary as plotted by the sixteenth-century geographers
from their reading of the Ptolemy figures.

The ancient name, adopted by a cottage at Poulton, eventually became the name of a modern town, so that it is easier to
suppose that the bay is named after the town than vice versa,
as is in fact the case, but until this recent evolution the full
extent of the bay as far as to the shore of Furness, was more
commonly realized.

To the Irish adventurers and merchants Morecambe Bay
presented a large open gateway into England, and so across
England to the Continent. You can plot their trade routes by
observing the distribution of the wheel-head type of carved stone
cross up the river valleys and along the hills; the bay's many
tributaries providing the most natural corridors of access to the
hinterland. When the trend of traffic came to be reversed it
was from this area that English ships began to sail to Ireland, as
they do to this day.

Between about 1670 and 1765 a group of Liverpool adventurers established themselves in Douglas to organize contraband
trade into England from the Isle of Man. This was possible
because the Isle of Man was the private kingdom of the earls of

Down to the sea in carts
The fishermen follow the tides

N. Wolstenholme

Derby and goods arrived there duty free. The East and West Indiamen, making for Liverpool and Bristol, found it worthwhile to call at the island with tobacco, silk, tea, linen, lace, muslin, rum, and brandy, and it was then a matter for local seamanship in small boats to deliver the goods on the deserted Lancashire and Cumberland beaches where there was a local community, including parsons and squires, willing to receive them. Graham Sutton tells a good story of these days in his *Shepherd's Warning*.

There are, as it were, two Morecambe Bays. When the tide is out you may walk away into a vast desert of sand, the wide circle of green and brown fells almost enclosing its yellow acres; although in the heat of the sun a veil-like haze rises from the moist ground, cutting off the surrounding land from view. Above and beyond the fells is a ragged frieze of blue mountains. Suddenly you find yourself on the edge of a river-course winding through the sand and, as you descend the ten or twenty feet to the water's edge, the outer world vanishes from sight and the silence is that unbelievable stillness of mountains and deserts.

The other Morecambe Bay is seen from the heights of Arnside Knot, Allithwaite, or Birk Rigg, when the tide is at the full and reflects the blue sky. Its character is thus utterly changed; the surrounding hills have a different appearance. No matter on what part of the bay you may be there is an entirely new outlook. That is why Morecambe Bay can provide continual interest for a lifetime, and if it had been in any other country than Britain it would have been 'discovered' long ago. In a selfish way I am glad that its charm remains for the solitary explorer. Turner and David Cox made numerous paintings in the area, displaying a variety of its moods.

Ahead of us is a twisting coastline incorporating innumerable creeks, small estuaries, and tiny villages where the men would die if separated from their boats and fishing. Even if fishing no longer provides a livelihood for so many of them, yet all are still quick to doff their overalls in the evening and don the blue jersey, and you may see them preparing gear or painting boats or hear the crack of a gun as they stalk wild duck in the estuaries. It is an old and traditional love which is bred in the bone and has been recognized as long as men have been inquisitive enough to keep records. Read Richard James, 1592–1638, in his *Iter Lancastrense*:

> Heere through ye wasshie sholes
> We spye an owld man wading for ye soles
> And flukes and rayes, which ye last morning tide
> Had stayed in nets, or did att anchor ride
> Uppon his hooks; him we fetch up, and then
> To our good morrowe, 'Welcome gentlemen,'
> He sayd, and more, 'You gentlemen at ease,
> Whoe money have, and go where ere you please,
> Are never quiett; wearye of ye daye,
> You now come hither to drive time away;
> Must time be driven? longest day with us
> Shutts in to soone, as never tedious
> Unto our buisnesse; making, mending nett,
> Preparing hooks and baits, wherewith to gett
> Cod, whiting, place, uppon ye sandie shelvs,
> Where with to feede ye markett and our selvs,
> Happy ould blade, whoe in his youth had binne,
> Roving at sea when Essex Cales did winne,
> So now he lives. . . .

Eighteenth-century John Lucas is very explicit about cockles: 'The places where they are found are called Cockle Skears, and they are got by treading or often by running over the Place which Motion works them up to the Top of ye Sand. The Cockles on these Sands are so excellent in their kind, and so much preferable to those on the East Shore of England, that they are carried 60 or 70 Mile Eastward.'

No matter at what part of the bay you may find yourself to-day, you will see the two-wheeled carts, each pulled by a horse, pursuing their lonely ways over the shining sands as they follow the tide. They have set out from Morecambe, Silverdale, Bolton-le-Sands, Baycliff, Flookburgh, and other villages to bring back shell-fish and flukes. As with so many old crafts and industries the trade is not such as the last century saw, but in villages like Flookburgh it is still the chief occupation.

I was fishing for eels in the river channel in 1940 when the time came for me to sign up with my age group. At the appointed hour I went to Grange-over-Sands (which is the only town on that part of the coast), only to be told that they had not got a Labour Exchange and that I would have to walk to Flookburgh, the infrequent bus having just departed. Flookburgh received its trading charters in 1278 and 1412 and bears the stamp of its local importance in its name, and continues some of the traditions of the functions of its status even though it has lost its protector, Cartmel Priory, and has been by-passed by modern transport. In the single street, and in the back yards of fishermen's cottages, are to be seen the special carts, nets hanging to dry, jumbos, and craams. At cottage doors or leaning on garden walls are the old fishermen with coppery faces and always wearing the blue jersey. They travel three or four miles across the firm sand of the bay in the carts until they reach their specially chosen sites. They spy out the small

Jumbo and craam used by the fishermen of Flookburgh

breathing-holes of the cockles in the sand and with one quick movement of the craam they bring them to the surface. The 'craam' (a Norse word) is like a three-pronged fork with a claw-like curve. Sometimes a 'jumbo' is used to bump up and down on the sand and so bring the cockles to the surface, although the process is damaging to smaller shell-fish. A jumbo has a heavy wooden base with two handles at each end by which it is raised to waist height. No more, however, will these men bring home to Flookburgh 3,000 tons of cockles per annum, selling at 48s. per ton, which were the regular figures for the last years of the nineteenth century.

Mussels are taken from the skeers (or skears). One method is to sail round them in a boat and rake them off with a twenty-foot-long mussel craam. Another is to walk out at low tide and pick them by hand. Baulks are built in zigzags where the mussels cling. Anyone may bait eels in the river channels and bring flat fish from beneath the sand by gently jumping up and down on it when it is wet. Occasionally a porpoise, sword-fish, or seal will venture too far and be caught, and on one occasion a fisherman friend caught a six-foot shark which we hung outside the cottage for the inspection of the village.

Sewage contamination has ruined the mussel industry and we saw, when visiting Lytham, what precautions have had to be taken.   You will find in Morecambe that more attention is paid to shrimps and prawns.   But even so the older generation will continue to go out with their carts and hand-nets, or spring the long curves of fluke nets across the channels.   They are not likely to be replaced by another generation.

The peculiarity of the Morecambe Bay water has resulted in the evolution through generations of a type of fishing-boat called the 'nobby.'   There are one hundred and twenty-five miles of open water between Morecambe and Ireland.   Across that space comes the full force of the south-west gales.   The shallow depth of the sea bed forces the waves into short lengths with steep sides which create a foul sea for a small boat.   Hence the cutter-rigged smack called the 'nobby,' which will meet any weather, manned by fishermen who are admired for their rough sea sailing on all the British and Irish coastlines.

The dangers of the Lancashire coast were even greater before the days of lighthouses, accurate charts, and navigation.   Year after year ships trying to make Liverpool were wrecked on the Fylde coast as the south-west storms blew them off their course and no other harbour was available.   Similarly if they missed Glasson or Sunderland Point they were liable to come to grief in Morecambe Bay.

Against this background the ancient pattern is still woven, although, as we follow the coastal route north from Morecambe through Bare and Bolton-le-Sands, we see, at first sight, only a modern veneer of red-brick houses.   There is another historic pattern woven on the hilly slopes to the sea.   In the thirteenth century Nicholas of Torrisholme held land there provided he supplied the larder of the king's castle at Lancaster.   Adam, son of Gilemichael, held land at Slyne for being the king's carpenter.   Roger de Gernet of Halton was the chief forester for the county, and also held land at Heysham on condition that he attended the king when he visited the county.   He had to meet the king on the border of the county with a horn and a white wand, remain with him while in the county, and conduct him safely back to the border.   The white wand was a symbol, the horn a warning, and both relics of the dangerous days of forest travel.   Alicia Gresingham was given land for breeding and rearing falcons and hawks out of Lonsdale for the king's use. When they were strong enough for service they were handed to the sheriff of Lancaster as you may read in the *Testa de Nevill* (1247).

Hest Bank had its pier in 1820 where vessels from Liverpool and Glasgow unloaded goods for Kendal and Lancaster, for it was on the main highway system. Out of Lancaster came the north road to Scotland, and from it branched that invisible road across the sands of Morecambe Bay which provided a short route to the isolation of Furness. The stage-coaches started from the King's Arms, or the Bear and Staff, at Lancaster, and threaded their way down the narrow, crowded China Lane and Bridge Street, crossed the river to Skerton, and so on to Hest Bank. At the Hest Bank Hotel was a room where a lantern was lit every evening at sundown to guide belated travellers on the sands.

The crossing was considered safe only when the tide had ebbed for four hours, or for two hours if the tide was coming in. This left six hours for the crossing. Even so, 'a reflection on the number of unfortunate people,' says the Dickson report, 'who are annually lost in crossing these deceitful sands, touches the nerve of humanity.' The danger consisted in crossing when the tide was coming in, or when there was a heavy sea mist, or when the three river fords of Kent, Keer, and Leven *en route* were not known, or when vessels had made holes in the sand.

The Keer channel lies about two miles out from Hest Bank, and until 1820 coach drivers chose their own crossing, after which date a guide was appointed to assist them. The next four miles leading to the Kent channel are easy going, but the channel itself is deep, always changing, and the flow very swift. The rest of the journey to the Guide's House near Kents Bank is easy, and the way lies overland through Flookburgh (and later also through Cark) to Sandgate (Sand Road) for the next crossing. The earlier crossing from Flookburgh reached the further shore between Conishead Priory and Bardsea; the later one led to the Guide's House at Ulverston.

Bearing the tides in mind it is an experience to walk out on the sands from Hest Bank to Silverdale, about five miles. On the way is Priest's Keer, mentioned by William Stout (see page 179) and so called because this is the way the monks of Furness

Abbey came to their salmon claim on the River Lune. The Keer channel can be crossed three hours after the ebb. About a mile out from Jenny Brown Point bear north for Silverdale. It is not safe to make landward between Keer and Jenny Brown Point because of the depths of mud. Maybe you will have the experience of eighteenth-century John Lucas: 'Whoever walks upon these Sands a little before Rain will hear a hissing Noise, occasioned by the breathing of innumerable little Bubbles, and will feel a noysom stinking Savour; the Reason of which I take to be, that the Pores of the Sand as well as of the Earth, are at such times unlock'd, and so steams of crude sulphur with a Mixture of Salts do breath forth and occasion this ungrateful Smell. This the neighbouring Inhabitants take for as sure a Progmastik of Rain. . . .' You will not be entirely alone on your journey, for in their season you will see shell-ducks, curlew, redshanks, herons, gulls, turnstone, knot, durlin, godwit, ringed plover, mallard, pochard, teal, widgeon, pintail, scoter, shoveller, and wild geese, all of which use the nearby marsh for feeding and some for nesting. You should also avoid Quicksand Pool, which is an area of loose, wet sand formed by a small stream which has not made a channel of sufficient depth to take away its surplus water. A compass is essential in case the mist comes down, and be sure of the timing of the tide!

Such an expedition will give you an appreciation of the history which has grown around the oversands route. A glance at the map (opposite) is sufficient to show the superiority of this route over the land routes, and will show also that the railway to-day, by going partly over the sea, is the closest modern approximation to this shortest distance route.

The obstacle to any easier land route was always a large peaty bog at the foot of Whitbarrow Scar and the nearest approach to one was the 1820 turnpike which did, in part, pass over the bog. The official route is revealed in the preamble to an Act of George III, 1763: 'Whereas the road leading from Kirkby Kendal, through Crossthwaite and over Bowland Bridge, in the county of Westmorland and from thence over Cartmel Fell to Newby Bridge, and from thence over Elingarth Brow to the market town of Bouth and over Pennybridge by Greenodd, a small seaport, and from thence on the east side of Arrad to Ulverston, out from thence through Lindal by Titup to Kirby

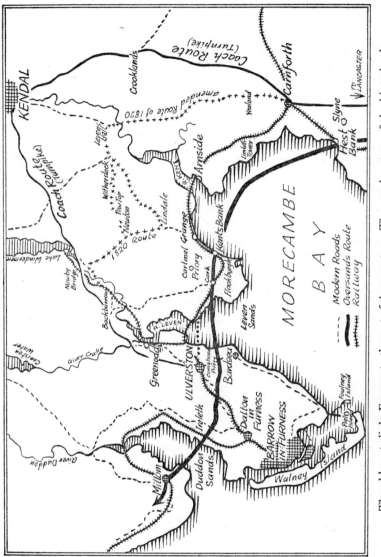

The old route links Furness to the rest of the country. The rough nature of the hinterland postponed further development until the nineteenth century.

Ireleth in the County Palatine of Lancaster is in a ruinous condition, and in several parts narrow and incommodious . . .' etc. The Kendal road was forty miles, the new turnpike of 1820 was thirty-four miles, and the oversands road only twenty miles long. Nor is there any record that the coaches ever used the land routes: they travelled over the sands.

Both John Fell and West write of a Roman road crossing the Cartmel peninsula which would link up with the sand route. West quotes from an ancient perambulation roll of Ulverston which says that the road left the sands at the Spina Alba, the whitethorn on Conishead Bank, proceeded west by Red Lane and Street Gate to the point where it was joined by the 1763 road, then turned south-west, heading for Lindal and Dalton. If we accept Roman occupation of Dalton, then it seems likely that we should also have to accept this road as Roman. But, Roman or otherwise, it is an ancient way. The age of documentary evidence begins with the guides provided since the foundations of Cartmel and Conishead Priories. Chapel Island in mid channel was a resting-place, where prayers for the crossings were offered by the monks who provided the guides. The first record dates from 1326 when Edward II asked for an inquiry to be made into the appointment of a guide on a petition from the abbot of Furness. This was granted. In the middle of the sixteenth century there was a dispute over the right of tenancy of 'Carter House,' and it was then stated that about the year 1501 a man called Edmondson held the office of 'Carter upon Kent Sands' as tenant right of the prior of Cartmel (Pape). In 1535 William Gate was the Cartmel Priory guide and John Hartley the Conishead Priory guide over Leven Sands.

Bruce's Scottish army, according to the Lanercost Chronicle, crossed the border on 17th June 1322 and burnt the bishop's house at Carlisle and plundered the monastery of Holm Cultram. He laid waste to Copeland and crossed Duddon Sands into Furness. The abbot of Furness Abbey met him and offered bribes if Bruce would pass by without destruction. His troops did burn and pillage to some degree, but on 24th June they crossed the Leven Sands to Cartmel, sparing the priory but taking cattle and burning farms. They then made the third crossing, over Kent Sands to Lancaster, where they were met by another advancing column which had come through Kendal. Four days in Lancaster saw the ruin of the town and the castle. Still southwards went the Scots destroying Skerton village and damaging Torrisholme, Halton, Carnforth, and Warton. They covered Wyresdale, Bleasedale, and the Fylde as far as Preston, which was sacked, while marauding bands struck out to Salmsbury and Healey Park. They returned to Scotland five weeks after first crossing the border.

The Scots paid other visits of the same kind, as Holinshed's *Chronicles* tell us, in 1316: 'The Scots having received the monie, turned their march towards the west parts, and journieing three score miles, came to Fourneis, burning all the countrie thereabouts, and took awaie with them all the goods and prisoners, both men and women which they might laie hands on, and so returned, rejoissing most of such iron as they had got in that journie, for they had great want in Scotland of that kind of metal in those daies.'

After the Dissolution the Duchy of Lancaster records take up the story: 'Office of le Carter's office of Leven Sands near Conyshed Lancashire, January 29 1548. The King, etc., all to whom greeting know ye that we by the advice and assent of our Council of our Duchy of Lancaster have given and granted and by these present do give and grant to John Harteley of Conyshed, yeoman, the office of keeper, conductor and governor of our sands near Conyshed aforesaid. . . .' For this service John Harteley was paid ten marks a year. But prior to the Dissolution he had been doing the same work for Conishead Priory for which he received fifteen marks a year, tips, and three acres of land. Nationalization did not pay good wages, but perhaps it was unwise to complain during the reign of Henry VIII.

In 1810 the Duchy of Lancaster granted £10 to Thomas Cooper, guide over Leven Sands, and paid £31 to repair his house in 1831. The Ulverston and Lancaster Railway Act of 1851 provides that a sum of £20 should be paid annually to the Leven Sands guide for the loss of fees or tips.

Also, in 1548, a keeper of Kent Sands was appointed, one Thomas Hogeson, who had previously been the guide for Cartmel Priory and he received £5 per annum, the Carter House, and three closes of land. The Carter House and the three closes of land are still in the occupation of the Kent Sands guide.

A little light is cast on the duties of a guide in the following petition for a wage increase by John Carter in 1715 (the guide now seems to have taken the surname which would commonly be ascribed by strangers to 'the man with the cart') : '... the petitioners father was for many years the carter, and had patent and salary paid him, and in regard to the smallness was allowed to sell ale in his house excise free ... that the petitioner is obliged for managing the said employ to keep two horses summer and winter, and being necessitated to attend the edy four miles upon the sands twelve hours in every twenty-four hours, his horses thereby and by often passing the waters are starved with cold and so often thrown into distemper that thereby and maintaining them he is put under a very great charge, and that the petitioner undergoes great hardships by his being exposed to the wind and cold upon the plain sands, and being often wett and he by seeking out new ffords every variation of the edy, and upon happening of ffogs and mist is often put in danger of his life. . . .'

To-day the salaries of both guides are received from the Duchy of Lancaster, although they are under the control of the Charity Commissioner. The chancellor of the duchy was one of the trustees until 1882 when three local trustees were appointed. No charge is made to the public for the crossing.

Official figures of the crossings made are compiled each year. The latest figures available are for the years 1945 to 1952 and are as shown on page 173.

In the early days the carter, mounted on a white horse, followed the ebbing tide to the channel, marking his path with branches of trees, a procedure called 'brodding' or 'brobbing' and this is still done by local fishermen. He tested the depth of the channel with a pole and, finding a firm bottom, he blew a loud blast on his horn and remained there until the flood-tide commenced. Then he blew another blast and returned to the shore. Edwin Waugh in one of his books tells of a gentleman who asked if any 'carters' were ever lost on the sands. 'I never knew any *lost*,' said the guide; 'there's one or two drowned now and then; but they're generally found somewhere i' the bed when th' tide goes out.' They were said never to have ended their days in their beds but always on the sands.

The overland route between the Kent and Leven sands leaves the sand at Sandgate, misses Flookburgh, and goes on to Cark.

CROSSINGS OVERSANDS ROUTE

METHOD OF CROSSING	FROM GRANGE								FROM ULVERSTON							
	1945	1946	1947	1948	1949	1950	1951	1952	1945	1946	1947	1948	1949	1950	1951	1952
Horses and Carts	5	20	12	6	4	10	12	6	23	18	14	18	32	27	32	24
Saddle Horses	6	2	—	—	1	5	4	—	3	4	8	6	7	8	4	6
Foot	151	120	316	136	241	30	279	566*	155	154	165	117	148	117	162†	113
Boat	—	—	16	20	6	30	28	—	48	64	33	31	44	79	51	33

* Includes a party of 450.
† Includes a party of 50 children.

Present guide at Cart Lane, Grange, is William Burrow, appointed early 1950.
Present guide at Canal Foot, Ulverston, is Alfred Butler, appointed September 1948.

The road leads to Headless Cross, a little nearer the shore than Cartmel Priory.   Here you will see stones built into the wall on the roadside which read 'Lancaster 15 miles over sands, Ulverston 7 miles, Cark, Holker, and Flookburgh.'   The Cartmel guide used to meet travellers here, and after prayers for a safe crossing they proceeded to Kents Bank and again overland.   The first ford is the channel of the Kent and Winster and three miles further is the small but treacherous crossing of the River Ken.   Dry land is reached at Hest Bank.   About three miles from here the River Lune was crossed by a bridge, and at Correll (Covell) Cross prayers were offered for a safe crossing.   (Thomas Corell (Covell) was a well-known local gentleman, born in 1561.)

John Lucas, writing between 1710 and 1740, tells us that the River Kent runs with incredible swiftness, is always muddy, and, where fordable, is of great breadth, the danger lying in the uncertainty of its bed ; what is a fair ford one day is impassable the next and to watch this point was the main duty of the carter. The River Keer, he remarks, has the danger of quicksands or 'syrtes,' and several little 'poos,' or rivulets, where quicksands are more frequent but can be detected by their smoothness and bright shining colour.   He remembers the local saying that 'he who rides over the Sands and does not gallop forfeits his horse to the King.'

When the channel has moved and the old river bed is not yet fully sanded and still bearing water it is called a 'lyring,' 'which is often more perillous to Travellers than the Ea full of water itself. . . .   At other times it removes gradually, when the stream, by inclining to one side, drives a Bank of Sand, sometimes of a considerable Height, and continually undermining, the Sand falls down into the River, in great Flakes with a hideous Noise.'

We now have at least a scrappy picture of the terrible nature of this invisible road which, for all its dangers, was preferred to any other land route because of the shorter journey.   Even so, the most terrifying danger of all has not been mentioned— that of mist and fog, which blots out all landmarks and render the immediate foreground as featureless as a desert, and even more treacherous, for to wander, lost, on the sands is to invite drowning by the incoming tide.

As parish registers have been kept only since the time of Queen Elizabeth it is impossible to compute accurately the toll of lives lost on the sands. The Cartmel registers alone record a hundred and forty-one persons, buried there between 1559 and 1880, who lost their lives in this manner. William Stout of Lancaster in his excellent autobiography tells us: '. . . sometime this year (1687) Christopher Harrys, a draper and grocer in Cartmell, of great business, but very penurious . . . who frequented our market at Lancaster, and usually to save the charge of carriage, brought one or more horses to carry his goods, but in crossing the sands some horse faltered and cast his loading, which he endeavoured to put to rights, was so long that the flood came, and he was drowned, notwithstanding several came by and saw him, but he would not call for assistance, otherwise might have saved his goods and his life.'

> 1821—Postchaise lost, close to Hest Bank. Occupant, postboy, and one horse drowned.
> 1825—Lancaster–Ulverston coach blown over in mid channel; passengers saved, one horse drowned.
> 1828—Lancaster–Ulverston coach suddenly sank in the sands, passengers saved.
> 1846—Nine young people returning to Cartmel from Ulverston Whitsuntide fair all drowned. Their cart went into a large waterfilled hole and other travellers on the sands did not even hear a cry.
> 1857—Seven farmhands going to Lancaster hiring fair found drowned the next day.

The list seems interminable. I believe it is Thomas Gray who tells the story of a fisherman who, with his wife and two daughters, set out to cross the sands and were overtaken by fog. Although he knew the sands well he was lost and left the cart and family to explore a little ahead, for he was sure he could find some guidance. But he had not returned by the time the tide changed and his wife would not leave the cart and return to safety while her husband was out there alone, for he might return at any minute and would then be sure to lose his life trying to find the cart. Eventually the two girls decided to go back to the shore, and although their horse was drowned they managed to swim ashore. At the next ebb the bodies of husband and wife were found on the sands not many yards from each other.

It is easy to see the reason for the local saying that:

The Kent and the Keer
Have parted many a good man and his meear.

(Note the similarity of this couplet to the equally ancient one about Martin Mere in south Lancashire, page 59.)

Even so there were many people who crossed the sands regularly in the course of their business. There was John Higgins, carrier, who went from Lancaster to Swarthmoor Hall with 'letters, iron ore, hopps, red-herrings, books, sugar, vinegar, meat, paper, oysters, phisicall things, and chocoletta.' And I seem to remember reading in Sarah Fell's *Household Journal* of a journey over sands to post an urgent letter at Lancaster! Also from Swarthmoor Hall in 1660 went George Fox, a prisoner, over sands to Lancaster Castle with sixteen troops of horse.

A letter from the Backbarrow Company to the Caton Forge Company, dated April 1782, says: 'You'll please to pay. . . . Six pounds Four shillings after they have sent all Margt. and Charles Taylor's Household Goods to Lancaster to the Care of Luke Barker Carr over Sands. . . .'

Here is just a private letter from a schoolboy, going back to school after the holidays:

'29 January 1786: Dear Mother, I arrived here (Lancaster) safe yesterday Evening about 7 o'clock after a rather disagreeable passage; it was very thick all the way, and crossing at the low Ford, there was no Carter, so the Driver was obliged to take a Horse and try the Ford, which was very deep for the Water was near a foot in the Coach, and after that the Sand was so exceeding heavy, that we were obliged to get out, and walk three or four miles. . . .'

In addition to the regular carriers there was a frequent service of coaches over the sands. The earliest type were called 'dillies.' They carried thirteen inside passengers and a heavy load of luggage and passengers on top, but they were heavy and frequently stuck in the sands, so they were superseded by smaller and faster coaches, as described in this advertisement from the *Cumberland Pacquet*, 11th September 1781:

'A Diligence or Chaise, which will carry three persons conveniently, will set out from Mr Stanley Turner's, the Sun

Inn, Lancaster, every Monday, Wednesday, and Friday, as the
tide will permit, to Ulverston, over the Sands, which is the
nearest and direct route to Whitehaven. And the same
Diligence will return to Lancaster from Henry Addison's, the
King's Arms, in Ulverston, every Tuesday, Thursday, and
Saturday. Each passenger to pay Five shillings on taking a
place for Ulverston or Lancaster. The proprietors assure the
public that they have procured a sober and careful driver, who
is well acquainted with the sands, and humbly hope that their
plan will meet with due encouragement, as this is the most
cheap, safe, and expeditious method of crossing the sands to and
from Ulverston.'

The coaches ran successfully until the opening of the Ulverston–Lancaster Railway in 1857. Often overtaken by the tide
or bogged in the sands they were recovered the next day,
cleaned out, and put on the road again.

From time to time notice is found of important personages
using the route, as in this letter to Sir Thomas Lowther from
his steward J. Fletcher:

'Honoured sir, On Thursday the 18th inst. (July 1728) I
waited on the Lord Bishop (of Chester) at Kendall, and on
Fryday he and his attendants came to Holker. On Monday
his lordship set forward for Whitehaven, and passed over the
sands at morning tide; called at Conishead, and stayed there
three or four hours and passed Duddon sands between twelve
and one o'clock. He lodged that night at Monchester. I am
etc., J. Fletcher.'

Thomas Gray came this way ten years later and writes of
passing Boulton on his way to Lancaster and that he 'had a full
view of Cartmell sands with here and there a passenger riding
over them, it being low water.'

He was not so descriptive as Wordsworth:

> . . . Over the smooth sands
> Of Leven's ample estuary lay
> My journey, and beneath a genial sun,
> With distant prospect among gleams of sky
> And clouds, and intermingling tops,
> In one inseparable glory clad. . . .

(Here describes the oratory on Chapel Island.)

> . . . Not far from that still ruin all the plain
> Lay spotted with a variegated crowd
> Of vehicles and travellers, horse and foot,
> Wading beneath the conduct of their guide
> In loose procession through the shallow stream
> On inland waters: the great sea meanwhile
> Heaved at a safe distance, far retired.   I paused,
> Longing for skill to paint a scene so bright
> And cheerful. . . .

Wordsworth passed on this cheerful spirit to Mrs Hemans
who visited him at Rydale in 1830 and wrote: 'I must not
omit to tell you that Mr Wordsworth not only admired our
exploit in crossing the Ulverston Sands as a deed of "derring
do" but as a decided proof of taste, the Lake scenery, he says, is
never seen to such advantage as after the passage of what he
calls its "majestic barrier."'

Another lady, Mrs Gaskell, writes in 1858: 'Looking down
on the Bay with its slow moving train of crossers, led over the
treacherous sands by the Guide, a square man sitting stern on
his white horse, the better to be seen when daylight ebbs. . . .
On foggy nights the guide (who has let people drown before
now who could not pay his fee) may be heard blowing an old
ram's horn trumpet to guide by the sound.'

On 6th June 1837 George Stephenson made a survey for
the proposed railway linking Barrow to the outer world.   He
travelled round Morecambe Bay, came round Humphrey
Head, crossed the Ulverston Sands, went inland to Coniston
and Windermere, and crossed the Duddon Sands to Whitehaven.   He recommended that the proposed railway should
travel from Lancaster to Poulton (Morecambe) across the sands
to Humphrey Head, then to Chapel Island, through Lindal
Moor to Kirkby Ireleth by tunnel, cross the River Duddon at
Dunnerholme and proceed along the coast to Whitehaven, so
giving a level route to Scotland instead of the Shap Fell route.
In addition such a railway would have put the iron-ore districts
on a main line, and the necessary embankments could have
reclaimed Morecambe Bay.

A meeting at the Sun Inn, Ulverston, in 1837 accepted the
idea.   It was opposed by towns further inland who also wanted
a railway.   Meanwhile the line from Preston to Lancaster was
nearing completion (1838).   A further survey was called for,

and John Hague, of Lincolnshire, who suggested the line should run from Poulton to Leonard Point, coming closer to Barrow and enclosing 46,300 acres and an additional 5,700 acres in the Duddon valley for reclamation. Meanwhile a parliamentary commission decided on the Shap Fell route for the Preston to Scotland railway, so that the plan for Furness became merely that for a branch line round the coast from Barrow to Carnforth, where it joined the Scottish line. The Furness Railway Bill was passed in 1844, the railway pier plans were passed in 1845, and the famous 'Copper Nob' engines and other rolling stock were ordered.

It was not long after the railway was in operation that it became apparent that Furness iron ore was not inexhaustible and that the town would never be a large port like Liverpool. If the original committee had not faltered, and relied on George Stephenson's prestige rather than obtain a second opinion, they would have secured a position on a through route instead of a side line, and had a chance to prosper from such a distinguished and important route.

While there is hardly a more picturesque road in the country than that from Hest Bank to Silverdale along the coast beneath Warton Crag, it is of more historical interest to travel round the back of the crag, by Warton village and the Yealand villages. This way also provides great beauties of rolling hills and wooded valleys. The first step is to climb Warton Crag and survey the whole sweep of the 'broad waters' of Morecambe Bay in the one glance. How little solid rock has been beneath our feet on this coastal journey is realized as soon as shoe-nails scrape on the slippery limestone where the ribs of Mother Earth show bare. Here are the aged, water-worn caves, peculiar to limestone regions, which provide such abundance of relics of our most ancient ancestors. On Warton Crag the Dog Hole (160 feet high), Badger Hole, and Fairy Hole have given up human and animal bones, together with implements. There are also some defence works and the foundations of five stone-walled huts, whose origin is dim and uncertain. There is too a local story of one three-fingered Jack who lived in a cave on Warton Crag, and made a living by robbing the travellers who crossed the sands. The village of Warton lies at the foot of its crag, its grey, lichened walls sparkling in the sunlight. This is certainly limestone country, and once more the countryside has changed its character.   The flat marshes and land below water level have given place to steep, jaunty crags, which climb and fall crazily to the sea in silver and green—the modern name of Silverdale close by was well and obviously chosen.

It is not surprising to find touring Americans in the church-yard, peering at a weather-worn coat of arms sculptured on the wall of the church tower.   It shows three mullets and two bars which in the more modern American version are just stars and stripes.   These people have come to see the origin of their own national flag as it was in the coat of arms of the Washington family.

The fifteenth-century church tower was built by Sir John Washington, the local squire.   A later John Washington sailed to the new country of America, as did many more Englishmen from these villages, and there his son, George Washington, was born in 1732.

Americans visit the ancestral home and the Shovel Inn where the Washingtons held court.   They also like to test a 'home-brewed' beer when they can find one.   One of them looked at his glass of beer against the light and said to the landlady appre-ciatively: 'What do you put in this wonderful home brew?'

'Nothing but malt and hops, sir,' she said.

'What about the water?'

'Oh, I forgot the water.'

'No, no,' said the American.   'I'll be damned if you did.'

There was also here a family named Kyston, who by trading with the new colonies waxed rich.   Sir Thomas Kyston had a daughter who married Sir John Spencer.   One of the male offspring of this marriage married a daughter of John Churchill, first Duke of Marlborough, and a sister of Sir Thomas Kyston married a John Washington, so it would seem that somewhere, springing from this tiny grey Lancashire village of Warton below the hill, there is an ancestral link between President George Washington of the United States of America and Sir Winston Spencer Churchill.

John Lucas (1710–40) gives a wonderful account of life in this far-away village when old pagan rites were still associated with the church into which they had become welded in the early days of Christianity.   The maypole was set up in Churchgate, the stocks and whipping-post stood next to the maypole, and the fish-stones were near by. The Ware was the name of a tarn at the lower end of the town, noted for its eels, and reflected in its still waters were Archbishop Hutton's almshouses. The archbishop also founded the local free grammar school in 1594. Its dated foundation-stone has been removed to a new building and the old school converted into two houses. To go there, follow the old road round Warton Crag from the Black Bull Inn and turn right along the track at the foot of the quarry. There you may perhaps recapture the scene with eighteenth-century schoolboys first playing a masterly game of football and then retiring to the ale-house to quench their thirst, or envisage them on Shrove Tuesday bringing 'Cockpennies' to the master, then taking the fighting cocks from beneath their jackets and spending the rest of the holiday in many a bloody battle of spurs. The Feast of Dedication was held on the first Sunday nearest the first day in August: '. . . and the vain Custom of Dancing, excessive Drinking etc., on that Day being, many Years since, laid aside, the Inhabitants and Strangers spend the day in duely attending the Service of the Church and making Good Cheer, with the Rules of Sobriety, in private Houses, and the next in several Kinds of Diversions, the chiefest of which is usually a Rush-bearing, which is on this Manner. They cut hard Rushes from the Marsh, which they make up into long Bundles, and then dress them in fine Linen, Silk, Ribbands, Flowers etc. Afterwards the Young Women of the Village which performs the Ceremony that Year, take up the Burdens erect upon their Heads and begin the Procession (Precedence being always given to the Churchwarden's Burden) which is attended not only with Multitudes of People but with Musick, Drums, Ringing of Bells, and all other Demonstrations of Joy they are able to express. When they arrive at the Church, they go in at the West end (the only publick use that ever I saw that door put to) and setting down their Burdens in the Church, strip them of their Ornaments and strew the Rushes in the Seats leaving the Heads or Crowns of them deck'd with Flowers, cut Paper etc. in some Part of the Church, generally over the Cancelli. Then the Company return to the Town from whence they came and cheerfully partake of a plentifull Collation provided for that purpose, and spend the remaining part of the

Day and frequently a great part of the Night also, in Dancing (if the Weather permits) about a Maypole, adorned with Greens, Flowers etc or else in some other place.'

The people kept the 'Arval feast' at a burying, and at the end of the harvest the sexton would go from house to house, receiving from each sheaves of corn which he claimed 'by immemorial custom' for his work in cleaning of the church.

If we continue along the road on the edge of Warton Crag there come into sight the three quiet, clean, and homely looking villages of Yealand Redmayne, Yealand Conyers, and Yealand Storrs, distinguished only by the names of their ancient lords and possibly by the excellent plums of Storrs. In 1228 Conyers was spelt 'Coyneres,' which is a little closer to the personal name of Roger de Coigniers, who came to England towards the end of the reign of William the Conqueror and received the local constableship from the Bishop of Durham. This family also gave its name to Howton Coigniers in Yorkshire. Henry Redmaine was the steward of Kendal in 1212. When William de Lancaster joined with the barons in 1215 and was taken prisoner by King John, Henry's son Benedict was demanded as the first of ten hostages by King John as a pledge of William's fidelity.

Generally speaking these villages are the quietest and trimmest under the sun. The Friends' Meeting-House (1697) and the tiny grass-covered graves set the key. The houses may hide shyly behind a screen of fruit blossom scattering white petals on the roadway, or if you come later in the year they will still be hiding behind wild and garden roses. The dry, red soil produced first quality hemp and flax, whose seed brought a high price on the market.

Standing on this ridge and looking across the green tree-clothed valley one has 'much pleasure of orchards,' sees fine country seats, rolling fells in blue and amber, the sparkle of sun on limestone, and gains a composite overwhelming feeling that this is English scenery at its best. The Great North Road with its whirl of traffic is out of sight and mind, and the eye is drawn to the stately calm of Leighton Hall.

But let us turn first to three record books in that quiet meeting house at Yealand. They are dated 1672. In the first of them is written: 'This is a true and certain Record, or Memoriall off the names off these worthy and faithfull sarvants and messengers off God who first brought the message off glad tydings amongst us, who was gathered to be a meeting, and am known or called by the name of Kellit or Yeland meeting.

'1st. George Fox and Richard Farnsworth was the first that brought the message of glad Tydings amongst us.

'2ndly. As to their sufferings att Steeplehouses Markett places or elsewhear, we have litell to say.

'3rdly. The first that received them and their message was

Robert Withers.	Thomas Chorley.
Richard Huberthorn.	Chris. Birsbrown and his family.
Thomas Leaper.	Francis Fleeming.
Robert Srout.	William Higingson.

'Richard Huberthorn who is deceased was a faithfull labourer, and one in our meeting whome the Lord called forth in one meeting to declare the message of glad tydings amongst us . . . after that he passed through severall parts of the nation, and cuming to London, wheer he had much exercise with the Kings and C.

'So after much labour and traviell in England and Wayles for 9 yeares time, he was imprisoned by Richard Browne, a great persecutor (Lord Mayor of London) in Newgate Prison whear he was thronged in the Heatt of Sumber, whear he finished his testimony, sealing it with his blood, dying a martor of Jesus the 17th day of the 6 month in the year 1662.'

This Richard Huberthorne must well have known the quiet beauty of Yealand's orchards. He was educated at Warton free grammar school of the fighting cocks and football. When the Scots came south in 1648 he joined with Cromwell and became a captain, returning to Yealand in 1650. Meanwhile a few thoughtful people were meeting monthly at Preston Patrick, three miles from Yealand. On the Wednesday of Whitweek, 1652, two of the leaders brought in a stranger. It was George Fox. The next day he went to Kendal, and later crossed the sands to Swarthmoor Hall in Furness. Richard Huberthorne (Hubberthorne) had several meetings with George Fox, became a Quaker, organized local groups, and laid a solid foundation for future generations. One morning in October 1653, when the harvest had been safely gathered in, he set out at twenty-five years of age on his first long journey, a journey which ended eventually in Newgate prison. This was the first impact of the stolid endurance and quiet faith of the Quakers upon the life of these villages—an outpost of a force which, for a long time subsequently, lit up these backwaters and has left enduring monuments in history.

Coming back to the coast over reclaimed Storrs Moss you pass the tarn of Haweswater (Haveswater—Hayeswater) upon the right, once well known for its char, a red-fleshed fish which pots well. 'Of these Pots, wch, they commonly call Char Pyes great quantities are yearly sent up to London from Kendal and Lancaster,' writes John Lucas; we shall have more to say about them later. Mention may here be made of the curious thirty-acre fresh-water lake in Challon Hall estate, on the shores of which are univalve sea shells, graduated in size down to perfect microscopic specimens.

Silverdale, despite its accretion of houses, is still a natural paradise of ferns, hazel woods, wild cherries, and its lily woods. An old resident remembers about a hundred acres of yellow lilies and lilies of the valley in this spot.

Lindeth Tower (four storeys of one room each) was called 'Gibraltar Tower' because it was built on a rock standing high and prominent from the seashore, and the name remains. The owner was a Mr Fleetwood, a banker of Preston. Mrs Gaskell often stayed here to write her books.

Not many yards along the shore is, or used to be, Arnset Well which marked the boundary of the town, the parish, and the county of Lancashire, for this is the point where Westmorland has that corridor to the sea which splits Lancashire into two portions, Westmorland taking the Kent estuary and Lancashire beginning again at Lindale across the water.

The path along the shore continues to the woods which are under National Trust protection, and can be followed at a low level or by climbing to the top of Arnside Knot for the sake of the view. On the landward side is the ruin of Arnside Tower, destroyed by fire in 1602, a Piel Tower which is a grim reminder of the interest taken in this district by the Scottish marauders. From here may also be seen the Piel Towers of Wraysholme, Hazelslack, and Baltham.

All paths lead into Arnside. It is quiet in the village street which leads down to the estuary, bringing perhaps a visitor, carrying a geologist's hammer and a rucksack and looking determinedly at his feet as by habit, who is certain to get a good haul of specimens from the limestone on the beach. A café is a good place to sit and watch the passing scene, much changed since Arnside was the port to Kendal. Now you look out across

Lindeth Tower, near Silverdale, where Mrs Gaskell
wrote some of her books

the road over a large waste of sand to the other shore which is Lancashire. There is plenty of time yet for the train which will take you there on Brunlee's viaduct across the estuary.

Castlehead can be seen across the bay and behind the viaduct. John Wilkinson lived at the house, the 'father of the iron industry,' manufacturer of flat-irons and iron coffins: more important still he floated the first model of an iron-built vessel in the River Winster which flows at the foot of the hill. He reclaimed the land hereabouts by building an embankment, and Mr Jenkinson of Yealand came to him with the idea of reclaiming Morecambe Bay. There have been many schemes for this project during the last two centuries, and still every few years another is put forward. The last I remember was in 1943, when Mr Ellis Smith, M.P., applied the idea of a miniature Tennessee Valley scheme to the area. He proposed a

N

causeway of reinforced concrete across the bay, giving a direct rail and road link from Lancaster to Barrow, which would at the same time harness the tides by means of three sluices to provide hydro-electric power for light industry to be developed in the area. The reclaimed bay, he suggested, would be an ideal site for a seaplane base and an aerodrome, and he saw Scotland brought so much the closer to Manchester (shades of George Stephenson!). The thousands of pounds of expenditure on the scheme contemplated and abandoned in the eighteenth century have now risen to millions, and Morecambe Bay still retains its own natural beauty. There is a monument erected to the memory of John Wilkinson in Lindale close by Castle-barrow.

Holme Island, on this side of the viaduct, was a barren rock until Mr Brogden, initiator of the Furness Railway, built his home there and covered the island with gardens and woods, joining it to the mainland by an embankment.

I was looking at the view from a farm on the shore one balmy evening when an old couple joined me. The man was a sailor retired from the sea, still bluff and hearty and unable to tear himself away from the salt breezes. 'That channel has altered course sin Ah wur a lad,' he said, pointing with his stick to the edge of the shore. 'Maybe the railway viaduct caused it. Before the 1914–18 war those viaduct pillars were tubular steel, but they had to be strengthened to carry th' heavy war traffic fra Barra, soashow they built a solid concrete base to each pillar, put some steel posts in and filled the whole thing wi' stone, and added a brick facing.'

'Passenger boats come to Arnside, I believe,' I said. 'Where was the quay?'

'Oh aye—th' old railway pier. Aye, it used to have good water, about twelve feet, and a booat came daily fra More-cambe. But that channel's silted down. That's bin t' fate o' many an old harbour on this coast. An' now, when t' flood-tide races, sand silts behind the viaduct pillars and has made them high sand-banks, and varra difficult they are for navigation.'

He had a far-away, wistful look in his eyes as, without taking them from the channel, he put his free hand over those of his wife and gently patted them.

'It was a wonderfully leisurely life in those pre-war days,' he went on. 'People had their own yachts, steamers, punts, and booats. There was always a sail in the estuary. Pleasure trips were planned to Morecambe or upstream to Milnthorpe and Haversham. There were regattas off Grange, an' trawlers fra Fleetwood, an' all ovver Morecambe Bay area took part.'

'There were few houses in those days,' his wife added. 'I lived on the top of the hill—that's where the old houses are—and when the boys were playing football and it rolled down the hill it never stopped until it reached the beach.'

'And now, you see, it's houses all the way.'

'An' if we wanted a doctor quick we had to go to Miln-thorpe. He came over on a horse in summer and a sledge when it snowed. Or you could hire a man from the Albion Hotel to take the message for 7s. 6d.'

'An' wi went nutting on Arnside Knott. It was covered thick wi' trees, and tall pines on the top such as tha couldn't see daylight through.'

'They were cut down in the 1914–18 war. 'Course they tried to replant later, but t' new trees wouldna tak hold. It's not bin t' same since.'

Suddenly we heard a distant and continuous rumbling noise. It was surely not of this earth? Ominous and threatening—yes—with a stored-up energy of which you could not guess the outcome.

The old couple looked seaward, and patiently waited as if to welcome an old friend. But the noise came nearer. It grew more distinct and even more threatening. Out in the channel the water was turning to flow upstream. Some of the sand-banks disappeared. Then a long white wave of water advanced up the channel from shore to shore.

Here at last was the cause of the long sustained roar—a white, curling, splashing wave swept all before it, a miniature of the Severn Bore. It passed under the viaduct and the full tide swept on behind. Another time one would be prepared for it.

The station is close by, and there are few that I know which have such a beautiful setting. The estuary narrows between the white limestone hills to a blue background of Lakeland giants. Ships used to sail up this broad estuary to Milnthorpe, Westmorland's seaport, until Mr Brunlees built his 1,300-foot viaduct in 70 feet of sand, an engineering feat in 1857.

The River Kent picks its way through the wet reflecting sand. Gulls fly low over the moss. A few duck cross in formation. A heron stands unconcernedly close to the viaduct. It is warm in the sunshine. No hurry for the train to come. Strange to think that I have left this station after breakfast, have been attending to my business in Manchester by half-past ten, and have been back picking blackberries in the lane to Arnside Knott the same evening after tea.

It would be a dull journey across the sands which did not afford the sight of herons, standing motionless in the channels. They come from the north Lancashire and Westmorland heronries which surround these Morecambe Bay feeding-grounds at fairly equal intervals of some ten flight miles. At last the train does arrive, and in a few minutes it has crossed the viaduct with a heavy rumble and stopped at Grange.

No longer ago than the middle of the last century, the approach to Grange was by coach over the sands (which accounts for part of the name Grange-over-Sands) and all that was to be found on arrival was a small group of whitewashed cottages. Among them was the Grange Farm, owned by John Brough, and so called because it was a grange, or granary, of Cartmel Priory. It stood on the site of the present police office and was substantial enough to give a name to the place in later years, when visitors and inhabitants had to have a tag to their name for the sake of convenience.

The Yewbarrow lane used to be hedged by thick walnut trees and the tide lapped gently against the roadside wall. One day the bore we have just been watching from Arnside (called 'Egor' here) came over the wall, through the front door of the dame's school and out at the back, carrying the school clock with it, an event momentous enough to be recorded by one of the scholars in later years.

The nearest butcher was at Cartmel, and the local carrier was a woman called Peggy Keith who brought provisions from Kendal over the turnpike, but you would have taken her for a man any day if you saw her in her trousers and jacket, smoking a small black clay. Many a time larders were empty and waiting for Peggy to come and fill them, so the villagers had to eat plenty of cockles, either fried in rows on a gridiron until they opened, or, for a change, boiled, shelled, and made into a *pâté*.

Grange-over-Sands, 'the Torquay of the North'

N. Wolstenholme

One might see Betty Bell, who caught salmon off Blawith Point and carried her fish balanced on her head above a sun-bonnet with her arms akimbo, coming down the lane. After having two children she said she had had enough, so she left her husband and went to live with her brother.

There was plenty of peat and wood to warm the small cottage rooms in winter, and coal too when a coal boat floated up on the tide. The water came from springs, particularly the one now in the small park by the side of the railway, but as it was covered by every tide, the villagers used to take a store of it between tides.

But now the railway has altered the scene. The village has grown into a small town, catering for 'select' visitors who appreciate the warm, relaxing air. They climb to the top of Hampsfell behind the town and enter the hospice there, which is a tower built by the Rev. Thomas Remington, one time incumbent at Cartmel. Over the doorway is an inscription in Greek which may be translated: 'To the rosy morn appearing,' and at more length inside an English versification, typical of the nineteenth century.

The view is admirable, for no matter which seaside fell around Morecambe Bay you climb, you will be rewarded. And looking landwards you will see Cartmel, neatly curled round the priory church like a grey kitten asleep on the hearth. This peninsula between the Kent and the Leven estuaries was dominated by the monks of Cartmel Priory just as the next, and largest, peninsula was governed by those of Furness Abbey. Most of the priory building survived the Dissolution because it was claimed as the parish church, and it makes a visit to Cartmel well worth while. The original stone-work is of the twelfth and fourteenth centuries, the roof is early seventeenth century, for much of the vast structure became roofless because the little parish could not keep up so large a building, and it was restored at that period by George Preston of Holker Hall, who also bought the gatehouse of the dissolved priory and converted it into a schoolhouse in 1624. The latter remains as an attractive feature of the village square, having been at different periods a dwelling for poor families, a Methodist chapel, a warehouse, a studio, and, since 1946, National Trust property. The huge east window in Cartmel church is made from Caen stone, which is a reminder of the greater ease of travel by water in those days as compared with that by road.

Cartmel looks well from the surrounding fells, pearl grey and green, hemmed in and embosomed in the valley of the Ea, with the priory outsoaring all its other buildings. And once within the village the first invitation is not belied. It is one of those places where you may still flatten your nose against genuine bull's-eye glass in a bay-windowed shop; where the village cross and pump, with the ancient priory for background, still obstruct the way of modern traffic yet none dare raise a protest, or else . . . !

There is a conglomeration of inns. If you visit one of these hostelries it will gladden your heart to hear the clink of boot nails on the slate floor and to find available the bread and cheese which is the right fare after a day on the fells. Its grey walls are a yard thick, it has a massive stairs door, studded with nails which would have served well in a castle, and the low-roofed bedrooms, twisty shaped to fit any odd corner, are made for candlelight. The landlord once told me a good deal about the local sport of hound trails. One tale I remember, about a skinny pup which seemed to have no chance against the geeàt hounds. 'No one would back it,' he said. 'Well, there was an iron geeàt on the trail, standing nine feet to an inch it was. The race was on, and t' lile pup ambled along oot of sight. When the hounds came to the geeàt they clammered and hollered and sprang about but couldn't manage it, but t' lile pup came trotting up and it was sa thin it just ran through the geeàt as though it were nivver theer and trotted home to win.'

The name 'Cartmel' suggests two items of interest which link with our story. First, the 'mel' is another 'melr' or sand-bank, as we noted in other places along the coast, the Cheshire 'mels,' Argameles, North Meols, among them, and many others. Secondly, 'Cart' (1187, Kertmel), it has been suggested, may be a derivation from Old Norse *Kerti*—signifying a candle or link used as guide, as at Becconsall, for the Ribble crossing. Possibly it is a new line of thought to connect the 'Cart' in Cartmel with the origin of the name of the oversands guide, for it will be remembered that he was traditionally called the 'carter,' and that this became a family name for the guide, who lived at the Carter House, and that his appointment, until the Dissolution, was from Cartmel Priory. I do not think that the guide would have a cart with him on this particular journey, and all the old reminiscences of him mention his white horse and his ability to marshal the straggling travellers in times of danger.

The other route out of Grange is by the coast, first on the esplanade by the sea, then by footpath interwoven with the railway, past the Carter House of which we learned in the oversands route, and so to the road into Kents Bank. Here

The crumbling battlements of Wraysholme Tower

the new building development appears to end, for only a few houses exist beyond the railway level-crossing, whence the road climbs away into the hinterland. In front of us lies the tempting shape of Humphrey Head, which can be reached travelling roughshod over the shingle or more smoothly by following the road to the Allithwaite cross-roads and thence doubling back by field paths.

There is nothing apparent of the old-established fishing industry, unless it be a sea-booted fellow strolling from an inn; but there is much land advertised for sale in building plots. The old farms, however, are still there, even though the cow byres are complete with electric milking-machines and tractors churn up the farmyard mud. These fields flood easily in wet weather. At the edge of the intake from the sea is Wraysholme Tower. It is a farm but an unusual one, for the broken castellated piel tower which has played its part in local history rises broad-ribbed and squat above the farm buildings. There has been a change of fortune in this fortified manor house since it was held by the Harrington family of Aldingham Castle, but there remains more than one legend about the place, the best known being that of the last wolf in England.

Briefly, this is a story of Sir Edgar Harrington, who swore to hunt and kill the last wolf in England, which lived on Humphrey Head that juts out into the bay close by. Sir Edgar had a niece called Adela, and promised half his lands, with Adela as bride, to the man who killed the wolf. It so happened that his son, supposedly killed while fighting abroad, appeared at the preliminary feast disguised and calling himself Sir John Delisle, and to complete the triangle there was also present one Layburne, a knight who was making little progress in the affections of Adela.

The stage was set for the hunt, and they chased the wolf all over Furness until it doubled back to Humphrey Head with Layburne and Delisle close behind it. Suddenly the wolf jumped a chasm. It was followed by the hounds and by Delisle but Layburne reined in on the brink.

Now it so happened that Adela was riding under that very cliff when the wolf appeared before her and 'bared his glistening teeth.' But Delisle was also there with his spear to settle matters with the wolf. It also happened that the prior of Cartmel was on the same path, on his way to drink of the Holy Well, and as the couple could not wait to publish the banns he married them there and then in the cave of the local fairies on Humphrey Head!

To follow in their footsteps to-day the imagination has to rid itself of the Furness railway line and the macadam surface on Adela's path to the shore, though it is still a pleasant lane, winding between hawthorn hedges and under the limestone crags where Delisle leapt and arrived at the base unscathed, although his Arab charger died in the attempt.

The road finally peters out in the sand. There are the marks of cart-wheels where fishermen go down daily into the channel, and under the cliff is the Holy Well of Cartmel, once much visited for the cure of gout, rheumatism, and bilious complaints, and especially by the Alston lead miners of Northumberland as it was supposed to be beneficial for certain diseases to which they became liable through their work. The old stone building has fallen down, although its outline can still be traced. In its place is the ugliest of corrugated iron shacks covering the stone trough where the water drips clear and cold.

Returning to the road across the marsh at Wraysholme one may see flocks of sheep wintering, and I have seen too a lonely plough, followed by seagulls in such numbers that the plough seemed to turn up a white plume wave which settled down behind the furrow, screaming continuously above the throbbing reverberations of the tractor.

Nearer Flookburgh are the ruins of a war-time aerodrome. It is hard to believe that its cracked and shattered concrete was in use such a little time ago. But the living quarters, iron and concrete igloos, are tenanted by a mixed crowd of people, chiefly foreign workers and their English wives, who work on the local farms or in Barrow and Lancaster. The village has changed little since it was rebuilt after the disastrous fire of 1602 and maintained its ancient market rights and its importance as a place on the main oversands route. A blue-jerseyed and grizzled fisherman in the street there told me recently that the cockling trade still averages ten bags per day per man. For some reason the modern builder has not been tempted to bring his semi-detached boxes to this place. The grey, seventeenth-century stones harmonize with the flat marshland, where the scream of the gulls and the whistling call of the waders are the only music heard above the constantly wuthering wind from the sea.

The Furness peninsula, the last foreland in Lancashire, lies across the Leven sands. Here again the railway crossing from Cark station saves a long inland walk. Out in the channel lies Chapel Island on the site of the oversands route, which here ran between Cartmel Priory's stewardship and that of Conishead Priory on the shore before us. The channel is only some 250 yards long by 50 yards at its widest. There are some sham ruins of a chapel on the island erected by Colonel Braddyl in 1823 when he was building his house, the new Conishead Priory, on the mainland, with the object of providing a picturesque view over the channel from his new home, a not uncommon practice in those days. Did we not see a replica of the vestal temple in the gardens on Holme Island?

As the train enters Ulverston we come to a 'big' town for the first time since leaving Fleetwood.

XV

FURNESS: (1) ULVERSTON

AT the beginning of the twelfth century the new Savignian order of monks was formed. They followed the rule of St Benedict with but slight modifications. Galfrid, the second abbot of Savigny, had been granted a strip of land on the banks of the River Ribble by Stephen, Earl of Boulogne. (What religious order did *not* have a strip of land on the Ribble!) Accordingly thirteen monks left France in 1124 to settle on that land, which was at Tulketh near Preston. They remained there three years and three days, after which they set out again for Furness, to a place they called Bekansgill, but which we call the Vale of Deadly Nightshade. Rather than embark on a discussion as to the origin of this translation (which appears to have been an error of West, the Furness chronicler) I will simply refer to the place as the Vale of the Nightshade and leave the question of its exactitude to those who are versed in such things, for it is of little importance. It is more to our purpose to remember that this place was also the property of the Earl of Boulogne, and this would seem to put an end to the usual legends of wandering monks who were given supernatural signs as to where they should settle.

Here the earl granted the monks of Savigny such extensive rights and privileges that, as the abbey grew through the thirteenth and fourteenth centuries, the reigning abbot became almost a king in his own isolated kingdom. His position was strengthened both by lack of interference from outside due to the isolation of Furness, and by the fact that his territory constituted a formidable bulwark and defence from the north, to the honour of Lancaster. His lands became recognized as a barony, and the abbot took his place among the barons at the court of the lord of the honour of Lancaster.

It was human, if not scrupulously within the rules of a

religious order, to put wealth before learning. The abbey collected royal subsidies, assisted the king's justices, had extensive interests in the Isle of Man, and owned the whole peninsula with one exception of the land round Aldingham which belonged to Michael le Fleming, who had brought his Flemish soldiers to the aid of William the Conqueror at the battle of Hastings.

Thirty years after the foundation of Furness Abbey a communication was received from the Savigny headquarters asking all dependent monasteries to change the rule of the Cistercian order. Following a meeting in the chapter-house it was agreed that the abbot, Peter of York, should go to Rome, and there the Pope agreed that the Furness monks might keep to the order to which they were accustomed. Peter of York began his homeward journey but was waylaid by the monks of Savigny, made prisoner, and compelled to resign from the abbacy of Furness and to become a Cistercian. Meanwhile in Furness a new abbot had been appointed and under him the monks agreed to become Cistercians. This accounts for the style of building you may still see in the Vale of the Nightshade on the outskirts of Barrow. The original Church of St Mary is represented only by the four piers at the transept, the lower parts of the west walls of the transepts, and the south wall of the nave. The building style and lay-out of the rest was carried out on the Cistercian plan.

In the Record Office in London is the valuable Furness Coucher Book, written by Richard Esk, one of the monks in 1412. It contains a history of the abbey, copies of charters and of bulls, genealogies and notes on the general business of the abbey. It has been published by the Chetham Society of Manchester.

With such complete autonomy, these men of the soil and the counting-house, these ironfounders and wool exporters, had need of a market town near at hand, and Dalton market became the centre of Furness activity until the Dissolution of the monasteries. This catastrophe took away the board of directors of this flourishing autocracy. An attempt to fill the vacuum was made by local men, but either their stature was too small or they had the wrong principles, such as greed and lust, at heart. William Sandys, the official receiver, was 'very

riotously and wilfully murdered at Conysheade' over a matter
of corn tithes; witnesses in the affair did not refrain their tongues
in his defamation, and we see here a glimpse of that deterioration in local affairs which generally followed the destruction of
revered authority.

The countrymen, however, going about their daily business,

The site of the Market Cross, Ulverston.   The Georgian
background remains

made their own changes in a gradual manner, and the one
which concerns us here is their abandonment of Dalton market
for the natural advantages of Ulverston.   A glance at the map
will quickly show that Ulverston is a natural focus of routes.
As so much of the trade was carried by sea it had an additional
advantage in its close proximity to the rivers which served the
hinterland of High Furness, as well as in its location on the vital
oversands route which joined Furness to the rest of the country.

So ended the period when all roads to Furness Abbey were
marked with crosses.   In Ulverston there was the district of
Little Cross, where Church Walk meets Soutergate and King
Street; there was Market Cross, Stone Cross, Cross-a-Moor,
Crossgates,   and   many   others.   Soutergate   was   once   an

Example of the rich wood carving in Cartmel Priory

important village on the west coast of the peninsula, and this road in Ulverston gives a clue to the ancient high road over the peninsula.

The town early showed traces of the beginnings of trade to replace that which had been formerly carried on from the abbey. For instance, before 1600 there are no surnames in the church registers suggestive of occupations connected with the sea, but thereafter they begin to appear, and it is interesting to note how many parents baptized their sons with the name of Christopher, who, says the legend, also lived on the banks of a stream and had the duty of guiding others across the water until, unknowingly, he one day carried the Child Jesus who, in the moment of danger, revealed Himself. Thus Christopher became the saint of dangerous crossings, the protector of sailors, and of all other travellers. What better place is there for St Christophers than in this perilous Morecambe Bay?

Ancient families now began to have their town houses in Ulverston, where they held parties, assemblies, and balls; there was a theatre, a cockpit, and a bull-ring. The leading shipbuilder of Furness was one Hart of Ulverston who had a new street named after him, which was later to be called Sunderland Terrace, after yet another local family. Here sea captains lived between voyages. One way down to the quay was by Ratton Row and Ellers. There was actually a rhyme which said that

> God mead (*made*) man
>   An' men mead money,
> God mead bees
>   An' bees mead honey.
> But the Devil mead lawyers an' 'tornies,
>   An' pleac'd 'em at Ooston an' Dotan i' Furniss.'

Now Ulverston was indeed the capital of Furness!

The shipping was dependent on local industries, and the port of Greenodd, further up the estuary, came now to be linked with Ulverston. In 1737, for instance, William White in his *Furness Folk and Facts* reports two hundred and thirty-one ships in the liberty of Furness. The iron ore from the Backbarrow and Cunsey furnaces was shipped on the Leven, and the quays at Penny Bridge and Greenodd were the ports for these two furnaces. (Penny Bridge takes its name originally from the

Penny family, who lived here for centuries and built the bridge to replace the old ford.)   Ore for the Leighton furnace was shipped across Morecambe Bay to Knowhill, Silverdale.   Ore was also shipped from Conishead Bank, Baycliffe, Wadhead, and Beanwell, for South Wales and Scotland, but at a slightly later date.   This Leven estuary showed a continual spread of

The old road disappears into the river at Greenodd.   The quayside is now a woodyard

canvas as the schooners and brigs went up to Greenodd for cargoes of copper and slate, or into Ulverston for iron ore.   As many as fifty 'flats,' schooners, sloops, and smaller craft would be anchored at one time at the Greenodd quays.   Only, however, if you have seen the present-day desertion and loneliness of Greenodd will you realize the significance of these facts by virtue of contrast.

Here once was the gunpowder magazine, near the Frith, with the *Low Wood* moored close by and loaded with explosives. Where are Roper Quay, Winder Quay, and Fell's Quay to-day? Low Quay may yet be traced—the loading place for Coniston copper ore.

The building of ships at Ulverston and Greenodd gave much employment to other quayside industries.   It was a big job in

1798 to build a vessel like the *Hope*, of 300–400 tons and mounting sixteen guns, for the West Indian trade. But this work finished in 1868 at Greenodd, and in 1878 at Ulverston.

The roads to the docks used to be red with the droppings of iron ore from carts going to the quays, and Greenodd inns were open all day, its quays a-jostle with seafaring men.

There was, of course, the usual drawback of this coastline—the silting up of Ulverston port by the sand. But Ulverston was not dismayed, and in 1796 a canal was completed, the shortest, widest, deepest, and straightest canal in England. On the beflagged opening day a London trader, the brig *Sally*, was the first to enter, with sails furled and bunting from every yard-arm. She was hauled along by the crowds and was followed by the *Valentine*, another London brig, and then a third. The fourth to enter was the sloop *Content*, laden with coal. She was lighter than the others, and her enthusiastic holiday hauliers passed the other ships so that she was the first to moor in the upper basin.

The first shipment of ore from Ulverston Canal was in 1799; the Newland Company built the Ore Quay, and Beanwell and Conishead Bank gradually declined. Even in that very year, only three years after the opening, we read that 'the channel has left the end of the canal, for some time past the larger vessels cannot get in.' Still, the best year was 1846 when the ninety-four vessels using the canal in 1798 had increased to nine hundred and forty-four, but soon afterwards it was bought by the Ulverston and Lancaster Railway, and its trade came to a gradual standstill. The Customs House, which had been established at Rampside in 1720, had been transferred to Ulverston. In the nineteenth century we see the stupendous growth of Barrow, with the anomaly of Barrow shippers going to Ulverston on Thursdays to complete their shipping business.

The railway then came to Furness—first to join the mines to Barrow quay, then to link that growing town with civilization, while a branch line extended past Greenodd to Coniston. Not only did viaducts seal the estuaries, but the trade was now carried by the new competitor. Liverpool and Barrow were the ports able to cater for the larger steam vessels of the industrial era. Greenodd has decayed, Ulverston has gathered other small industries within herself, and Barrow is near enough

to any part of Lower Furness to attract skilled labour. Moreover it remains an important market town, and for that we may
be thankful.

Thursday is market-day at Ulverston, when all roads into
the town are full of slowly moving flocks of sheep and clumsy
cows, for there are still many farmers who do not use the motor
and trailer. Those that do so, as I one day saw for myself,
were in town quickly and had the animals deposited and packed
into the auction stalls long before the walkers came into sight.

The womenfolk, meanwhile, took their places in the market,
where long narrow benches were waiting for their merchandise,
which on that day was very meagre, sometimes nothing more
than a plucked fowl or a bunch of flowers. Young master
Edward was taking the sheep down from his father's farm on the
edge of the rigg. He was only ten years old but could handle
sheep with the best. His skin had the hue of autumn gold,
matching his strong light curls and deep blue eyes. All he
wore was a faded khaki shirt, open at the neck all three buttons,
and a pair of his father's riding-breeches. They stretched from
his shoon to his arm-pits, yet he was not ungainly. A button
was missing at the back, so that a brace stuck jauntily into the
air like the cock of a thumb. Down the narrow centre streets of
Ulverston he came at a rapid pace, with the sheep so close you
could have spread a sheet over them and had all under cover.
When he came into the square his dog ran round and round,
and Edward struck hard at any sheep that tried to leave the
closely packed circle. Then he raised his hand to stop the
traffic ; motors drew to a standstill—Edward gave an order and
the sheep darted forward and were safely on their way to the
auction. Afterwards the motorists continued their interrupted
journeys, smiling at the confidence the wee lad had displayed.

Edward was well known at the auction rooms. His elder
brother, a man of nearly thirty, was already in the ring, buying
new stock. With the sheep safely penned and marked, Edward
went into the ring to watch developments. The auction room
was small, comprising a centre ring covered with sawdust, and
rising tiers of seats in two sections opposite one another. The
auctioneer and his clerk sat in a tall box facing the two gates by
which the sheep entered and left the ring. The room was full
of farmers, and such variety of character and of dress it would be

Canal Foot, Ulverston
Starting point to cross the sands

hard to better anywhere. A thick blue tobacco haze filled the air, already smelling vile from the warmth and stench of animals.

The auctioneer was a live wire. He was tall and lean, with shirt-sleeves rolled to the elbow and a well-worn trilby pushed to the back of his longish head. His eyes were never still. Like quicksilver they darted continuously all over the room, observant of every bidder, until he banged down his walking-stick on the desk at the highest price. His gabble was incomprehensible to a stranger, yet the men in the ring played their parts without the least sign of strain.

The gate opened and three ewes were shooed out of the ring, while at the same time three more were pushed in as the other gate was opened. Those were three of Edward's flock. Interested bidders rushed forward to feel at them. 'Three fine ewes,' shouted the auctioneer, 'who'll start a pound, who'll start a pound, a pound, fifteen, fifteen-fifteen, sixteen-sixteen-sixteen, sixteen half, sixteen half, sixteen half, seventeen . . .' The rises in price occurred as the auctioneer noted the wagging of a finger, of a hand, the winking of an eye or the nodding of a head. It was a continuous, quickfiring explosion of figures which ended as suddenly as it began with a crack of the walking-stick on the desk. The buyer took a scrap of paper from his overcoat pocket and made a note. Edward ran under the exit gate with the sheep, and the auctioneer began asking for bids once more.

Edward's father was in the next auction room, a little further down the same street, where calving cows were being sold. There were some first-class cattle in the ring and he had his eye on one particular beast. He is a man who makes broth once a week to last all week, agreeing that it has a scum of fur on top by the end of the week, but maintaining it is all the better for that —mix it in and it puts a kick in the broth!

Buying cows is a slower business than buying sheep. The farmers took their own cows round the ring, passing laudatory remarks when the bidding was not so brisk. Outside, even by noon, there was still a bustle of arriving cattle, which three hours later would have changed hands and be on their way once more through the streets to their new homes. Beneath the ancient oaks in the street stood blue and red painted farm

o

machinery, and Irish cattle. Here the buying was a more intimate affair, with high offers and low, a long-drawn-out process, ending in a fair price and the signing of a cheque.

Crowds of people thronged the open-air stalls overlooking the rose gardens, farmers' wives handling yards of curtains, fingering table-cloths, and tapping crockery. Groups stood

Swarthmoor Hall

gossiping while the motor-buses came in continuously, dropping their loads of people before setting out once again into the surrounding countryside. Later in the afternoon this order of things would be reversed, until Ulverston returned once more to the quietude of its everyday life.

Swarthmoor Hall, near Ulverston, has become deservedly famous as the centre from which George Fox spread his gospel of Quakerism. He was able to do this through the generosity of the owner, Judge Fell (who never became a Quaker) and his wife, who later married George Fox. Sarah Fell, one of her daughters, took charge of the household, particularly when her mother was busily engaged in furthering the new approach to religious matters, and kept a household account book which supplied a wealth of information on the mode of life in those days in such an isolated district. Lancaster was twenty miles

away by the oversands route, and one entry shows a payment of
2s. 6d. 'for going with a letter to Lancaster to the post, that
required haste.' Normally the Fell household had to wait for
the post, which came every Thursday with John Higgins the
carrier who visited Ulverston market. The account book tells
of a 'whitesmith' called John Fell, who repaired surgical
apparatus, 'blooded' animals, and attended to clocks and
watches, and of one Thomas Wilson and his men who 'sowed'
a tree into bedsteads and boards, and made ploughs, yokes, and
a 'great firrdale chaire.' We learn that when peat was cut for
the fires it was called 'graveing.' The brick-shaped pieces were
spread out to dry; 'footing' was leaning them against each
other, and 'windrowing' meant arranging them in heaps so
that the wind could blow through the pile. 'A cartfull of
peats' cost thirteen pence.

George Fell of Trinkeld near Ulverston, weaver of 'Ulverston
checks,' who 'rose to great affluence,' wove for the family on his
hand-loom '9 ells of Kearsey, 18 ells blankettin, 48 ells of teare of
Hemp Cloth, 18 ells of feather-bed ticking, and 13 ells of fine
cloth.' William Hobson of Cartmel wove 19 yards of 'hugga-
backe' for 4s. 6d.

In 1682 tobacco halbs were imported from Virginia and used
to cure scabbed sheep and horses. These were the days when
butter and fat were used for wheel grease and 'quicksilver,
gunpowder, brimstone, hogs lard,' and such items for scabbed
horses. An entry reads: '1717, paid for tarring the backs of
Galloways [pack-horses] paid for brandy for horses backs.'

Around the hall was a daily scene of much activity. Besides
the cutting of peat from their own mosses there was bracken to
fetch from the hills for cattle bedding, and not only for bedding.
When ferry and bracken were mown green and burnt, their
ashes, containing a higher percentage of salts than those of any
other vegetable, were mixed with lime and tallow to produce
the soap of the period. Strewn in the lanes and farmyards the
bracken was crushed in with the manure and provided an
excellent compost for arable land, while poor people used it to
thatch their houses.

There is an old superstition that faery power is at its height
on the eve of St John (23rd June), and that if the stem of the
bracken, which is regarded as almost a sacred plant, is cut

across on that night, the cut surface will show the outline of the sacred oak-tree.   On this evening bracken rises to the height of its power and sends out a tiny blue evanescent flower, of which the seeds are already ripe by midnight and must be gathered as they fall, to make one invisible to mortal eye.   To-day we have forgotten that the young tips of ferns were squeezed and rubbed between the fingers to produce a scent and that otherwise prepared they gave an oil and a salt, while the roots provided a styptic and bitter concoction.   Heather ling was used in some places to preserve beer.

There was always spinning and weaving to be done, hose knitting, walling, 'swingling' (flax and hemp), muck spreading, harrowing and dressing meadows, picking and pulling flax and hemp, riddling beans and ploughing.   There was the gathering of orchard fruits, sheep-shearing, and preparing the meat of animals.

Nails and ironwork for carts and repairs could be purchased from a local manufactory, or if, like the Fells, a family were financially interested in one of the furnaces, they could provide their own.

There were salmon and sea trout to be had from the river estuaries, and crabs and cockles from Morecambe Bay.   Herbs were grown for food and medicine, and the household grew its own parsnips, carrots, onions, turnips, cabbages, radishes, and strawberries, while the orchard provided apples, pears, plums, and damsons.   From the marsh and its own woods came geese, woodcock, teal, tufted duck, pigeons, partridge, and snipe. The brew-house produced ale and cider, and the kitchen home-made fruit wines, only white wines, brandy, claret, and port being imported when trade with France was stable.   Whisky was run contraband from the Isle of Man and landed locally without much trouble.   Bee's honey was collected for sweetening before the introduction of sugar, and beeswax used for wax lights.   The best shoes came from Kendal, but for workaday life clogs were worn, made sabot fashion, as learned from Huguenot immigrants.   Leather tops were added later, the materials coming from the family's own cattle and being tanned with their own oak-bark.   Items that had to be bought in Lancaster included ink, sealing-wax, scissors, knives, special leathers, silverware and pewter ware, drinking-glasses and flagons, pens and kettles, looking-glasses, clocks, and some medicines, particularly for horses.

At harvest time every village hired a fiddler who went from field to field to play to the reapers (musick while ye worke). For the harvest home the local landowner provided the malt

Craftsmen of the Lancashire countryside. Shaping clog soles, basket making, and slate cutting

for the liberal supply of ale required, and dancing took place in the village street just as you may find it to this day in isolated Spanish villages of the Pyrenees.

Homespun was the wear of 'everyman.' It was an old tradition of Blawith in High Furness that every cottage had at least three spinning-wheels. Flax and hemp produced the linen and finer wear for the gentry, and nearly every farm had one field called 'hempland.' The weaving of wool called for fulling-mills to finish the cloth produced. There were corn-mills, eel dams, and salmon fishing to provide the staple diet, the corn-mills producing more oatcake (or havercake) than wheaten loaves.

From the rivers came 'pow seaves' (cut rushes) for bottoming chairs, sand for rough-casting, and waterdubs for watering skins for the tanners, who used oak-bark for tanning until the process was replaced by the introduction of cheaper, imported, chemically tanned leather.

Homespun, havercake, rough-cast, and whitewash—these made the background of the Furness folk who, despite their industry, remained poor. The tale is told of the Blawith parishioners, wishing to add a steeple to their church, but being obliged first to sell some of their land to raise the necessary funds, and then to build it with their own labour. It is recorded in an eighteenth-century rhyme:

> Blawith poor people,
> An auld church and new steeple,
> As poor as hell,
> They had to sell,
> A bit of fell,
> To buy a bell,
> Blawith poor people.

The clergy were as poor as the rest. To make a living it was a recognized custom for them to teach in the schools, for which service they received board and lodgings, turn and turn about in the various houses in the parish. This custom was known as 'whittle gate.' Clark's *Survey of the Lakes* (1789) tells us that 'Whittle Gate is to have two or three weeks victuals at each house according to the abilities of the inhabitants, which was settled among them, so that the parson should go to his course as regular as the sun, and compleat it annually. Few houses having more knives than one or two the pastor was obliged to bring his own (sometimes it was bought for him by the chapel wardens), and march from house to house with his whittle seeking fresh pasturage . . . a parson was thought a proud fellow that was not content without a fork to his knife. He was reproved for it, and was told that fingers were made before forks.' He was also allowed to have a '*darrack* of peats,' or as much as one person could cut in one day; the 'harden sark,' a rough, coarse linen shirt provided by the parishioners; and 'goose grass,' which was the right to pasture geese on common land.   In return the clergy did the services of an educated man for an isolated community, such as acting as lawyer to its inhabitants.

The classical example of the perfect clergyman is that of the Rev. Robert Walker of Seathwaite in the Duddon valley.   He was born there, at Undercrag, on 21st December 1709 and took his first curacy at Buttermere about 1732.   He was appointed to the church in his native village in 1736, and died in 1802 in his ninety-third year.   He became the father of eleven children. He was granted the customary whittle gate, goose grass, harden sark, and a darrack of peats.   To this he was able to add a labourer's wages by working in the fields at harvesting, mowing, ploughing, planting.   He tended sheep on the hills, sheared and salved them.   He spun flax and wool, knitted his own stockings, and made his own shoes.   He collected tithes in kind, and as his pupils were too poor to pay him they helped him in the fields, and as he was also the doctor they gathered herbs for him. All conveyancing and writing of letters was left to him.   He worked late at night and rose early, eating chiefly oatmeal porridge night and morning, with dried beef and bread for dinner.   In summer he added vegetables, milk, and cheese. On this he raised his large family and left a fortune of £3,000.

While its natural iron-ore resources were the foundation of Furness industry, the iron could not be separated from the dross without charcoal, and charcoal demanded a plentiful supply of wood.   From the twelfth to the early eighteenth century that supply was provided locally, but by that time wood had to be imported to the district.   For example, Leighton Wood was purchased in 1713 for £2,300, for use as charcoal, for the building of vessels (including the sloop *Leighton* at Arnside) and for 'wheel timber, spade shafts, axletrees, clogsoles, coffin boards, heart and sap laths, spikins, ship nails, barrel staves, and many other articles.'   Holly-trees were bought for their bark and the wood sold to calico printers who used it to make wooden designs for cloth printing, and to cabinet makers for veneers. Oak was sold to ship carpenters on the River Crake, where many a vessel was launched in the seventeenth century.

A commissioners' report on Furness Abbey in 1537 gives a further list of the local usage of wood: '. . . Also there ys another yerely p'fytte comying and growing of the same woodes called Grenehewe Bestyng Bleckyng byndyng makyng or Sadeltrees, Cartwheles, Cuppes Disshes and many other thyngs wrought by Cowpers and Turners wt makyng of Coles and pannage of Hogges according as hath always been accustumed to be made in the said woodes to the yerely valewe by estymacyon of XIIjLi. vj. vij.'

Another document refers to 'two little houses called Easinge Harthes wth the brusinge wood and the Ealinge Asshes, . . .' and Alfred Fell suggests that the ashes were used as a substitute for fuller's earth in the fulling-mills where woollen goods were cleaned and prepared for use. It is evident that much wood was used, not only for making charcoal, but also as raw material for those craftsmen in wood who provided the daily requirements of home and industry. Was not Cartmel Fell Chapel 'a place for prayer and poetry,' dedicated to 'St Anthony of the Fells'? St Anthony is the patron saint of hermits, herders, basket-makers, charcoal-burners, and other lowly folk, and incidentally the local surnames of Tyson and Towson are corrupt forms of his name.

Speaking first of charcoal manufacture, this is a skilled industry based on the simple scientific idea of driving out the moisture, and all other constituents of wood except carbon, by heat. The process carried out in the open air of the fells has varied little since the earliest times. The charcoal-burner regulates the supply of air to the wood so that only enough oxygen is admitted to allow combustion but not to cause flame. The place in the woodland where this is done is called a pit ring or pitstead. The wood is cut up in spring and summer and stacked for burning in the autumn. The shallow, circular pit is some 15 feet in diameter with a stout stake set up in the middle. The wood to be burnt is leant against the stake to form a cone about 6 feet high. The first beams are set almost vertically, the angle being increased until the edge of the circle is reached. Another layer is added and wood is also laid horizontally, closely packed, and with no gaps. The stack is finally covered with grass rushes and marl, with perhaps the addition of a windward protective screen of interlaced twigs. The central stake is then taken out, dry wood is dropped in its place, and the opening finally sealed. The fire is started from a twig fire laid at the centre through a temporary opening. It takes about twenty-four hours to complete the making of a stack of charcoal.   A further layer of marl may be added, and water poured on the top which sends steam into the stack to cool the charcoal: slow burning gives better results than a fast burning.

The greener the wood the more charcoal it yielded was the common belief.   Certainly charcoal (unlike coke) is almost free from sulphur, and its use facilitated the toughening and hardening of iron into steel of the highest quality.   It was also used in the making of gunpowder at a time when the local iron industry also supplied cannon and shot for the Napoleonic wars.   W. T. Palmer in *The River Mersey* (1944) calls to mind the red-flagged hulk off Dingle, where explosives were stored before being exported, and tells how he remembers as a boy coastal vessels bringing their cargoes of gunpowder from the Elterwater factory to the River Leven to this place, and going from there to the West African coast, the kegs being marked with a red hand or a black Negro's head.

The varieties of wood manufactory which were once carried on in Furness are too numerous to be described here in great detail.   While the oak was stripped of its bark for the tanneries of Lancashire and Cheshire until fifty years ago, the smaller branches were used for cask hoops and swills (or strong baskets). Still smaller branches were sent to the Potteries to be made into pottery crates.   Birch twigs were tied into besoms (or garden brooms) and these are still obtainable.   Larger stems of all varieties went for the manufacture of bobbins for the cotton-mills and for cotton reels.

Hoop making was a cottage industry.   The smaller branches of summer-felled oak, still full of sap and pliable, were cut and trimmed in the correct lengths and then bent, their circular shape being preserved by tying them with rope.   The bending or coiling frame was like an eight-armed windmill with holes pierced in the arms at prearranged distances.   Stout pegs were driven into these holes and wooden strips were soaked in water and bent around the pegs.   The chief market for these hoops, as also for swills, was Liverpool.   The swills were made of long thin strips of oak, first soaked in water and then boiled, after which they were bent round an oval frame of ash or hazel and interlaced.   The men who made them were called swillers and the centre of the trade was the village of Finsthwaite.

The copse wood which supplied the raw material for these crafts was naturally carefully preserved. The wood was cut when fifteen to sixteen years old; eighteen years was considered too long, as by that time the undergrowth decays. There was a local saying that to have wood you must cut wood, more new shoots springing from a young stub than from an old one. Another way of judging the time to cut was when the main stems had a diameter of five to six inches. Cutting was usually undertaken from 10th May to 5th July, after which the workers sorted, peeled, tied, and hauled until the autumn. Oaks to be stripped of bark for tanning were left until the sap began to rise, because this made the bark-stripping easier. The word 'tan' originally meant a young oak-tree and trees were stripped for 'tan-bark.'

It required a lot of wood to produce, at the turn of the last century, 30,000,000 bobbins a year, and this was but one item. 'Hoopstuff is sold by the 100 or 1,000 at six guineas,' Dickson reported in the early nineteenth century; 'poles for carpenters' use by the foot at one shilling; swillwood by the cord, 8 feet by 4 feet at sixteen shillings; roods by the hundred at eight shillings, charcoal by the tub at twenty-five shillings the dozen; oak bark at £20 a ton for tanning leather.' He complained that not enough use was made of elder wood, as it made the best poles 'whereon to hang cotton yarn to dry, that wood acquiring a fine polish by frequent use, nor does it splinter by exposure to the weather, and its bark also sells at nearly one penny the pound as an article for dye.' It gave a red dye selling at £6 a ton.

Not very long ago, the fresh-water Fishery Research Station at Wray Castle, Windermere, potted char, caught in the lake, and this unusual fish had provided a notable industry in times past. It appears to be confined particularly to Coniston, Windermere, and Haweswater near Silverdale, although a species of char, has, I believe, been found in some of the Welsh lakes, and is known in high altitude lakes of Switzerland and Austria. Even so, it is in Windermere and Coniston that the particular industry seems to have been popularized.

The name 'char' seems, without doubt, to have come from old Celtic 'ceara,' which means blood-colour, and described the flesh tint of the fish. All species of char differ from trout and salmon in teeth formation. In the spawning season upper parts of the fish are a brownish green and the under surface shades from orange to vermilion, gradating from throat to pelvic fins, where it is most intense. The sides are adorned with round spots, varying between white and red. The dorsal fin has black markings, while the pectoral and pelvic fins are a brilliant red. Char are rarely more than eight or nine inches long, and in deeper water the colours are more subdued.

Any reading of Furness life will show that char was looked upon as a delectable luxury with an export value. The iron-masters found that the most acceptable gift they could send to their customers and friends was a pot of char, many being obtained either from 'the House of Mrs Petty at Kendall,' or in Ulverston, where they were made up in three sizes, selling at 10s. 6d., 15s., and 21s. In 1784 the fish were selling at 8s. a dozen unpotted. Many of the pots, by the way, were made by Zachariah Barnes of Liverpool.

On 2nd July 1701 Dame Elizabeth Ottway of Ambleside let to George Braithwaite of High Wray her privilege of fishing on Windermere, with the privilege of plying a boat with any goods for one year for a payment of 5s., reserving for herself the twenty chars which the fishermen were to give her every year.

The Furness monks had twenty nets on Coniston and Winder-mere. In the eighteenth century Windermere was divided into five districts by imaginary lines recognized by land features. As the fish moved in shoals, one fishery might have abundance while another had none. In the nineteenth century the division was recognized as three 'cubbles,' each cubble consisting of four fisheries.

Nets were used until 1823, at which date Otley writes that 'of late [in Coniston Water] several have been taken by angling, with a hook baited in a peculiar manner with a minnow.' And so char fishery moves out of the field of food production and industry into that of sport.

For the sportsman it is well to remember that from the end of March to the beginning of May the char will be in ninety feet of water: from the end of July they come to the top of the water, then go down slightly until September, when they come nearer the shore in shoals ready for the October spawning.

And what about char pie? Celia Fiennes in 1695 made a

note on her journey, 'to get some clean, fresh mutton fat, hot it till it almost boils, take your char by the tail and slowly dip it in, having floured it first, turn it round in your fingers 2 or 3 times, take it out, bread crumb it, and eat it as soon as you can.' About the same period, Daniel Fleming of Rydal's account book (1664) prescribes 'eleven dozen of charres from Conni-stone for four pies'—that is thirty-eight fish per pie, and if they averaged three to the pound it would make 13 lb. of fish for each pie.   He sent a pie, however, to his Aunt Dudley in London on 23rd March 1662 which weighed 36 lb.! 'Item for the carryage of a Charr-pie vnto my Aunt Dudley in London at 2d. per lb. 6s. 0d.'   Pennant, on his tour (1772) records char selling at 3s. 6d. per dozen a few years ago, 'but thanks to the luxury of the times are now raised to 8 or 9 shillings.'   In Sir Daniel Fleming's time a char pie cost 33s. for the fish.   But the demand from London for char pie, baked in pots and well seasoned, was great, for it was considered the height of luxury. The Fell family of Swarthmoor preserved and seasoned their pies with mace, cloves, nutmegs, cinnamon, and black pepper.

It was the Swarthmoor account books which prompted this dissertation, and we must return to the hall, the home of Thomas Fell, barrister-at-law of Gray's Inn. He married eighteen-year-old Margaret Askew of Marsh Grange, whose family were renowned throughout the district for their hospi-tality and piety.   Small wonder, therefore, that when George Fox was travelling north through Lancashire in the year 1652 he should be directed to Swarthmoor Hall, where all religious people were sure of a welcome. On the Sunday following he went to Ulverston church with Margaret Fell and asked permission to speak, as was commonly done in those days.   His speech caused him to be thrown out of church, but a more important result was that Margaret Fell became convinced of the truth of his words, and so began fifty devoted years for the work of George Fox and the Quakers.

George Fox rode thence to Aldingham, where he preached one morning, and at Rampside in the afternoon, and Thomas Lawson, then minister there, became a Friend, leaving every-thing like the disciples, and was later imprisoned for his faith. Fox went on to Dalton, Walney Island, Baycliff, Gleaston, and other villages before returning to Kendal and Sedbergh to meet the antagonism being there raised against him by 'Priest' Lampitt.

His friends Nayler and Farnsworth, who were following his trail, had by this time arrived at Swarthmoor Hall, and were there when Judge Fell came home from his Welsh circuit. The judge was partly prepared, for as he crossed the sands he had been met by Lampitt and his friends, but he nevertheless seemed 'afflicted and surprised at the revolution in the religious principles of his family.' After dinner Judge Fell saw George Fox alone. They were then joined by the rest of the family. Margaret Fell reported later that 'if all England had been there, I thought they could not have denied the truth of those things. And so my husband came to see clearly the truth of what he spoke, and was very quiet that night, said no more, and went to bed.' Lampitt came the next day to follow up his exhortations, but the judge told the Friends that they could hold their meetings at Swarthmoor Hall. So it was that next Sunday they met in the large hall, and continued so every Sunday until 1688 when George Fox gave a meeting-place to the society.

Judge Fell himself continued to go to Ulverston church with his clerk and groom for the next two years, after which he took to sitting at home in his parlour, leaving the door ajar the better to hear the meeting of the Friends in the hall. He died in 1658 and left money to found a school at Ulverston. This was well known as Town Bank School, and is now the Ulverston Grammar School. It is interesting, in noting the reversal of importance in towns and villages, that at that date there was only one grammar school in the whole of Furness, and that was at Hawkshead (where Wordsworth was a scholar). There was a small free school at Urswick.

The first meeting-place for the Society of Friends was given by George Fox in this manner. In 1687, when he saw that religious toleration was to be allowed, after forty years of persecution, he wrote from London to Thomas Lower of Marsh Grange saying that he gave up 'freely to the Lord for the service of His sons and daughters and servants, called Quakers,' the three-acre property called Petty's, not far from Swarthmoor Hall. He had bought it from Susannah and Rachel Fell a few years previously. Now he instructed that the house and barn should be made into a meeting-house and put in good repair;

that the land and malthouse were to be let to maintain the meeting-house; and that a 'poor honest Friend' could live in the cottage.   He asked for a porch, with seats, to be built and an orchard and fir-trees to be planted.   The carved stone over the door was placed in position: 'Ex dono G. F. 1688.'   He also gave his 'ebony bedstead with its "Pintado" curtains, a large elbow chair, a great sea-chest "with bottles in it," all to be heirlooms,' so that Friends might have a 'bed to lie on, a chair to sit in, and a bottle to hold a little water to drink.'   Margaret Fox gave a Cromwellian oak arm-chair, and George Fox's 'Treacle bible.'   After that date stables and a mounting block were added, for, as you may see in all such remote churches, there had to be accommodation for the necessary horse.   In 1710 a burial-ground on the other side of the road was brought into use; it makes a lovely picture in spring when the daffodils are in bloom.   An earlier burial-ground is hidden away on the top of Birk Rigg, close by Sunbrick.   Never have I seen a lonelier or lovelier place, and there lie the remains of Margaret Fox.

XVI

FURNESS: (2) THE SOUTHERN SEABOARD

THE coast road from Ulverston to Barrow is a comparatively recent innovation and the bus service even more so, but 'Johnson's' bus to Bardsea (as it may still be called although Mr Johnson has now retired), which gives a three-mile lift on the way, has been running since the First World War and is a typical village service. I have no idea how far afield the Ministry of Transport extends its functions, but there is still a smack of the old village life in the Thursday market crowds which tend to bulge the tinplate and to overflow the seats with their number and their crowded baskets; or when the village exodus to the Ulverston cinema on a Saturday has to be accommodated somehow on the last journey home. The only time I have known Mr Johnson fail me was when I wanted him to carry myself and my wife and a perambulator complete with baby. He could only take my wife, and so I settled down alone to that enjoyable walk out of Ulverston, past Conishead Priory, and over the hill into Bardsea.

It is only a few minutes' journey to get clear of the town and on to the country road, shaded by ancient trees. Once in the open pasture and close along the shore, the huge mansion of Conishead Priory comes into view, and at first glance is a shock for the historian who is only prepared to see the small priory, founded by Gabriel de Pennington, with the consent of his overlord William de Lancaster, in the reign of Henry II. De Pennington built a hospital for the relief of decrepit persons and lepers and endowed it with all the lands on both sides of the road from Bardsea to Ulverston, 'and from the great road to Trinkeld and the sea banks,' which was later converted into a priory, holding the church of Ulverston, some forty acres of land in that town, a saltworks on the coast near by, and other properties. It suffered at the Dissolution along with Furness Abbey, and it is believed that a house was built on the site from the monastic stones soon after the Dissolution.   William Sandys lived here, whose name occurs often in early records of the forest and bloomeries (bloom is the product of iron), for he was the official receiver.   We have learned how he died, and those who like to pursue matters to the bitter end may see his tomb in Ulverston church graced with an effigy in Elizabethan armour (see also page 228).

The present mansion, begun in 1821, was designed by Philip Wyatt and is recognized as an early example of the Gothic revival.   In 1878 it was turned into a hydropathic sanatorium and it is now a welfare home for miners.   You will meet the patients, easily recognizable by their cloth caps and blue-scarred skins, taking a constitutional anywhere between Ulverston and Bardsea and will always find them willing to talk about their mining experiences.

A little way past the priory the 'new' coast road goes down to the shore round the outskirts of Bardsea village, while 'Johnson's' bus takes the tree-shaded lane over the hill and into the village.   The first houses to be seen are modern enough and represent the overspill which is common to most English villages to-day.   They extend into the grounds of Bardsea Hall.   This is no violation, for it has been a ruinous heap for long enough. There was a family named de Bardsey living here at one time who received their grant of land at the Conquest or soon after-wards.   Adam de Berdsey was a witness to the charter of Ingelram de Ghuyres to the burgesses of Ulverston, and in Drydale's *Monastica Anglicanum* there is reference among grants and endowments to Conishead Priory to William, son of Roger de Berdsey granting an oxgang of land in Berdsey, with a croft in which stood the house of the hospital of St John of Jerusalem, with eight acres of land in Berdsey.   The last of the line seems to have been one Nicholas de Bardsey, who is men-tioned in a trust deed for the free school at Urswick and who died in the reign of James I.

Beyond the site of the hall is the village street lined with old limestone cottages, and passing Bardsea church (1843) on the crown of the hill, whose spire is a landmark for miles around. It is higher than anything else, dwarfing the village.   The newer stone-work is in contrast to the aged stone-lichened houses, huddled together for comfort when harsh weather

Furness Abbey

N. Wolstenholme

comes. Such strength may well be its weakness, for to stand aloof from one's brothers is not the best way to obtain their friendship. Also, in this case, the ecclesiastical roots of the village are buried in Urswick church three miles away inland, where Saxons and Normans have left their more venerable handwork. At the date when Bardsea church was built there

The main road to Barrow sweeps round the bay at Bardsea. The packets used to tie up by the hill in the middle distance

were hardly two hundred people living in Barrow, six miles away, and the railway had not come to the peninsula.

My best memories of Bardsea date from before the last war and the era of rationing, when there were still cottagers who had been in service to the gentry and who were still in a position to feed you on chicken and gooseberry flan from a grossly over-loaded table.

The Ship Inn is as much a farm as a pub, and is a reminder of the days when sailing ships called here at the quay and unloaded from the Fleetwood packet passengers from the Isle of Man and 'furrin parts,' and when many of the villagers were seafaring men, and the schoolmaster a retired sea captain.

The old quay has now disappeared, or is only occasionally

P

revealed by the shifting sands.   I can envisage the romance and
adventure in a journey a hundred years ago, from Preston to
Fleetwood on the newly opened railway line, then by paddle
steamer to Bardsea, where 'the inelegant tub-car and the much
more picturesque Donkey Shandry cart, were awaiting the boat
to take passengers along the country lanes to Ulverston.   Or
the traveller could sit on the shore and see ships sailing across
the bay, with coal for Greenodd, to be distributed as far as
Coniston and Hawkshead in High Furness; with sulphur and
nitre for the gunpowder works at Low Wood and Black Beck;
with copper from Coniston for South Wales; with iron ore,
hides, tanned leather, and slates from Coniston.

It was in a cottage here that I first met an old lady, sitting
upright on a kitchen chair and dressed in a long black Victorian
dress which somehow suited her perfectly.   Plainly she was
more interested in the past than the future, and finding a willing
listener she spoke feelingly of her girlhood days spent aboard
local schooners, for her father was an old sea salt whose ship
was the last wooden hulk to be repaired in Barrow.   It was a
coastwise trade in which he was employed.   Yes, she remembered how they carried gunpowder in one-pound kegs to Liverpool where it was reloaded into African service boats.   They
also carried granite for the Liverpool streets, and ore to
Swansea, returning to Ulverston with cargoes of flour and
general merchandise.

It was in pre-war days that my wife and I were first invited
to a pil-gil.   This, we found, was a dance held in a malt kiln.
Since the war there have been further village activities in this
malt kiln and the dances are now more like those elsewhere,
but we still would rather see the youths dressed in their best
Sunday tight-fitting trousers, and wearing heavy, but highly
polished boots, their red necks bulging from unaccustomed
collars, and becoming, after a round of lancers, even redder!
Those lads used to be late starters, but in the early hours of the
morning it was hard to stop them, for they were beginning to
enjoy themselves.

The village is separated from the seashore by a few fields,
with deep-hedged lanes growing with wild flowers such as the
glaucous yellow sea-poppy and the purple thyme which are
alternately warmed by the sun and kissed by the sea spray.

To the north lies Sea Wood, a last remnant of the forests of
Furness, whose trees sweep down to the edge of the shore.
Countless times have we gathered dead wood in its glades to
light a fire on the beach and to spend the day without seeing
another soul.   Only at week-ends do visitors come for the day,
and then an itinerant ice-cream vendor sets up shop for a few
hours.   Close to the shore is the old corn-mill, now a tea-room,
and you may see some of the millstones under the large tree on
the shore.   If you go to the other end of the small bay and
beyond the promontory you will find the remains of the quay.

The tide comes in here silently and swiftly over the mud—a
mere lurking creepiness, where the pulse of the sea is too feeble
to be felt.   There is no depth, no opposition, to the swirling
lines of ooze: as imperceptibly as it becomes high tide it returns
to low tide, and there is only the wet shimmer of miles of open
silt and sand to show you where the tide has been.

Some distance off-shore runs the deep channel of a stream,
behind a small, long skear, and when the tide is out we go there
to catch blennies left in the pools and to lay lines for eels to be
collected after the next tide.   Standing there you may see the
two-wheeled carts going out from Baycliff for the fishing.   The
horses plod on the soft sand, lifting their legs high until the water
is too deep for such action; then they stand with the sea up to
their bellies while the nets are cast.

Behind the village is the hog's back of Birk Rigg, rising to
over four hundred feet immediately above the sea.   Sweet-
scented hawthorn hedges give place to woodland, and then to
gorse and bracken, rising over the grey limestone, which shows
its ribs here and there.   Peewits are constant company, crying
plaintively overhead, while larks sing thrillingly the whole of the
day.   The top of the rigg is covered with bracken and festooned
with brilliantly green lanes, linking and diverging endlessly.
The views over sea and country from here are worth any
exertion in the climb, and you will not be disappointed by the
atmosphere of the lonely Stone Circle up here, or of the first and
simple burial-grounds of the Quakers at Sunbrick at the other
end of the common.

I was walking up here one Saturday afternoon when I met
Sam.   He could tell me the names of all the birds that lodged in
the bracken, and of the wild flowers in the woods below.   We

sat on the close-cropped greensward, chewing grass and looking over the bay to Morecambe on the other side. Ulverston lay like a grey handkerchief dropped on the patchwork arable land.

'Can ta see John Barrow's monument on Hoad Head?' Sam asked.

There it was, standing about as high as we were above sea level.

'Ah reckon it about a hundred years old,' he went on. 'Mi fadder has a book 'at says it were built in 1850, an' that it coast £1,250, has walls 12½ feet thick at the bottom, that there's 112 steps inside, and it's a model of Eddystone lighthouse. It's all in t' book.'

'You're an Ulverston man, Sam?' I asked.

'Aye, born and bred in Lile Ooston,' he said. 'Fadder were a farmer and Ah had mi hand to plo' as soon as Ah could walk nearly. After schoàl I went to Barra shipyards. Ever sin a lanching?'

'No,' I confessed.

'Goo this Thursday then,' he said. 'There's a P. & O. boat being lanched at three o'clock. It's well worth seeing.'

I promised to go to the 'lanching.' We were silent again, then Sam suddenly said: 'It's not offen a church is sold by auction, is it?'

I waited for him to continue.

'Colonel Braddyl fra Conishead Priory laid t' foundation-stone of Bardsea church an' began building in 1843. Then he failed. The church had not been consecrated so it was sold by auction in Lonnon. A minister called Petty bought it an' endowed it wi' a farm on Walney Island. It was finished in 1853. Then when Vickers Maxim Ltd, at Barra, wanted to build a model workmen's town on Walney Island they bought t' farm. It was a good thing for Bardsea church——'

He broke off and sat upright, pointing speechless down the pasture below us. I followed his direction, but only saw two men walking towards Ulverston.

'They're laying th' aniseed trail,' he said.

'What does that mean?'

'It's a trail hunt.'

He lit a cigarette and I filled my pipe.

'This will be a good place to see 'em.   They'll come ovver
t' park yon, under t' lea an' o'er t' rigg.   Ast ta sin 'em mak'
trail rags?'

I hadn't, of course, being from the south of the county.

'We getten a few owd stockings an' soak 'em in water for
twothri days.   Then we add a touch o' paraffin, a touch o' fish
oil, an' a bottle o' aniseed essence.   It's mixed in a bottle an'
t' rags are well soaked in it.   As them fellas go they keep dipping
t' rags in it to freshen like.   Better when it's donk [damp].
Ah've backed "Dean Swift"—it's owned by a local bookmaker.'

At that moment I saw a hound coming down the hillside
behind us.   As soon as it got the whiff of the trail it was over
the wall as fast as it could go.

'That's "Royal Oak,"' Sam shouted, jumping up.   'A
conny hound, he wur favourite in t' last race.   Someone's bin
holding 'im.   Leàk where he's geàn, doon looàn!'

Trail hunting is open to many unorthodox tricks such as this,
to prevent certain dogs winning the race.   Even scouts placed
specially to prevent such occurrences are unable to watch every
part of the course.

Just then we heard the noise of bracken being crushed and
turning round we saw a man running quickly down the scroggs.
He knew Sam and they greeted each other.   Then they drew a
little to one side, where I saw them talking in undertones and
gesticulating, until they went together down the aniseed trail
and were soon out of sight.   I had been forgotten in the excite-
ment of the race.

It may be said by some that I have made but a poor trans-
cription of the local dialect.   My answer to that is that I have
never tried!   An odd word here and there must suffice, or
Sam's conversation would seem a foreign language to strangers.
If I had said, for example, 'Does it ever rain here?' then Sam's
answer might easily have been : 'Why it dizzles and donks and
dozzles and duz, and sometimes ge'es a lile bit of a saifter, but
it nivver cums i enny girt pell.'

You see what I mean!   But this north-country dialect, with
its strong Norse and Anglo-Saxon, has a throbbing life which
turns our watery modern speech into a simper.

'"Hod ta noise, thoo bellerin coaf," thundered fadder as he
gat oot o' patience . . .' is an example.

Can you not feel the ancient icy wind from the tundras in 'blea' (as in Blea Tarn)? Or picture the 'borrans' (rough craggy places) and the 'varra brant' (or steep places)? This is the country where you 'brast his hide' and 'brost the door oppen.' And does not 'clag' seem 'to stick,' and does not the porridge seem to 'sotter' when it is slow boiling? Among the 'sl' words is the richest storehouse, as slaa—slow; slair—to move around indolently; slamp—soft and loose; slape—mouth, slippery, or bare; slocken—to cool hot iron or quench a thirst.

'Strang' seems stronger than 'strong,' 'steean' more stony than 'stone'; 'thrang' more bustling than 'busy.' And the slim, slender length of 'wandle' or the weak instability of 'wankle' has a far stronger music for my ears than any of our Mediterranean or French importations.

Great Urswick lies on the other side of Birk Rigg. A pleasant up-swinging and down-swinging moorland road joins the two villages, and it was on the way down it that I saw one day new cart-wheels, painted a daring red, standing against a wall, telling me that here lived a local craftsman in the old tradition. Later I found that the hymn and psalm boards and the literature table in the church were made locally. The altar-piece ('The Last Supper') was painted by a local artist, John Cranke the Elder, who was born in 1707.

The village snuggles close to the shores of a tarn, and because this is unusual it has a legend attached which runs somewhat as follows. At a time of drought, long ages ago, when the wells had dried up, the womenfolk of the village conceived the idea of asking the parson to make practical use of his religion by praying for rain. He obliged them, and a copious stream was born which cut a way through the fertile fields and found an outlet to the sea. But when the winter rains came the stream muddied to such an extent that the women could not wash their clothes nor the cattle drink the foul water. So the women went again to the vicar, asking if he was playing tricks on them. What they wanted was a full, copious supply, so copious that mud and dirt would settle and leave the water clean.

The vicar argued with them in vain, suggesting that they should count themselves blessed that they had been vouchsafed a regular supply. Finally he promised to give them a day and a night in which to change their minds. But these obstinate women would have none of it and at the expiration of the time limit the vicar prayed again.   This time the result was a terrible storm, out of which came a great wall of water which blotted out the entire village, including the obstinate women.   Only the church remained after the deluge, as you may see, but where the houses stood is now a peaceful sheet of water.   And you will be told that on a calm evening, if you take a boat to the middle of the tarn, you may hear the sounds of the drowned village. A wag at the General Burgoyne Inn told me it was the women you could hear, but that is merely his private opinion.

Be that as it may, the legend goes that 'Ossick' women for a long time after the deluge were quiet spoken and good wives, but that the lesson was forgotten and the ducking-stool had to be once again brought into common use.

Birk Rigg and the hills around Urswick have an affinity with the Silverdale, Warton, and Heysham coastal ranges as burial-grounds and living places of our earliest settlers.   Every cave has produced its relics, and stone circles, camps, and tumuli are strategically placed in these higher regions, all of which command the bay.

Urswick adds to the list a series of terraced stone dwellings of various shapes and sizes, with two enclosures built of un-mortared limestone blocks which, in excavation, brought to light a few pieces of bronze dating from the first and second centuries B.C.

More modern history has left its traces in the church, where a portion of a Viking cross was found in the north wall of the chancel and another in the south wall of the nave.   Presumably these represent the beginnings of religion in this area.   Just as Heysham was important enough to receive its earliest of chapels, so pioneers of the Faith came to Urswick, where civilization already existed in some form of settlement.

It is also interesting to note that when the Savigny monks were at Tulketh, and before they moved to Furness to found the abbey there, they claimed Urswick church.   The first recorded vicar is one Daniel le Fleming, son of Michael, about A.D. 1150–60.

Of the present church there is probably no part older than the thirteenth century, which is represented by the south wall of the chancel, the lower part of the tower, and the nave.   The windows, with the exception of one Early English example on the south wall of the chancel, are of later date.   In two of the windows is some ancient stained glass, possibly of the fourteenth century.

The tithe regulations for Urswick have been preserved, and the following extract (1778), referring to lambs and calves, shows an interesting method of computation:

> 15. The whole Parish pays wool and Lamb in Kind, but a Modus on Calves.
> 16. The custom of Tithing Lambs in our Parish is as follows. (viz.) a Half Penny p. Lamb is due to 5 Lambs, so that if a Person has but 4 Lambs he is chargeable only 2 Pence.   If he has 5 Lambs or half a Lamb, Half of the agreed price of a Lamb is payable.   All above 5 Lambs to ten is a whole Lamb, only abating a Half Penny for every Lamb short of ten and so in same Proportion for any greater quantity of Lambs.
> 17. A Tith Calf in our Parish is fixed at four Shillings.   Two pence p. Calf is due to five Calves.   Five Calves pay 2 shillings or half a Calf.   Six whole Calf abating Two Pence for every Calf short of ten; in same manner as for Lambs.   For a Cow that give Milk, but has not had a Calf within the Year; called a Strip Milk Cow—due one Penny.
> 24. The Vicar has a right to put any Goods he keeps on any Common in the Parish.

Money was accepted instead of kind in 1849.   About Easter time the custom was for the tithers to lunch at Hawkfield and dine at the present vicarage, then a private house.   The difficulties of assessment were thrashed out at these meetings.   The vicar would collect a sum of about £50.

Poor law overseers arranged for very poor people to have their children put out by the parish as apprentices, and we read, for instance, in the records:

> 23. August 1769: Margaret Waller, Daughter of Fras. Waller of Bardsea plac'd apprentice to Thos. Fell of Little Urswick.   Apprentice aged 11 Years or thereabouts.
> 23. August 1769: June Blacburne, Daughter of Chr. Blackburne aged 7 years or thereabouts to Mr. Tho. Petty for Wellhouse.

Vagrancy was discouraged 'as we do not apprehend that such Kind of Relief can properly be deem'd an Act of Charity, but rather an Encouragement to Laziness and Vice.'

Here and there in these records is mention of items of village life which passed unnoticed by the outside world. The February of 1739 was so cold that a sheep was roasted on the ice on the tarn. In January 1763 a bull was roasted on the tarn and races and country dances took place on the ice. In 1769 a swan swallowed a 'Pike Hook at a float.' The year 1770 was a wet summer and grain lay out of doors in November, and 1762 was, on the other hand, an exceedingly dry summer, and the tarn was almost dry at Candlemas in 1768.

Urswick folk were fond of cock-fighting, and it was usual amongst them to keep a couple of hens and a cock, rearing the best cockerels for fighting and eating the rest. The remains of a cock-fighting ring are still to be seen on Urswick Green. The referees for cock-fighting were the same men who were chosen as captains for the annual football match. William Ashburner, who was vicar from 1788 to 1800, also presided at the cockpit on occasion, complete with gown.

Although Rushbearing came to an end in 1826 the custom is still commemorated in September by a children's procession through the streets, carrying rushes and flowers, and preceded by the Rushbearing banner. They enter the church, strewing rushes as they walk to the altar where the vicar receives their flowers, which are afterwards placed in the 'Children's Corner.'

The next coastal village is Baycliff, which remains a small fishing-farming community. A living is eked out with the help of the few select visitors who have discovered the quietness of this coastline, and a modern inn caters for those who do not wish to depart altogether from the amenities of civilization. I certainly have reason to bless this particular inn, for I was fed there when I was hungry and my parched throat eased when an unreasonable boarding-house keeper failed to provide enough victuals to keep body in line with soul.

Although one is more likely to remember this coastline for the silent creeping of its tide, I have walked from Baycliff to Aldingham to the accompaniment of far-flung spray and battering waves, the more impressive as the approach to Aldingham is through a heavily tree-shaded by-lane, and suddenly there is the church on the seashore, with its graveyard acting as a breakwater. You may look in vain for a village, for as with so many places in Furness it exists now only in tradition, which in this case tells us that the church was once the centre of a village. The immense tidal storm of 1553 has left only the church. This is hardly as old as Urswick church and lacks the weathering and hoary-aged features whose uneven lines delight the eye, for it was largely renovated in 1932, the walls being plastered with concrete and new doors fitted to porch and organ loft. The ravages due to its open-sea position had made this work necessary. Incidentally, I have nothing but praise for the Sunday-school building which faces the sea and has one wall of glass which can be opened on warm days. The first recorded rector is one Daniel le Fleming of about 1180. It will be remembered that Urswick church claims him from 1150 to 1160 and that these were Fleming lands, the only portion of Furness over which Furness Abbey had no jurisdiction. Moreover this is a St Cuthbert church, one of the places of which it is recorded that the saint's body rested here on its journey through the north of England to escape the clutches of the Danes. So it would appear that once again we are following the old-time line of civilized settlements.

The fabric of the church is not very informative owing to the many alterations it has undergone. The Transitional south aisle and the Early English priests' doorway are the oldest parts. There was a rebuilding of the chancel and south aisle in the fourteenth century, a tower was added in the fifteenth century, after which nothing changed for two centuries unless it were the purchase of two bells about 1550 which were hung along with 'one great bell . . . in the steeple of the said pyrshe Chirche.' Then came the devastating tide of 1553 which wiped out not the church but the congregation. It was only just over a hundred years ago that the north aisle was built, windows were renewed in the south aisle, the south porch pulled down, and the west door reopened. In 1922 the chancel was restored, the ceiling removed, and the walls stripped and recovered with plaster. There can be little remaining of the more ancient church. But in all this time the feet of masons and carpenters have been walking on the thirteenth-century altar slab at the west end of the south aisle upon which is inscribed 'Hic jacet Goditha de Scales'—Scales, it may be noted, being a tiny village lying between Aldingham and Great Urswick.

XVII

FURNESS: (3) BARROW TO DUDDON ESTUARY

'**B**ARROW is the youngest child of England's enterprise,' said Gladstone in his speech at the opening ceremony of the first dock there in 1867. Yet in 1799, it is reported, not more than a cargo or two of coals could be sold in a season, so little was the consumption apart from lime burning.

To find the reason for this nineteenth-century growth—the reason why a town was required at all in this remote corner of Lancashire—we must outline the history of the Furness iron industry.

There are no records of the Romans having used the iron-ore deposits. The earliest mention of iron ore here is that of William de Lancaster (1220–46) when making a grant to the prior of Conishead of 'one acre of land next the stream which runs next the house of Ricardi le Tournour for a forge with a yard and for building other houses there necessary to it. The mine in Plumpton. . . . Dead wood in Blawith to burn coals wheresoever they may be found' (Patent Roll 12. Edw.). Further evidence is provided in 1346 by records of the death of William de Coucy who was seized of one moiety of the vill of Ulverston where 33s. a year profit was made on iron.

In the taxation rolls of Pope Nicholas (1292) there is an item, 'de mineria ferri deductis necessariis et expensis £6 12s. 4d.'

The Furness Abbey Coucher Book, which supplies a good deal of information, mentions Orgrave, Alinschales (Elliscales), and Merton (Marton) as having mines. In this same thirteenth century certain individuals such as Roger, son of Orm de Ograve, Gilbert, son of Roger de Orgrave, and Orm de Kellet were assigning claims for mining rights to Furness Abbey for a handful of silver, after which there is an absence of written records for a hundred and twenty-seven years, until the Dissolution in 1537. The abbey lands were then sold and the first mining licence was granted to William Sandys in 1544. It was 1609 before another was issued and this was never renewed. The name of Sandys occurs throughout the centuries of the Furness iron trade and must be noted by all who wish to study the peninsula and its folk. When visiting Ulverston church you may see a monument to the son of the aforesaid William Sandys, another William. The first William Sandys was Receiver General of the lordship of Furness after the dissolution of the monastery. He formed a partnership with one John Sawrey and worked the three bloomsmithies which had formerly belonged to the monastery. Sawrey died in 1547 and William Sandys shortly afterwards, when the smithies passed to the latter's eldest son, William, and his fourth son, Christopher. The son William succeeded his father also as receiver, and his is the monument in Ulverston church. He purchased the Conishead Priory estate from the Crown in 1548, and on 10th September 1558 he was 'very riotously and wilfully murdered at Conysheade.' An inquiry was held at Preston, and one witness said that he had been murdered on account of certain corn tithes which he possessed and which the sons and servants of William 'Bardseye' attempted to carry away. We learn further from evidence of witnesses that William Sandys was unpopular in the district because of his actions as receiver. The leases of the iron mines passed on his death to his brother Christopher who, we are told, willingly surrendered them.

Furness Abbey had used the mines for its own local requirements. William Sandys and John Sawrey did the same, for in 1545 we find John Preston writing to William Sandys about repairs to Dalton Castle: 'Half a ton of iron must be bought for the stayngers for the windows, hinges for doors and spykyns, or maybe for the flooring, which iron may be bought in the country for about £4.'

The development of the iron-ore industry had been seriously hindered by lack of suitable wood. Although Furness had been covered by woods at the time of the Domesday survey, the early charters of the abbey report wood only in the north of Furness. Tenants were allowed wood for all uses, and their cattle and sheep browsed among the young shoots—a practice which prevents the growth of woodland. Several Acts were passed in the sixteenth century to protect the forests from being used as fuel. In 1558, for example, trees were protected for an area of one foot square at the 'stubb end growing within fourteen miles of the sea.' In 1546 bloomsmithies on the Furness fells were abolished because complaints about the shortage of wood had been made by tenants in Colton and Hawkshead. Twenty pounds had to be paid out of the manor of Hawkshead in lieu of the bloomsmithy rent lost to the Crown, but this was eventually commuted to twenty-five years' purchase. The scarcity was not peculiar to Furness, for John Evelyn wrote that it would be better to purchase our iron from America than to exhaust our homeland woods.

At the dissolution of Furness Abbey the commissioners reported that 'there ys moche wood growing in Furneysfells in the mounteynes there as Byrk, Holey, Ashe, Ellers, lying lytell shorte okes and other Undrewood but no timber of any valewe wherein the Abbots of the same late Monastery have been ascuctomed to have a Smythey and sometyme two or thre kepte for making of Yron to the use of their Monastery. And so now the said comyssyoners have letten unto William Sandes and John Sawrey as moche of the said woodes and other underwoodes as wyll mayntenye iij Smytheys for the which they ar content and agreed to paye yerely to the Kinges Highnes as longe as hit shall please his grace they shall occupye the same. . . .'

From then onwards many licences were granted for 'ealing' hearths, which were exempt from bloomsmithy rent. Tenants were allowed to make iron, but only for their own use. By 1657 a stocktaking of the woods was more reassuring and the Crown thought the tenants could spare 'six hundredth seme of coals' to be delivered near the shores of Windermere. But as the woodlands were the chief source of supply for the livelihood of the tenants nothing could in fact be spared and the strictest supervision was required. As in so inaccessible a part of the country this was not possible, the woods were denuded not many years after the Dissolution.

The charcoal industry is first mentioned in the Furness Abbey Coucher Book, and there are many entries of 'colliers' in parish registers. Anthony Collett in *The Changing Face of*

England reminds us that 'the name "collier" meant a charcoal-burner until the men in the north began to ship south that black "earth" called sea coal'; that the Weald has its Collier's Hatch, and that Collier's Wood is now a station on a tube line. The shortened form of charcoal was 'cole' or 'coal,' and so it was but a short step to name that equally black substance dug from the earth for burning 'coal,' and the men who dug it 'colliers.'

H. S. Cowper in his *History of Hawkshead* mentions a supply of charcoal, that in 1662 'Mr Thomas Mussock, chirurgion, the day and yeare abousaid have sold fourteene wainloads of charrecoales to be delivered at Boweth unto William Rawlinson of Graythwt for XIXs a loade at pitteing. . . .

The remains of old bloomeries have usually been found on the banks of small streams.   Others which have been found on the high fells, apparently remote from wood supplies, may have been following the disappearing tree line or using the wind as a natural blower.   These were followed by the bloomsmithy, a combination of bloomery and forge, the product of which was a beaten bar of iron.   In the early seventeenth century the making of iron for trade and profit recommenced, and a study of local records, such as the Duchy of Lancaster MSS., books, and special commissions, shows not only the gradual growth of the industry but also the search for wood.   In 1623, for example, all oak and timber trees growing upon the ground called Hackett in Little Langdale were sold for £250.   Cunsey and Force Forges were built.   Bloomsmithy records mention expenses for fetching coals out of woodland by night to keep the furnace going. About 1780 woods were bought in Scotland and the charcoal shipped from Galloway to Greenodd.   The furnaces employed wood agents to buy timber anywhere they could.   Furness iron has been found on the site of bloomeries in Rossendale in the Lancashire Pennines, and this has been taken as evidence that in this instance iron was sent to the place where wood was obtainable.   Later, when coke furnaces were built, supplies of wood were obtained from as far away as Germany.

After the erection of the first furnace in 1711 licences were freely granted in lieu of a royalty of 1s. 6d. for every ton of 21 cwt.   In 1748 3,629 tons were produced, and by 1790 the total had reached 12,491 tons.

The chief mines, in order of opening, were at Hills Pit (1713) (now Old Hills near Whiterigg), Crossgates, Heaming Wood, Whiterigg, Wardclose, near Whiterigg, Lindale Cote, and Elliscales.

The Whiterigg mines were nicknamed the 'Peru of Furness' and were at one time the richest in England. The ore 'was not so deepe buried by nature in the entrailes of the earth, nor so closely couched amongst the rockes but that desire of gaine with instruments of art can digge them up.' In 1723 the 'instruments of art' brought a Dr Wright ten shillings fee 'for curing Oliver Crek of the wound he got by blasting with powder.' The ore was found in veins, some a mere trace, others as much as from forty to fifty yards in thickness. One was found upwards of 1,200 yards in thickness, though only in parts of its length. Fortunately it was all found near the surface. The ore was mined at first by individual miners, and later the furnace owners acquired the mines. Pennant, on his way to Scotland in 1772, noted the mines around Whiterigg and wrote: 'The iron race which inhabit the mining villages exhibit a strong appearance: men, women, and children are perfectly dyed with it, and even innocent babes do quickly assume the bloody complexion of the soil.' Even a century later there was a local saying that a miner had 'ta'en his degrees i'th'Red Lone college.'

The Force Forge I have already mentioned ceased to exist as a bloomery on the introduction of furnaces. It was rebuilt in the new mode in 1713, but operated only until 1744. Cunsey was already being worked in 1675, but in 1711 the Backbarrow Company was formed and Cunsey, together with other forges in the district, was taken over. The Cunsey lease expired in 1715 and it ceased work as a bloomery. It had been let as a farm to Daniel Cotton and Edward Hall on the formation of the Backbarrow Company, and obtained a new lease of life when these two men rebuilt the furnace. They worked it until 1750 when it passed again to the Backbarrow Company, 'together with the Liberty of free passing and re-passing of boats for the carriage of any material whatsoever to and from the said premises in and upon the water or meer commonly called Windermere.' Bought out by its all-powerful rival, Cunsey was left to decay, and was dismantled ten years later.

There was once a bloomery forge at Coniston, on Church Beck. All that now remains is the name of Forge Cottages. Hackett forge was on the River Brathay about half a mile above Colwith Force, by the side of the road to Little Langdale. Another was erected at Burblethwaite on the River Winster near Bowland Bridge. At Cartmel there was a forge in Cark Shaws Wood. The forge site at Burnbarrow was later covered by the Low Wood furnace, afterwards by the gunpowder works.

Spark Bridge forge stood on an island on the River Crake, north-west of Spark Bridge. Like many other forges it was built on the site of a fulling-mill, for iron manufacture replaced that of cloth in Furness and fulling-mills were mostly closed from the middle of the eighteenth century. Stony Hazle, erected about 1720, is regarded as the last bloomery forge to be erected in Furness. It was bought by the Backbarrow Company in 1725 and they paid for the lease until 1822, although it never worked again.

The Force forge was at Milnthorpe, just below the waterfall on the River Kent. Gray in his *Journal* described his visit there : 'The calmness and brightness of the evening, the roaring of the waters and the thumping of huge hammers at an Iron forge not far distant . . . I went on down to the forge and saw the demons at work by the light of their own fires.'

Some of these forges worked for nearly a century on methods differing little from those of the earliest times. By the middle of the eighteenth century there were signs of improvements in manufacturing technique. Backbarrow was the last example of a charcoal forge in Great Britain, Alfred Fell tells us, and was also the first smelting furnace in the north.

There was a furnace of the new type at Leighton Beck, two and a half miles from Arnside, until it closed in 1806. Ore came to it from Yealand Redmayne Common and across the bay.

John Lucas (1710–40) in his *History of Warton* tells us that, after gently seasoning a new furnace, 'in about three weeks Time the Fire will be so intense that they can run in a Sow and Pigs once in about twelve Hours.' The sow is a long funnel made through a bed of level sand below the mouth of the furnace and out of it, on each side, eleven or twelve smaller for the pigs. They become moulds for the liquid iron. When the redness goes from the iron and it begins to look blackish on top 'then they break the Sow and Pigs off from one another, and the Sow into the same lengths with the Piggs'—and so we find the origin of the term 'pig-iron.'

There is an interesting history behind the Newland furnace at Ulverston. In 1746 a very ancient water corn-mill was sold to one Agnes Bordley, sister of Richard Ford (a well-known name in the local iron trade), 'commonly called by the name of Newland Miln situate standing and being upon the Common or Pasture near the King's Highway leading from Ulverston to Arred Foot.' A lease was obtained for a furnace which was worked until 1891.

An agreement between Richard Ford and John Bigland to build Low Wood furnace was made in 1728, but it was twenty years later before it was erected on the site of the old Burnbarrow forge. On the deaths of the partners, the Backbarrow and Newland Companies obtained the lease. In 1799 gunpowder works were built on the site. An interesting sidelight on the fuel difficulty is afforded by the company's right to obtain peat for the use of the furnace, and to call on workmen out of the mosses belonging to the lessor. The partners paid three halfpence for every common cart-load of peat, 'such carts to be drawn by one horse.'

The last of the light furnaces to be built in Furness was Penny Bridge. Again the struggle for fuel is realized when it is noted that this furnace was built by William Penny and other wood-owners in retaliation against the ironmasters, who had combined to force down the price of charcoal. However, production had hardly begun when William Rawlinson retired from the Backbarrow Company, and the wood-owners accepted a share in the Backbarrow furnace. In 1805 the Penny Bridge site was taken over by a paper-mill. A measure of comparison is provided by John Lucas, who computes a minimum of 130 furnaces and hammers working at this same period in Sussex, and consuming 94,900 loads of charcoal annually.

The interdependence which linked the Lancashire coastline with Ireland is again exemplified in the early Furness iron industry. Even in 1672, Alfred Fell tells us, there were in Ireland some 2,000 men and women employed in the industry, and at least 6,600 smith's forges employing 22,510 men and women.

Q

It is not surprising therefore that a certain Christopher Burns should have come from Ireland in October 1711 to erect and supervise the first furnace at Backbarrow.   And with him came Irishmen to work it.   These intermarried locally, so that we find Irish family names to-day such as Bevins, Leonard, Cavannah, Druit, Jordan, Mayberry, and many more.

Backbarrow furnace

The cast-iron work came from Ireland, the bricks from Liverpool, the sandstone from Heysham, and the shaft for the wheel from Barton Park near Lancaster.   The old account books make strange and interesting reading to-day.   Two hundred and forty years ago they were using butter as a lubricant at $2\frac{1}{2}d$. per pound; otter, sheep, and hare skins were employed for putting round bellows pipes, and the bellows were made from tough bull hides, bought in Yorkshire and tanned locally, fifteen or eighteen being required for one pair of bellows.   Eventually there was a change in the industry from bellows to iron cylinders, but Backbarrow was the last to convert.   The first 'blow' was on 7th June 1712, and, writes Alfred Fell, 'from that time to the present (1938) this furnace has a record of continuous and successful work, probably unique in the annals of iron making'—to which we can add another fifteen years, for this furnace is still working night and day.

Prior to 1721 cast-iron 'pot' ware was imported into Furness from Bristol, but in that year some 'potters' were induced to come north and production began at the Leighton furnace. Isaac Wilkinson came to Furness to be employed as a 'pot founder,' assisted by his son John, the self-styled 'father of the iron trade.' According to Stockdale, Isaac Wilkinson came to Backbarrow in 1740 and obtained leave to carry metal out of the furnaces to a cowshed across the road in which he made flat-irons and smoothing-irons. On the other hand, Alfred Fell quotes *The Lilies of Boulton and Watt* in which Wilkinson tells of advances he received from his masters, from 12s. per week to a guinea. Concluding that if he was worth a guinea per week to the masters he was worth a guinea a week to himself, so he began a business on his own account, dispensed with leather bellows and made them from iron, and finally used a steam-engine to blow them. Stockdale dates his break away from Barrow in 1748. The new forge was erected at Wilson House, near Lindale. A canal was built into the peat and a boat used to carry this fuel to the furnace. The venture was, however, a failure, and when twenty-eight years old John Wilkinson went to Staffordshire, where he was ultimately to own many large ironworks and to become the greatest name in the iron trade at that time.

Richard Ford, who began at Nibthwaite on the Crake, founded in 1735 the Newland Company, which eventually absorbed all the furnaces and forges in the district as well as acquiring mines. Nibthwaite, Newland, and Backbarrow became centres for the manufacture of cannon balls and shot. Inventories at Nibthwaite for 1745 show machines for producing guns and trucks, gun frames, gun boring, gun carts and car-riages, swivel guns, six-pounder guns, and so on. Much of this material was for men-of-war. The material was boated down the River Leven from Backbarrow to Hammerside Hill to be shipped to Portsmouth. Thousands of rounds of shot, for from three to thirty-two pounders, were shipped from Ulverston to the Office of Ordnance at Woolwich. However, the staple war manufacture was cannon balls and this trade lasted from the Seven Years War to Waterloo. The bulk of the remaining iron went to Liverpool for ship chains, anchors, and shipbuilding.

The decline of the Furness iron trade is accounted for in an unusual manner: it was too good for the job. Later inventions produced cheaper grades, and steel became cheaper than charcoal bars. By the middle of the nineteenth century the iron bar which had given Furness a proud name was no longer required. It was at this point that certain Furness 'men of iron' had the courage and ability to adapt themselves to the new era. They concentrated their energies on the natural harbour at the very corner of the peninsula, and less than a hundred years ago the town of Barrow was carved out of the sand-hills and rabbit warrens.

It was the Backbarrow Company which arranged the first 'mine floor' on the shore where Barrow now stands. The ore was brought down here from the mines and stacked on the coast to await shipment. Previously ore had come from Elliscales to Palace Nook, a herdsman's hut close by. Ore from Wetflat was stacked for shipment at Louzey Point, and the Duddon Company arranged shipments from Ireleth Marsh to their Scottish furnaces. All the above places grouped together found a natural focal point in the Barrow area, and in 1780 the Newland Company purchased land at Barrowhead, including the Barrowhead Inn built by James Hoole about 1745 for the use of sailors, later to become the Ship Inn, and there they built the first quay.

We may get some picture of the birth of Barrow from Alfred Fell, who tells us that a sign-painter received half a guinea for his work there and that 23 feet of stone and five pillars were provided for a seat in front of the inn, which was the centre of festive drinking to celebrate the opening of the new quay (1782) and to christen the birth of the new town, although the pioneers could have had no idea of the enterprise which was to be shown at this point in the future. From that stone bench they looked back into history. Out in the sea stood the ruins of Piel Castle, or the Pile of Foudrey, built by the Furness monks in the reign of Edward III to guard the entrance to their harbour and to be a place of refuge for them during the border wars. History was turning a full circle. A report at the time of the Spanish

Armada had said that 'between Mylford Haven in Wales and Carliell on the borders of Scotland there is not one good haven for greate shyppes to londe or ryde in but one which is in the furthest part of Lancashire called Pylle of Fodder. The same pyle is an old decayed castle, parcel of the Duchy of Lancaster, in Furness Fells, where one Thomas Preston (a papyshe Atheiste) is a deputy steward . . . what the Spanyerd mean to to, Lord knowes; but all the countrye beinge knowne to doctor Allen (who was born hard by the Pyle) and the inhabytents thereaboutes, all ynfected with his Romish poyson, yt is not unlyke but his directione will be used for some landings there.' And the modern shipbuilders of Barrow were forestalled in 1667 when a government survey reports 'ye Place where we proposed to build a ship or ships for ye King's service, which to all intents does give great sattisfaction,' while in 1565 the ports of Lancashire are listed as Cockersande, Cartmeale, Kirkeham, and Pile of Foderye (Liverpool was included in Cheshire), but the Pile was never developed because there was no connection for trade with the hinterland.

Holinshed landed at Rampside after his tour of the Isle of Man and mentions the fine islands, the Pile of Foudrey, and Walney Chapel (which we know was in existence in 1577). Then we find the parliamentary fleet sailing from here after their local defeat in the Civil War of the seventeenth century. It was the surprise route for adventuring warmongers, such as Martin Swartz. Otherwise the area was the home of peaceful agriculturalists who were not even troubled by the iron industry until the middle of the eighteenth century. Rampside even showed possibilities at one time of becoming a bathing resort, but it was too far away from civilization and the railway came to it too late. It is interesting to note, however, that in 1800 the village had ninety-four inhabitants and Barrow but sixty-five. By 1801 there were eleven dwelling-houses in Rampside. Nine years later one Anthony High was in business there as a tailor, and in 1814 there was a schoolmaster, a schoolmistress, and a pilot. A blacksmith then came twice a week from Hawcoat, and was not resident until 1822. The first school was a converted pigsty. In 1815 Captain James Barrow converted it into a dwelling-house, although, he said, the tide flowed through it when it was high.

By 1830 there was a population of a hundred and thirty people who obtained a living from the new port. Tom King's farm stood at the present junction of Dalton Road, Church Street, and Duke Street. The Free Trade Hall now stands on the site of Tom King's barn, and the Bull Hotel on his granary. In 1876 William Fisher, another farmer, still farmed in Dalton Road opposite the Albion Vaults. Joseph Fisher's malt kiln stood on the site of the High Level Bridge, and served also for sheep slaughtering, for Joseph Fisher worked in the new town as farmer, lime burner, and coal dealer, and naturally also had a hand in the iron-ore business. Peggy Creary was breadmaker, Thomas Hodgson coastguard, John Smith shoemaker, Captain Barrow shipping agent, pilot, schoolmaster, and unofficial postmaster. The postman was one Tom Shaw who came from Ulverston to Barrow every day, calling at all the villages and walking some thirty miles.

It was a happy community which lived and worked in close neighbourly fashion. If anyone was poor enough to be hungry there were always potatoes kept in the malt kiln for the asking, and there was a 150-yard draw-net for any fisherman who cared to use it. Everyone went fishing in the summer. When the harvest was safely home any six people could man a boat and fish in the Bars Pool. When the village had taken what it wanted the rest of the catch was salted down for the winter. The townsfolk grew their own wheat, oats, and barley, and shipped the surplus to Preston. The barley provided work for twenty malt kilns around the coast, some 72,000 bushels a year being exported to south Lancashire, and cattle were driven oversands to the Manchester market.

Meanwhile the people watched the iron ore coming down to the piers from the Dalton mines. Sometimes there would be a convoy of horses and carts stretching for two miles, and as many as a hundred sailing ships lying off the shore waiting to have their bottoms filled for the voyage to South Wales.

The completion of the Furness Railway in 1846 was the first step to greater expansion. This meant the creation of docks. Then, in 1855, Bessemer's steel discoveries ended the iron age. The change of direction found Barrow just at the right stage of development, with the raw material on her doorstep. Two years later Schneider and Hannay decided to manufacture at the growing port of Barrow, which now became an industrial town.

Behind all these interdependent movements towards the creation of a new town lies the work of James Ramsden. He came to Barrow at the age of twenty-three in charge of the engineering department of the new Furness Railway. His abilities were rewarded when he was made manager and eventually a director of the company. He persuaded the dukes of Buccleuch and Devonshire and other capitalists to build docks, to use the new Bessemer steel process, and to build iron ships. He was behind the town's incorporation as a borough, became its first mayor, and was knighted.

Throughout this period of enthusiastic and well-planned development, factors were already in being which were to stop the process. As the local iron industry grew, so it took more and more of the local iron ore, until shipments not only ceased but supplies had to be imported. To-day all iron ore is imported. Then the mistake of not accepting George Stephenson's plan for a railway to Scotland passing close to Barrow became apparent, when the more powerful railway groups accorded the Furness line no more than local line status. The 1923 grouping of railways (which also controlled dock facilities) gave Heysham and Fleetwood the trade, cut out all sailings from Barrow, and further increased her isolation. There remains to her, however, the firm of Vickers, which carries on the original work of Schneider and Hannay, whose engineering contracts, especially shipbuilding, have brought prosperity to Barrow in good years but only lean fare in times of trade recession.

Although, as you approach, you can see the cranes and girders of the shipyards before you see the town itself, it is a pleasant surprise to be greeted by clean buildings and tree-lined boulevards. (Is not the main street the longest tree-lined street in the country?) There is a local saying that Barrow has only three ancient things—'Copper Nob' (the railway engine in a glass case at the station), the Pile of Foudrey, and the Lancashire tongue.

I have already given the names of a few people who lived in the early village of Barrow: I might have given the name of every man and of his job, for that is how it has been throughout the town's development—the incoming workers from all over the country joining in the enthusiasm and optimism of a growth inspired by leading men whom they knew and respected. There was pride here, in the town, in the steelworks, in themselves. The tradition of ironworking remained a family heritage, as in the old days of small companies, and workmen sent their sons into the works to continue the tradition. The town became a magnet, drawing workers from every corner of the peninsula. To-day we see its growth limited by its isolation, but it can still keep to a certain level of prosperity if trade remains good, and there is no other industrial town in the kingdom which can offer such a delightful surrounding countryside for the homes of its workers.

Nearby Dalton is built in an amphitheatre of small, rounded hills from which the inhabitants have, in these past centuries, derived their living—from red earth and red iron ore. As the bus from Barrow climbs to the rim of the hills, you may see below lines of small grey cottages. It is a disappointing aspect. As one of the oldest centres of Furness life I had always expected it to be a small Shrewsbury or a little Worcester. Instead it is a miniature mining village, showing an entire lack of imagination in the reconstruction and renovating of the older houses. The remains of the castle in Skelgate (an air raid warden's post during the last war) are, however, a focus of interest, and have a history more colourful than the present. The monks of Furness built the castle, for Dalton was the last habitable place before the crossing of the Duddon Sands into Cumberland. There was already an established Roman road from Maryport to Lancaster, across the peninsula to Conishead, when the monks from Savigny arrived in the Vale of the Nightshade and accepted the gift of this land, and a castle was a necessary guardhouse, on such a border route, to protect the riches of a prosperous abbey.

The Dalton fairs of 1239 and 1245, granted to the abbot of Furness, have been proclaimed from the market cross for these five hundred years, and it always seems remarkable to me to hear the proclamation read on behalf of the steward of the 'lately dissolved Monastery and Manor of Furness, and Liberty of the Same' (I think it was so worded) and asking persons visiting the fair to keep the peace, every knight upon pain of

£10, every esquire or gentleman upon pain of £5, and every other person upon pain of forty shillings, and that no person have or wear any habiliments of war such as jack, steel coats, bills, or battle-axes.

We must now return to Conishead Priory for the last stage of the old route across Lancashire—the crossing of the Furness peninsula.

In a grant to Conishead Priory by William de Lancaster, confirmed by Edward II in 1307, there is mention of all the land on both sides of the road which leads from Bardsea to Ulverston, and from the great road to Trinkeld, and from thence to the sea bank. The 'great road' would be the northward route reaching, at the edge of the marshland, the solid cliff upon which Conishead Priory was built. Its continuation across the peninsula to the Duddon crossing may be traced to-day by the line of the most ancient settlements—that is by Urswick, along the edge of the drainage area to Kirkby Treleth, one of St. Cuthbert's resting-places. (Could it be that the monks made the journey from Aldingham to Ireleth where they rested to await the tides for the crossing?)

Another peninsula crossing ran from Conishead, and later from Ulverston, over Pennington Moor to Soutergate and Sandside. Gamel de Pennington, owner of this land, gave the church of his village, on the high road, to Conishead in the reign of Henry II. In 1902 a tympanum was discovered over the doorway of Beckside Farm, upon which, around the centre carving, are these words: 'Kamail seti these kirk Hubert mesun vanm'—'Gamel founded this church; Hubert the Mason built it.' The date of this dedication was 1160, so that even as late as the twelfth century we find this corruption of the old Norse language in use.

The commercial roads which developed within the peninsula from the twelfth century onwards were connected with the vast domains of Furness Abbey. The Coucher Book has such entries as: 'Richard I—1195-6 Abbot and Gilbert Fitz Reinfred: The latter granted free passage to the monks and transit for themselves and all their goods by the way leading from the Abbey of Furness, through Ulverston, and so through Craikeslith as far as the fishery of the Crake, and so on their lands where they will, because the said Monks and their goods have

sometimes been disturbed on their way there.' Again, '7 Oct.
1318. Abbot and William de Pennington : the latter granted to
the abbey a certain way of the breadth of 50 feet through the
middle of the moor and pasture of the said William in Pennington; that is to say, the way which is the upper way towards the
Water of Doden beginning at the land of Merton of the same
Abbot and Convent and so going along to the metes of
Ulverston.'

But, as I have said, this is but the beginning of another
fascinating subject, and already we ought to have followed one
of the ways over the peninsula to reach the crossing of the
Duddon Sands. As this is the twentieth century I shall choose
to go by the Soutergate in Ulverston, and to climb over the
ridge of moor behind the town. Some say that 'Soutergate'
means the 'road of the leather makers,' but I can only say that it
always gives me a thrill to leave a town by a road which tells
me of the place I am setting out to see. Soutergate lies there,
at the end of the road, by the shores of Duddon estuary. The
more common name for the terminus is now Sandside, but it
was once Sandgate (the sand road) and this is what we are
seeking. There could be no scene of quieter beauty than these
last shores of Lancashire, with their acres of samphire and
shining wet sands, reflecting green woodlands and blue mountains.

> . . . Duddon water a brave River where the
> famous cockles of all England is gathered in
> the sands scraped out with hookes like
> sickles, and brave salmons and flookes
> the bravest in all England hang'd up
> and dryed like bacon and as good
> feeding as Iseland saltfish.[1]

A caterpillar-like train under a banner of white cloud
slowly crosses the viaduct over the smooth flat sands and then
over the river, 'gliding in silence with unfettered sweep.'

But for the hesitations of Barrow and Ulverston men that
train might have been an express to Scotland, following the plan
of George Stephenson and the course of that padded track which
had been in use 'tyme out of mynd of man.'

[1] From Sandford's *Antiquities and Familyes, Cumberland* (1675).

BIBLIOGRAPHY

Battle of the Land and Sea, by William Ashton.

The River Mersey, by W. T. Palmer.

Lancashire and Cheshire Antiquarian Society, 1886, by William O. Roper.

The Merchant Schooners, by Basil Greenhill (1951).

Antiquities and Familyes of Cumberland, by Sandford (1675).

History of Warton Parish, by John Lucas (1710–40). First printed 1931.

'Early History in Furness,' by J. Melville and J. L. Hobbs. (Cumberland and Westmorland A. and A. Society, *Transactions*, vol. xiii, 1951.)

Shepherd's Warning, by Graham Sutton.

The Household Account Book of Sarah Fell of Swarthmoor Hall, edited by Norman Penny (Cambridge, 1930).

Margaret Fell, by Isobel Ross (1949).

Chronicles of Town and Church of Ulverston, by Thomas Wareing Bardsley (1884).

'Notes on the Wilkinsons, Ironmasters,' by Francis Nicholson. (Manchester Literary and Philological Society, *Transactions*, vol. xlix, Part III.)

Amounderness Survey, by Mawson. (Fylde Regional Committee, 1937.)

Kirkham in Amounderness, by Cunliffe Shaw (1949).

Leaves from the Annals of a Mountain Parish (Torver), by T. Ellwood (1888).

The Place-Names of Lancashire, by Henry Cecil Wild and T. Oakes Hirst. (Constable, 1911.)

The Yellow Rock, by Peter Donnelly. (Eyre & Spottiswoode, 1950.)

A Glossary of the Words and Phrases of Furness, by J. P. Morris.

The Road goes on (anthology), by G. W. Scott-Giles.

Notes on the Agriculture of Lancashire, by Jonathan Binns. (Preston, 1851.)

Marina (a Sea-bathing Companion, 1829), by P. Whittle (Preston).

The Land of Britain, by Dudley Stamp. (Longmans, 1948.)

History of the Fylde, by John Porter (1876).

These Charming Acres, by Peter Nodin.

History of Over Wyresdale, by D. Schofield (1909).

Baines's *History of Lancashire and Cheshire* (1876).

Fairie Land, Song, edited by Drayton (1622).

The Natural History of Lancashire, Cheshire, and the Peak in Derby-shire, by Dr Leigh (1700).

British Canals, by Charles Hadfield.   (Phoenix House, 1950.)

Furness Abbey Coucher Book, Chetham Society, Manchester.

Formby Reminiscences, by Catherine Jackson, *née* Formby (1897).

Seas and Shores of England, by Edmund Vale.   (Batsford.)

'The Rise of Morecambe, 1820–62,' by R. G. Armstrong. (Lancashire and Cheshire Historical Society, vol. c, 1948.)

Short History of Heysham, by F. Whewell Hogarth (1934).

Annals of Southport and District, by E. Bland.   (Abel Heywood & Son, Manchester, 1886.)

The Lancashire Recusants, by J. Stanley Leatherbrow.   (Chetham Society.)

Chetham's *Historical Geography of South-West Lancashire*, vol. ciii (1939).

The Early Iron Industry of Furness and District, by Alfred Fell (1908).

'Some Glimpses of the Fylde Country,' by G. A. Wood. (Burnley Literary and Scientific *Transactions*, vol. xxxviii.)

Old Catholic Lancashire, by F. O. Blundell (1938).

Industrial Revolution in the 18th Century, by Paul Manoux (1928).

The History of the Business Man, by Miriam Beard.   (Macmillan, 1938.)

Milestones of Marketing, by George Burton Hotchkiss.   (Macmillan, New York.)

Through England on a Side Saddle, by Celia Fiennes.

General View of the Agriculture of the County of Lancaster, by John Holt (1795).

The Battle of Land and Sea on the Lancashire, Cheshire, and North Wales Coasts, by William Austin (1909).

'*Burscough Priory*,' by F. H. Cheetham (*Southport Visitor*).

Windmill Land, by Allen Clarke.

The Heronries of an Estuary, by S. Moorhouse.   North-Western Naturalist (1940).

Lancashire, its Puritanism and Nonconformity, by Robert Hully.

The Sands of Morecambe Bay, by T. Pape (1947).

INDEX

Main references are given in italic figures

Walker, Rev. Robert, 207
Walney Island, 24, 212, 220
Wardleys, 6
Warrington, 4, 7, 21, 56
Warton, 171, *179–82*, 183, 223
Windy Harbour, 89, 90, 116
Wordsworth, William, 177, 178
Wraysholme Tower, 191, 192

Wrea Green, 89, 92, 100
Wyre, river, 6, 7, 86, 87, 88, 89, 90,
103, 116, 117, 118, 119, 121, 129

Yealand Conyers, 182
— Redmayne, 182, 232
— Storrs, 182